The Doctrine of
Eternal Life

*A Civil-Minded Study of Calvinism and
Arminianism in the Light of Scripture*

PASTOR KEVIN KLINE

ISBN 978-1-64569-659-9 (paperback)
ISBN 978-1-64569-660-5 (digital)

Christian Faith Publishing, Inc.
832 Park Avenue
Meadville, PA 16335
www.christianfaithpublishing.com

Printed in the United States of America

CONTENTS

PREFACE

I have endeavored to write this book in the spirit of kindness, not judgment. The purpose of this study is not to attack Calvin, Arminius or any other person, living or not. We will examine the doctrines of man in light of Bible truth. The reader is invited to decide for himself which doctrines are of God and which are of men. We should never hate those with whom we disagree, but rather each individual should form and/or change his view based on his understanding of scripture. God hates sin, but loves the sinner. In truth, we are to love every brother while hating every false way.

"Thy word is very pure: therefore thy servant loveth it" (Ps. 119:140).

"Through thy precepts I get understanding: therefore I hate every false way" (Ps. 119:104).

PASTOR KEVIN KLINE

Paul said that there were heresies among the Corinthians (1 Cor. 11:19), yet Paul loved them and showed them the truth. Whether you identify yourself as a Calvinist, hyper-Calvinist, 2.5-point Calvinist, non-Calvinist, Arminian, Biblicist or other, my goal is to assist the reader in understanding the reasoning behind these various views. We all should learn from scripture and change our views based upon our understanding and spiritual growth. Those who never change, never grow, for growth is a series of changes. We must, however, be assured that our changes are based on truth and not religious dogma or pressure to conform to man's religion. In plain English, something isn't true just because many people believe it or because we wish it to be true.

My burden is to challenge the reader to think. Do you believe what you do because you were taught it, because it seems to make sense to you or because you have read the entire Bible numerous times and use scripture to answer scripture without adding, diminishing or changing Bible words and their meanings? A true student of the Bible doesn't reject a teaching because it doesn't "fit" with his preconceived ideas, but rather because it violates the clear teaching of scripture. It's helpful to keep in mind that just because one side of any issue is wrong, it doesn't necessarily follow that the other side must therefore be correct. I have been studying the doctrine of eternal life as understood by Calvin and Arminius for almost forty years with the premise of allowing the Bible to speak for itself without putting words in God's mouth. If I can help clear up even a small portion of confusion in the reader's mind, surrounding the teachings of Calvin and Arminius, all the writing effort will have been worth it.

Perhaps a brief personal testimony might be appropriate here. I grew up with no church or religion. When I was twenty-two years old, I decided to read the Bible for myself to see if there was anything to it. I said in my heart something like this, "God, if you're real, help me to understand your Bible." Not long after, I became a born-again Christian by receiving the free gift of eternal life. You do believe that eternal life is a free gift and not a payment for doing good works, don't you?

> "For the wages of sin is death; but *the gift of God is eternal life* through Jesus Christ our Lord" (Rom. 6:23; emphasis mine).

I will admit that I was confused by the plethora of Christian denominations and sects and set out to learn what made each distinct. Intuitively and meticulously, every doctrine was examined through the light of scripture, the same scripture which had led to the salvation of my soul.

> "Wherefore lay apart all filthiness and superfluity of naughtiness, and receive with meekness the engrafted word, which is able to *save your souls*" (James 1:21; emphasis mine).

Dear reader, please let scripture alone direct your doctrine and not preconceived ideas, popular opinion, organized religion or rationalization, and you will have a special peace that intellect alone will not allow. Literally, thousands of Bible verses have been referenced, examined, cross-indexed, and prayed over in order for this book to be in your hands. Please be willing to follow truth wherever it leads, while keeping in mind two things. One, truth usually lies between the two extreme viewpoints and two, following man is easy; following truth requires work!

"Study to shew thyself approved unto God, a workman that needeth not to be ashamed, rightly dividing the word of truth" (2 Tim. 2:15).

My personal experience has been that most Christians defend the Bible doctrine of salvation and eternal life not with scripture, but with human reasoning. The Arminian usually defends his belief by saying something like, "You mean to tell me that if I become a Christian and go out into deep immoral sin that I'm still going to heaven?" Their argument being based on that which makes sense to their human reasoning and not on scripture. Likewise, I've been told by Calvinists that Calvinism must be true because "many great and famous men were Calvinists!" Again, this is a rationale based on human reasoning and not on Bible fact. If Bible facts agree with either Calvin or Arminius, then accept the part which agrees with scripture and discard that which disagrees. Truth is never based on human reason nor on popular opinion. Does John 3:16 really make sense? Is it reasonable that God would be willing to leave heaven, become a man, be born of a woman, suffer, bleed, and die to redeem any sinful person?

> "And without controversy great is the mystery of godliness: God was manifest in the flesh, justified in the Spirit, seen of angels, preached unto the Gentiles, believed on in the world, received up into glory" (1 Tim. 3:16).

When anyone says that the preceding verse doesn't apply to Jesus Christ, I ask them to whom then does it apply? The verse is written in the past tense, so if God was not revealed in Jesus Christ, then please tell me, in whom was God revealed?

Is it reasonable that God in the person of the Holy Spirit would possess any fleshy body other than that of his Son, Jesus Christ? Yet we read in Romans 8: "But ye are not in the flesh, but in the Spirit, if so be that the Spirit of God dwell in you. Now if any man have not the Spirit of Christ, he is none of his" (Rom. 8:9).

Is it reasonable that the Lord himself will one day descend from heaven and suddenly snatch away millions of people from the earth in an instant?

> For the Lord himself shall descend from heaven with a shout, with the voice of the archangel, and with the trump of God: and the dead in Christ shall rise first: Then we which are alive and remain shall be caught up together with them in the clouds, to meet the Lord in the air: and so shall we ever be with the Lord. (1 Thess. 4:16–17)
>
> In a moment, in the twinkling of an eye, at the last trump: for the trumpet shall sound, and the dead shall be raised incorruptible, and we shall be changed. (1 Cor. 15:52)

I question whether or not any one of these examples is reasonable; yet each is true and we believe them solely based on scripture. Human reason should never be the final basis for truth; the Bible is true whether we believe it to be reasonable or not and whether we understand it or not.

A brief summary of history:

John Calvin was a theologian who lived from 1509 to 1564. Some of his core beliefs were the doctrines that God chose some persons for heaven and some for hell, and that those whom God chose would persevere unto the end. Calvin believed and expanded the works of Augustine who lived in the fourth and fifth centuries.

Jacobus Arminius who lived from 1560 to 1609 reacted against Calvinist doctrines by believing that God did not foreordain people to heaven or hell and popularized the belief that a child of God could lose eternal life. It is the doctrine of potentially losing one's salvation, which most clearly defines Arminianism. Others such as Martin Luther, who lived from 1483 to 1546, also held the belief that it was possible for a child of God once saved to become unsaved. Most of those groups, which separated from the Roman Catholic Church, were and still are Arminian in doctrine. It is noteworthy that while both Calvinistic and Arminian doctrines came out of the Roman Catholic Church, the

Baptist, Anabaptist, Waldenses, and several other groups were never a part of the Roman Catholic system. It may not set well with the reader that John Calvin, Martin Luther, and Jacobus Arminius were Roman Catholics, but their doctrines cannot be condemned because they were once a part of the Roman Catholic system; neither are their doctrines vindicated as pure because they separated from the system. Each doctrine must be accepted or rejected in light of the totality of scripture. Historically speaking, both Luther and Calvin did a great deal of good backing the reformation by exposing the corruptness of the Roman Catholic Church. It may be helpful to the youthful scholar to be reminded that the correct view of any controversy is usually between the two extremes.

When I was asked by several different individuals to write this book, the Lord reminded me that "we see through a glass darkly" (1 Cor. 13:12). In other words, no one has perfectly flawless doctrine. The dark lens can be preconceived ideas from our own human reasoning or the paradigm of what we have been taught. Both Calvin and Arminius sought to explain the Bible to the best of their abilities, and no mortal can do more. It is, however, the methodology we utilize in truth seeking which becomes extremely important. An extremely intelligent person using a flawed methodology will probably arrive at some wrong conclusions, while a person of average intelligence, following a superior methodology, is more likely to arrive closer to the truth.

Some further thoughts:

1. This book is meant to be used as a study guide for further reference.
2. To avoid confusion, all scriptures are from the authorized King James Bible.
3. Let scripture be the final authority.
4. Be intellectually honest; don't change or add Bible words to support a particular view.
5. Please forgive me for being redundant, slow, and plodding. There is a reason for this and if the reader skims, I guarantee that he will misunderstand points and be confused.
6. Please pray now and ask God to show you what is true and be willing to go where God's truth, not Calvin's truth, Arminius' truth, or the author's

truth, but the Bible truth takes you. There is a saying that goes something like this: The greatest hindrance to truth is the perception that you already have it. Indeed, if we believe we hold ultimate truth, we will defend the truth we hold without considering a deeper way of looking at that truth. Let's look at an easy and quick example. Some folks may believe that money is the root of all evil and as such, they may live a meager existence because of their belief. However, we know that the Bible doesn't teach that money is the root of all evil, but rather, the love of money or avarice is the problem.

"For the *love* of money is the root of all evil: which while some coveted after, they have erred from the faith, and pierced themselves through with many sorrows" (1 Tim. 6:10; emphasis mine).

The point being that the problem wasn't what the Bible said, but what some individuals thought it said, and this is the polarizing factor underlying many doctrinal differences.

Yet another hindrance to truth is that of taking our stand with less than all the facts. Here is a simple example. If we ask a hundred people, "What is the city of David?" Some would turn to Luke's gospel and read.

"For unto you is born this day in *the city of David* a Saviour, which is Christ the Lord" (Luke 2:11; emphasis mine).

"And Joseph also went up from Galilee, out of the city of Nazareth, into Judaea, unto *the city of David*, which is called *Bethlehem*; (because he was of the house and lineage of David)" (Luke 2:4; emphasis mine).

Very often, when Christians find a single corroborating scripture, they are satisfied that they have arrived at truth! The Bible scholar, however, must exhaust the scriptures on any given subject before he's satisfied. For example, if we stop with our search for truth and say the Bible says that

Bethlehem is the city of David and reject all other possibilities, we then are doing truth itself a disservice. How so? Another person, not knowing your truth, puts forth his truth and declares that Jerusalem and not Bethlehem is the city of David.

> "And his servants carried him in a chariot to *Jerusalem*, and buried him in his sepulchre with his fathers in *the city of David*" (2 Kings 9:28; emphasis mine).
>
> "Then Solomon assembled the elders of Israel, and all the heads of the tribes, the chief of the fathers of the children of Israel, unto *Jerusalem*, to bring up the ark of the covenant of the LORD out of *the city of David*, which is Zion" (2 Chron. 5:2; emphasis mine).

Now what do we do? Who is correct? Is there a contradiction in the Bible? No, it's never the right answer to suggest that there is a contradiction in the Bible. That is, of course, if we adhere to the traditional texts and the authorized version. Who then is correct? The answer is both and neither. How can this be? If the first person believes that Bethlehem is the city of David to the exclusion of all other possibilities and the second person believes that Jerusalem is the city of David to the exclusion of all other, then both individuals are wrong. However, if both persons take the position that they only know what the Bible says in some scriptures, but there may be more possibilities, then they are both correct. Both cities are called the city of David. Bethlehem, because it was David's birth town, and Jerusalem, because it was a stronghold in which David captured. We can now see how very easy it is for all of us to hold to one truth so strongly that we reject other facts that are equally true. All scriptures are true and are in harmony with all other scriptures when they are rightly divided. It's perfectly fine, however, for us to say we don't understand how two or more scriptures or Bible doctrines agree.

1

Let's Consider Twenty Questions

Questions for those of the Calvin and Arminian faiths.

Twenty questions for those who follow the teachings of Calvin:

Do you consider yourself to be a Calvinist? Would you make an honest effort to answer all of these questions using scripture?

1. Why was Paul willing to endure all things for the elect's sake so that they may obtain salvation if the elect were already saved?

    "Therefore I endure all things for the elect's sakes, that they may also obtain the salvation which is in Christ Jesus with eternal glory" (2 Tim. 2:10).

2. If no one can resist the grace of God, then why aren't all men saved?

   "For the grace of God that bringeth salvation hath appeared to all men" (Titus 2:11).

3. If no one can resist the Holy Ghost, why then did Steven, who was full of the Holy Ghost in Acts 7:55, say in Acts 7:51, "ye do always resist the Holy Ghost"?

   "Ye stiffnecked and uncircumcised in heart and ears, ye do always resist the Holy Ghost: as your fathers did, so do ye" (Acts 7:51).

4. If man has no free will, then why did the Lord Jesus say he does?

   "Then said Jesus unto his disciples, *If any man will* come after me, let him deny himself, and take up his cross, and follow me" (Matt. 16:24; emphasis mine).

5. Does God's will always overpower man's will?

6. If God is only the Saviour of the elect (or a chosen few), then how do you explain 1 Timothy 4:10, which says that God is the Saviour of all men?

"For therefore we both labour and suffer reproach, because we trust in the living God, who is the Saviour of all men, specially of those that believe" (1 Tim. 4:10).

7. Is either the word sovereign or sovereignty found in the Bible?

8. Does sovereignty mean that God forces some people to be saved and others not to be saved?

9. According to the Bible, is it God's will that only some men be saved or all men?

10. If God only wants a select few to repent and be saved, why would God command all men everywhere to repent?

"And the times of this ignorance God winked at; but now commandeth *all* men every where to repent" (Acts 17:30; emphasis mine).

11. According to the Bible, for whom did Jesus die?
12. If God chooses people for heaven, why is it the Comforter's (the Holy Ghost's) job to reprove (convict) the world of sin and not just the elect?

Nevertheless I tell you the truth; It is expedient for you that I go away: for if I go not away, the Comforter will not come unto you; but if I depart, I will send him unto you. And when he is come, he will *reprove the world* of sin, and of righteousness, and of judgment. (John 16:7–8; emphasis mine).

13. Does the Bible teach that believers must persevere in order to be saved?

14. Does man's total depravity to save himself from hell mean that he can't repent and believe the gospel? If so, why did the Lord Jesus tell people to do something that he knew they could not do?

"And saying, The time is fulfilled, and the kingdom of God is at hand: repent ye, and believe the gospel" (Mark 1:15).

15. Is God's election of man for salvation or service?

16. What crucial Bible point did Calvin overlook relating to the election of man?

17. Did Calvin believe in the doctrine of the limited atonement of Christ?

18. Can you explain the difference between Calvinism and hyper-Calvinism?

19. A follower of Calvin may claim to be a one, one and a half, two, two and a half, three, three and a half, four, four and a half, or five-point Calvinists. Why are there so many variations on Calvinism?

20. If election is for salvation, and God only calls the elect to be saved, and no one can resist God's call-

ing, then *every* called person must be God's chosen, right?

I invite you to make an honest effort to answer these questions using scripture. The answers from scripture will appear in a later chapter.

Twenty questions for those who follow the teachings of Arminius:

Do you believe that eternal life can be lost? Can you answer these questions using scripture?

1. What is the Bible definition of eternal life?
2. Is eternal life given by God as a gift or as a payment for doing good works?
3. Does the Bible teach that born-again believers keep their salvation or that God keeps the believer?
4. Is it possible for a child of God to have no rewards in heaven?
5. Can God lie?
6. When does a believer in Christ receive eternal life?
7. What does the Bible phrase "never perish" mean?

8. Can a person pluck himself out of God's hand?

9. Can a believer in the Son of God know that he has eternal life?

10. What does the word "redeemed" mean?

11. Did God buy us just to throw us away when we fail?

12. Did Job and Paul guess, hope, feel, or know that they were saved?

13. For which category of sins did Christ die: past, present, or future?

14. Is there a difference between sins before salvation and sins after salvation?

15. What is threefold sanctification?

16. Does the Bible make a distinction between salvation and service?

17. Does the Bible make a distinction between being delivered from hell and discipleship?

18. What does it mean to become a child of God?

19. Can a child once born become unborn?

20. Is our will greater than God's promise?

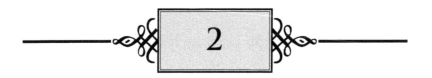

Coming to Terms

If you have not read the preface, please do so. Each part of this book builds upon its previous parts. This is the "line upon line, precept upon precept" teaching design of the Bible known as cognitive scaffolding.

Below is a list of common words and terms in alphabetical order. Which of these terms and words are found in the King James Bible and which are not?

1. atonement
2. depravity
3. elect/elect's/election
4. eternal security
5. foreknowledge/foreknow/foreknew
6. grace
7. irresistible grace
8. limited atonement
9. perseverance

10. predestinate/predestinated

11. saved

12. sovereign/sovereignty

13. total depravity

14. total inability

15. unconditional election

Space to write your answer.

These terms/words are found in the Bible:

- atonement
- elect/elect's/election
- foreknowledge/foreknow/foreknew
- grace
- predestinate/predestinated
- saved

These terms/words are not found in the Bible:

- depravity
- eternal security
- irresistible grace
- limited atonement
- perseverance
- sovereign/sovereignty
- total depravity
- total inability
- unconditional election

At a glance, we can see that the Bible words and terms are far outnumbered by man-made terms and non-Bible words. Let me assure the reader that I believe in all the Bible terms listed above; however, it is Calvin's explanation of these terms that we will examine in the light of scripture. As we go through our study, we will define all of these terms, especially these five common non-Bible terms used to explain Calvinism and hyper-Calvinism:

1. total depravity
2. unconditional election
3. limited atonement
4. irresistible grace
5. perseverance (of the saints)

Rather than clutter our thinking with a pile of definitions, we will define these terms as needed while moving deeper into our study.

Below are some important rules that will assist the reader to come to logical and biblical conclusions by defogging and defining confusing words and terms.

Rules used to help determine truth:

1. Don't force people into a theological dichotomy of camps.

2. Use Bible words and terms whenever possible.

3. Always define the terms.

4. Let the Bible define the words or terms by comparing scripture with scripture.

5. Let the Bible define the words or terms by their context.

6. Draw your conclusions based on logic, not emotionalism.

7. Don't forget to pray.

Rules and examples:

1. Don't force people into a theological dichotomy of camps.

   In other words, we must not assume every issue is an either/or proposition.

   Example: We would be wrong to assume that a person is either a Communist or a Capitalist. There are many other options; here are a few:

a. Socialist

b. Free enterprise system

c. Democrat

d. Representative Republican

e. Monarchist

The United States of America did not begin as a pure democracy, but rather as a representative republic and a free enterprise system. If politics confuse you, don't worry, because many politicians are confused also. My only point here is that we must not stick an oversimplified label on our system of government and by the same token, we must not be too quick to label people as either Calvinist or Arminian. A person may not believe all of what Calvin wrote, yet he may still label himself as a Calvinist. Another person may believe that his soul is eternally secure in Christ, with no chance of losing eternal life, yet he may choose not to use the Calvinist label. The point is that it's not necessary to believe all that Calvin wrote or all of what Arminius wrote. Let's believe all that God wrote and let God himself explain the Bible by comparing scripture with scripture.

Although many Christians label themselves as belonging to the camp of Calvin or Arminius, remember Christianity predates both men. How would you label Christians who never heard either man's explanation of the Bible? The most common misunderstanding is to label anyone who believes in the Bible doctrine of eternal life as a Calvinist.

2. Use Bible words and terms whenever possible.

    The Roman Catholic church mixes Bible and non-Bible terms to the point that Bible scholars unfamiliar with Catholic jargon cannot communicate effectively with a Catholic. Catholics also redefine Bible terms, causing greater confusion. Here are a few commonly used Catholic terms; which of these are Bible terms and which are non-Bible terms? Are these Catholic terms or Bible terms?

    a. Absolution
    b. baptism

c. confirmation

d. dispensation

e. Eucharist

f. mass

g. penance

h. purgatory

i. rosary

j. sacrament

k. saint

These terms/words are found in the Bible:

- baptism

- dispensation

- saint

These terms/words are not found in the Bible:

- Absolution

- confirmation

- Eucharist

- mass

- penance
- purgatory
- rosary
- sacrament

The Bible terms above are indeed found in scripture; however, the "Catholic" meanings are changed and varied from the true Bible meanings. Let's examine one of these terms. Arguably, the most misunderstood Bible term in the English language is the term "saint." Here is the word "saint" in the official Catholic dictionary.

Saint: A name given in the New Testament to Christians generally (Col. 1:2), but early restricted to persons who were eminent for holiness. In the strict sense, saints are those who distinguish themselves by heroic virtue during life and whom the Church honors as saints either by her ordinary universal teaching authority or by a solemn definition called canonization. The Church's official recognition of sanctity implies that the persons are now in heavenly glory, that they may be publicly invoked everywhere, and that their virtues during life or martyr's death are a witness and example to the Christian faithful. (Etym. Latin sanctus, holy, sacred.)

Do you see what happened? The meaning of the word *saint* was changed from the Bible meaning of any Christian in general to some kind of super Christian. These "saints" can be "invoked" or prayed to in public! According to scripture, any living person praying to any dead person is a necromancer; a practice forbidden in the Bible. Unfortunately, the Catholic rather than the Bible definition of the term *saint* has permeated our society. We hear in our society, even from professing Bible-believing Christians, the phrase "I'm no saint!" which, because of the Roman Catholic Church, carries with it the connotation of sinless perfection or a miracle worker. The unbiblical practice of invoking and worshipping "saints" compounds the confusion. The light of scripture declares that no "saint" is to be worshipped, but God only.

"Then saith Jesus unto him, Get thee hence, Satan: for it is written, Thou shalt worship the Lord thy God, and him only shalt thou serve" (Matt. 4:10).

This truth is repeated in Luke 4:8. In truth, every born-again believer is a saint. The unnecessary confusion surrounding the term saint was caused by changing the definition of a Bible word to a man-made definition and term. As we will see, this very practice of changing the meanings of Bible terms causes confusion and is at the heart of our study.

3. Define the term. (The general term as opposed to the specific term)

Much confusion and waste of time can be avoided by defining the terms of any subject before any discussion of that subject. Even the difference between the general definition of a word or term and the specific can cause chaos.

Example 1: A woman goes to a lawyer and asks for a restraining order against her husband. The lawyer asks, "Do you have any grounds?" To which the woman replies, "Yes, I have forty acres!" The lawyer replies, "No. I mean, for example, does your husband beat you up?" The woman says, "No, he never beats me up. I'm up at five every morning and he gets up at six." Ha! So, until the terms are defined and both parties understand what is meant by the terms "grounds" and "beat you up," there is no use in discussing the subject.

On a more serious note:

Example 2: If we choose to study evolution, we must distinguish between the general and specific meanings.

a. General definition of evolution: Change over time.

b. Specific definition of evolution: Changing from one kind of animal into another.

Everyone will agree with the general definition of change over time. Everything in the material world (not God or his Word, etc.) changes over time. It's the second law of thermodynamics, the law of entropy, or in Bible terms, the heavens and earth wax old like a garment. Yes, material things do change over time and if you're still not sure, check out your waistline; gravity always wins! Notice that the natural change over time is to devolve, not evolve. All things tend toward chaos or disorder. I would agree that generally, people and animals change over time, but I would disagree that lower forms of life evolve into higher forms of life. Fish don't turn into birds and monkeys don't turn into humans.

"All flesh is not the same flesh: but there is one kind of flesh of men, another flesh of beasts, another of fishes, and another of birds" (1 Cor. 15:39).

Simply put, Bible believers accept the general definition of evolution while rejecting the specific.

Now let's apply this same distinction of a general term as opposed to the specific Bible term.

Consider the Bible word "church." What does it mean? *Generally*, the word *church* means "any called out assembly." However, *specifically*, there are no less than seven different meanings based on the context in which the word is used. We'll consider all seven contextual definitions later, but for now, let's briefly look at three definitions and see how those various meanings can affect doctrine.

Example 3: The church of Moses.

a. The general definition of the word *church*: a called-out assembly

b. Specifically: An Old Testament called-out assembly comprised of believers and non-believers or a *professing* church; a mixed multitude.

"This is he, that was in the *church* in the wilderness with the angel which spake to him in the mount Sina, and with our fathers: who received the lively oracles to give unto us" (Acts 7:38; emphasis mine).

Here, the Bible is referring to the church of Moses in the wilderness, which is separate and distinct from any New Testament assembly.

Example 4: The local or *professing* church of today.

a. The general definition of the word church: a called-out assembly
b. Specifically: A local New Testament called-out assembly comprised of born-again believers and un-regenerated persons or a *professing* church; a mixed multitude.

If we ask the question, "To whom is the book of Revelation written?" how would you answer?

If you answer, "The church," then we must ask, "What do you mean by church?"

- Born-again believers only (the possessing church).
- The local churches (the professing church).

Please take some time to consider your answer. The book of Revelation is not written to born-again believers only, but also to the local churches!

"John *to the seven churches* which are in Asia: Grace be unto you, and peace, from him which is, and which was, and which is to come; and from the seven Spirits which are before his throne" (Rev. 1:4; emphasis mine).

Why is it important to know whether the book of Revelation is written to the professing church or the possessing church; to the local churches or the born-again body of Christ? The answer is one of context. If we don't know the proper context of a passage or book, we will misapply the scriptures. Any local church may consist of saved and unsaved persons; those who have been born again as well as those who have never been saved. It should be noted that while every believer possessed by the Spirit of Christ should profess Christ as Saviour, some may not. Also, a person may profess Christ as Saviour and may not be a possessing Christian because he was never born again. Moreover, it's not one's profession that makes someone a believer, but rather being possessed by the Spirit of God.

"Now if any man have not the Spirit of Christ, he is none of his" (Rom. 8:9b).

A great deal of doctrinal confusion has resulted simply because scholars often neglect to rightly divide the word of truth by recognizing that the *specific* context of the book of the Revelation of Jesus Christ is to the *professing* local churches and not the possessing church of born-again believers. Again, John tells us that the book is addressed to "the seven churches which are in Asia" (Rev. 1:4), which were local churches. The point once more being that in any local church, we expect to see a mixed multitude of saved and unsaved souls. This is what is often referred to as a professing church because there may be persons therein who claim or profess to be saved but are not possessed with the Spirit of God. Further, this is why we find in Revelation 3, written to a single local church, such opposing language as "He that overcometh, the same shall be clothed in white raiment" and "thou art wretched, and miserable, and poor, and blind, and naked." This only makes sense if we realize that Revelation is written to the local or professing churches made up of *both* saved and lost.

At the risk of being redundant, Christ specif-ically addresses the "clothed" and the "naked" in the same chapter because he is addressing the *professing* local churches comprised of both saved and lost. Revelation is not written to believers only, i.e., the born-again body of Christ, but to believers and unbelievers within the local churches. Are you still unconvinced? Consider this question, "If the book of Revelation is written to born-again believers only, then how do we explain Revelation 22:17?"

"And the Spirit and the bride say, Come. And let him that heareth say, Come. And let him that is athirst come. And whosoever will, let him take the water of life freely" (Rev. 22:17).

If the book of Revelation is only written to believers possessed by the Spirit and belonging to the bride of Christ, then why would the bride invite the bride to come? This would make no sense and is not what's happening. In this text, the bride of Christ (those born-again persons, possessed by the Spirit of God as a single body) is inviting unsaved persons within the *professing* local churches as well as others outside the professing local church (whosoever is reading) to become part of the bride of Christ, which is sometimes referred to as the *possessing* church. Understanding that the book of Revelation is not written to born-again believers only, but to all professing persons in the local churches, both saved and lost, makes its contextual doctrines much less confusing and much more understandable. Please notice that Christ addresses "he that overcometh" and "him that overcometh" in *each* and every one of the seven local churches! Why? Because he knows that there are Spirit-possessing, born-again believers in each. Here is a Bible definition of an overcomer:

"Who is he that overcometh the world, but he that believeth that Jesus is the Son of God?" (1 John 5:5).

Born-again believers are overcomers and comprise the body of Christ; also called the *possessing* church. These believers exist within the local churches or *professing* churches made up of both saved and lost. Notice that Christ makes promises to all of the overcomers in each local church.

Ephesus = "To him that overcometh will I give to eat of the tree of life" (Rev. 2:7).

Smyrna = "He that overcometh shall not be hurt of the second death" (Rev. 2:11b).

Pergamos = "To him that overcometh will I give to eat of the hidden manna" (Rev. 2:17).

Thyatira = "And he that overcometh" (Rev. 2:26).

Sardis = "He that overcometh, the same shall be clothed in white raiment; and I will not blot out his name out of the book of life, but I will confess his name before my Father, and before his angels" (Rev. 3:5).

Philadelphia = "Him that overcometh will I make a pillar in the temple of my God" (Rev. 3:12).

Laodiceans = "To him that overcometh will I grant to sit with me in my throne" (Rev. 3:21).

The local church at Laodicea is perhaps the clearest example of a mixed multitude consisting of redeemed and unredeemed souls in the same local assembly. Christ is seen on the outside of the local church, knocking to get in! Please note how Christ addresses both the redeemed and unredeemed groups.

A. Christ's language to the overcomers, i.e., the saved and Spirit-*possessing* individuals within the local church at the Laodicean church.

"To him that overcometh will I grant to sit with me in my throne, even as I also overcame, and am set down with my Father in his throne" (Rev. 3:21).

B. Christ's language to the unsaved, non-over-comer, *non-possessing* individuals within the same *professing* local church.

> So then because thou art luke-warm, and neither cold nor hot, *I will spue thee out of my mouth*. Because thou sayest, I am rich, and increased with goods, and have need of nothing; and knowest not that thou art wretched, and miserable, and poor, and *blind*, and *naked*. (Rev. 3:16–17; emphasis mine)

When the spewing out of verse 16 is applied to salvation, (as followers of Arminian doctrine do) it must be applied to the un-regenerated *professing* Laodicean church members who were never born again and not the born-again *possessing* church members. Please realize here that these *professing* church members are *spued out* because they are spiritually "blind" and "naked" not because they stopped believing, fell from grace or stopped doing good works. To be clear, when the spewing out is applied to individuals, the context reveals that these "naked" and "blind" persons were never born-again or truly *possessing* believers at all. These persons within the local church of Laodicea were merely *professing* believers. In simple terms, the "spewing out" has nothing to do with a saved person becoming unsaved, but rather it is the unsaved professing person being rejected for being spiritually blind and having not the Spirit.

Once again, we must never make the mistake of assuming that because this book is written to the churches that it is written to believers only. Moreover, the most wonderful and absolutely beautiful part of God's love is seen in the fact that even *after* the Lord declares that he will spew out the naked and blind ones, Christ himself proceeds to offer them raiment (clothing) and eyesalve to cure their naked and blind condition! Thank God for his mercy and grace! Observe Christ's rebuke and counsel to the lost within the professing church.

Because thou sayest, I am rich, and increased with goods, and have need of nothing; and knowest not that thou art wretched, and miserable, and poor, and *blind*, and *naked*: *I counsel* thee to buy of me gold tried in the fire, that *thou mayest* be rich; and white raiment, that *thou mayest* be clothed, and that the shame of thy nakedness do not appear; and anoint thine eyes with eyesalve, that *thou mayest* see. As many as I love, I rebuke and chasten: be zealous therefore, and *repent*. (Rev. 3:17–22; emphasis mine)

Christ's promises to those within any church, willing to repent and allow him into their heart.

Behold, I stand at the door, and knock: *if any man* hear my voice, and open the door, *I will come in* to him, *and will sup with him,* and he with me. *To him that overcometh will I grant to sit with me in my throne,* even as I also overcame, and am set down with my Father in his throne. (Rev. 3:20–21; emphasis mine)

The only way that the language to the churches of Revelation makes theological sense is to realize that Christ is speaking to both the saved and lost within the local churches. This is exactly the same language expressing that some will hear and some won't that is demonstrated in chapter 3 verse 22.

"He that hath an ear, let him hear what the Spirit saith unto the churches" (Rev. 3:22).

Not surprisingly, we clearly see the Holy Spirit acknowledging both the saved and unsaved in the final two chapters of Revelation. The born-again believers or overcomers are encouraged via a reminder of their inheritance and standing in Christ, while the unsaved or non-overcomers are invited to become part of the bride of Christ.

To the believer in Christ: "He that overcometh shall inherit all things; and I will be his God, and he shall be my son" (Rev. 21:7).

To the would-be believer not yet saved: "And the Spirit and the bride say, Come. And let him that heareth say, Come. And let him that is athirst come. And whosoever will, let him take the water of life freely" (Rev. 22:17).

We must conclude that the context of the book of Revelation is to the professing local churches made up of saved and lost souls and not to born-again believers only. Understanding this fact yields great dividends relating to other very important doctrines as well.

Example 5: The born again or possessing church.

a. The general definition: A called-out assembly.

b. Specifically: A New Testament called out assembly comprised of born-again believers only, those possessing the Spirit of God, or simply the *possessing* church.

"And he is the head of *the body, the church*: who is the beginning, the firstborn from the dead; that in all things he might have the preeminence" (Col. 1:18; emphasis mine).

Here the Bible is referring to Christ as a single head of a single body. This verse does not say that Christ is the head of the bodies, plural, but the head of a single body. There are indeed many local churches containing many believers, but the body of Christ transcends all local churches and includes all believers in a single body.

> "For by one Spirit are *we all* baptized into *one body*, whether we be Jews or Gentiles, whether we be bond or free; and have been all made to drink into one Spirit" (1 Cor. 12:13; emphasis mine).

This verse is not referring to a single local church body for several reasons:

- The Spirit of God doesn't baptize persons into a local church.
- All believers are not baptized into the same local church.
- All Jews and all Gentiles are not baptized into a single local church.
- The Bible here is referring to a spiritual baptism, not a water baptism.

Note: If this verse were referring to water baptism, it would read something like, "For by one pastor are we all baptized into one local fellowship."

The important lesson to remember is that we have seen that a general definition for a word such as "church" is not always sufficient in some cases. A more specific contextual definition is needed to differentiate between any general called-out assembly and a specific called-out assembly. In other words, the church of Moses is different from the New Testament local churches and the born-again church of all New Testament believers, is distinct from the local churches. The local or professing churches are populated by saved and lost persons while the born-again church is comprised of saved persons only. We will refer to the former as the professing church and the latter as the possessing church. Failure to make these distinctions, regardless of which terms are used, is to wreak havoc on clear Bible doctrines.

4. Let the Bible define the words or terms by comparing scripture with scripture.

    Most of us are probably familiar with the technique of comparing scripture with scripture.

    Example 1: The parable of the sower in the gospel of Matthew.

> Hear ye therefore the parable of the sower. When any one heareth the word of the kingdom, and understandeth it not, then cometh the wicked one, and catcheth away that which was sown in his heart. This is he which received seed by the way side. But he that received the seed into stony places, the same is he that heareth the word, and *anon* with joy receiveth it; (Matt. 13:18–20; emphasis mine)

    What in the world does the word *anon* mean? Do we need a Greek scholar or a computer program to tell us what anon means? No, we simply compare scripture with scripture. Here is the parable of the sower in the gospel of Mark.

> Hearken; Behold, there went out a sower to sow: And it came to pass, as he sowed, some fell by the way side, and the fowls of the air came and devoured it up. And some fell on stony ground, where it had not much earth; and *immediately* it sprang up, because it had no depth of earth: (Mark 4:3–5; emphasis mine)

The simple process of comparing scripture with scripture teaches us that *anon* means "immediately." Here is a fun and important example that the Lord showed me one day while having my devotions. What is the Bible definition for the soul?

Example 2: The soul of man.

> "For what is a man profited, if he shall gain the whole world, and

lose *his own soul?* or what shall a man give in exchange for *his soul?*" (Matt. 16:26; emphasis mine).

The parallel account in Mark.

"For what shall it profit a man, if he shall gain the whole world, and lose *his own soul?* Or what shall a man give in exchange for *his soul?*" (Mark 8:36–37; emphasis mine).

The same parallel account in Luke.

"For what is a man advantaged, if he gain the whole world, and lose *himself*, or be cast away?" (Luke 9:25; emphasis mine).

We have here a great example of the synoptic gospels. That is to say, we have three gospels telling the same story in a slightly different way, but it is the subtle difference which defines our term. Notice that Matthew and Mark use the term *his own soul,* but in Luke, the term is *himself.* The Bible definition therefore for the *soul* is a person's own *self.*

Another way to compare scripture with scripture to define words is to understand the Bible use of Hebrew poetry. Much of the Old Testament is written in a poetic style of Hebrew. In this poetic style, the writer of scripture uses rhyming thought patterns instead of rhyming word patterns as is common in English. This very important teaching will be used more extensively later in our study, but let's consider a few examples now.

Example 3: Lamp and light.

"Thy word is a *lamp* unto my feet, and a *light* unto my path" (Ps. 119:105; emphasis mine).

Note the matching or rhyming themes of God's word being both a "lamp" and a "light" unto the psalmist's path. A lamp, of course, is a type of light, thus the matching theme.

Example 4: Zion and Jerusalem

"Rejoice greatly, O daughter of *Zion*; shout, O daughter of *Jerusalem*: behold, thy King cometh unto thee: he is just, and having salvation; lowly, and riding upon an ass, and upon a colt the foal of an ass" (Zech. 9:9; emphasis mine).

We see several rhyming thought patterns; one being that Zion is another name for Jerusalem.

Example 5: Israel and Jacob.

"O ye seed of *Israel* his servant, ye children of *Jacob*, his chosen ones" (1 Chron. 16:13; emphasis mine).

Here, Israel is matched with Jacob; Israel and Jacob being the same person with Israel being the name given by the heavenly Father and Jacob given by the earthly.

Example 6: Seed and children.

"O ye *seed* of Israel his servant, ye *children* of Jacob, his chosen ones" (1 Chron. 16:13; emphasis mine).

Using the same verse again, we can see a deeper level of truth in the words seed and children. If someone asks, "What does the Bible mean when it says Jacob's seed?" we can here teach that Jacob's seed is a reference to his children.

Now let's look at a couple of New Testament verses to see how the Bible defines itself without using poetry. If someone asked you for a Bible definition for love, what would you tell him? I encourage you to stop reading and try to use the Bible (or Bible computer program) to come up with a definition that defines love before you continue.

Example 7: The Bible definition of love.

"For God so loved the world, that he gave his only begotten Son, that whosoever believeth in him should not perish, but have everlasting life" (John 3:16).

Did you see the Bible definition in the text? How about now?

"For God so *loved* the world, that he *gave* his only begotten Son, that whosoever believeth in him should not perish, but have everlasting life" (John 3:16; emphasis mine).

The Bible definition for love is giving. Still not convinced? Please consider example 8. Try again to find the Bible definition for love in the next example.

Example 8: Another Bible definition of love.

"Husbands, love your wives,
even as Christ also loved the church,
and gave himself for it" (Eph. 5:25).

Was it easier that time? The Bible definition for love is giving.

"Husbands, love your wives,
even as Christ also *loved* the church,
and *gave* himself for it" (Eph. 5:25).

We give our time and ourselves to the things we love and for the ones we love. A person who says they love their spouse, but never gives of their time or self has no love. We have shown that Bible words or terms can often be defined by comparing scripture with scripture.

Let's squeeze in one more!

Example 9: One last Bible definition of love.

"He that loveth not knoweth not God; for *God is love*" (1 John 4:8; emphasis mine).

The Bible declares that God *is* love which means He is *all* love or as we would say "God is all loving." Since God is *all* loving and love is giving, we should see this giving love expressed to *all*.

God that made the world and all things therein, seeing that he is Lord of heaven and earth, dwelleth not in temples made with hands; Neither is worshipped with men's hands, as though he needed any thing, seeing he *giveth to all* life, and breath, and *all* things; (Acts 17:24–25; emphasis mine)

5. Let the Bible define the words or terms by their context.

Since we have studied the word "church" in part already, let's see how this word can be defined by its context. As was mentioned previously in section 3, there are no less than seven different meanings of the word "church" based on the context in which the word is used. Here is a brief overview of the seven various meanings of the word church.

The seven different meanings of the word "church" in the Bible.

a. The general term for any called-out assembly.

b. The called-out assembly of Moses (Acts 7:37–38).

c. The called-out assembly of John the Baptist.

d. The called-out assembly that the Lord Jesus started before Pentecost consisting of saved and lost including Judas Iscariot.

e. The local assembly point, gathering place or building used by professing believers.

f. The local called-out assembly of the professing believers (a called-out assembly consisting of both saved and lost).

g. The called-out assembly of born-again believers only.

Let's now define the word "church" by its context. The church of born-again believers did not exist before Pentecost in Acts 2. Yes, the Spirit of God existed, worked, moved, and filled persons before Pentecost, but the Holy Ghost never permanently sealed believers prior to Pentecost. Today, all born-again believers are permanently sealed with the Spirit of God; something that never happened before in history and will never happen again or be duplicated on earth after the possessing church of Christ is removed. Generally speaking, most Bible references of the word "church" before Acts 2 are not referring to the born-again church because no one was born again or sealed with the Holy Ghost before Acts 2.

An example of the church definition 1: Any called-out assembly.

All references of the word "church" generally refer to any called-out assembly.

An example of the church definition 2: The called-out assembly of Moses.

> This is that *Moses*, which said unto the children of Israel, A prophet shall the Lord your God raise up unto you of your brethren, like unto me; him shall ye hear. This is he, that was in the *church* in the wilderness with the angel which spake to him in the mount Sina, and with our fathers: who received the lively oracles to give unto us: (Acts 7:37–38; emphasis mine)

This is an example of how a New Testament passage after Acts 2 clearly defines itself as an Old

Testament assembly because of the reference to Moses.

An example of the church definition 3: The called-out assembly of John the Baptist.

> "Then came to him *the disciples of John*, saying, Why do we and the Pharisees fast oft, but thy disciples fast not?" (Matt. 9:14; emphasis mine).

Although the word "church" is never used in the Bible to directly refer to John and his disciples, John clearly had his own "church" or called-out assembly, separate and distinct from Christ and His disciples (Matt. 11:2, Mark 2:18, Luke 5:33, Luke 7:18, Luke 7:19, Luke 11:1, John 1:35, John 3:25, John 4:1).

An example of the church definition 4: The called-out assembly that Jesus started before Pentecost.

"And if he shall neglect to hear them, tell it unto the *church*: but if he neglect to hear the church, let him be unto thee as an heathen man and a publican" (Matt. 18:17; emphasis mine).

Please remember that Judas Iscariot was a hand-picked, called-out disciple of the Lord. He was within the local assembly and part of the ministry.

"Jesus answered them, Have not I chosen you twelve, and one of you is a devil?" (John 6:70).

"That he may take part of this ministry and apostleship, from which Judas by transgression fell, that he might go to his own place" (Acts 1:25).

Again, Matthew 18:17 is not referring to the born-again body and bride of Christ because believers were not born again or sealed with the Holy Ghost until Acts 2 and the day of Pentecost. Chronologically speaking, Matthew 18 is not only before Pentecost, but also before the death, burial, and resurrection of our Lord. All New Testament scripture written before Acts 2, although physically contained in the New Testament, is written on Old Testament ground before the birthday of the born-again church. There are a few references before Acts 2 alluding to the yet future possessing church, which we will consider later.

An example of the church definition 5: The local assembly point, gathering place or building used by professing believers.

"But if I tarry long, that thou mayest know how thou oughtest to behave thyself *in the house of God*, which is the *church* of the living God, the pillar and ground of the truth" (1 Tim. 3:15; emphasis mine).

In a physical way, the church building can be referred to as the house of God, the outward visible meeting place of the believers. I do realize that there are several deeper applications to this verse as well, but let's agree that when we want children to behave in God's house, we use this verse!

An example of the church definition 6: The local called-out assembly of the professing believers.

And unto the angel of the *church* of the *Laodiceans* write; These things saith the Amen, the faithful and true witness, the beginning of the creation of God; I know thy works, that thou art neither cold nor hot: I would thou wert cold or hot. So then because thou art lukewarm, and neither cold nor hot, I will spue thee out of my mouth. Because thou sayest, I am rich, and increased with goods, and have need of nothing; and knowest not that thou art wretched, and miserable, and poor, and blind, and naked. (Rev. 3:14–17; emphasis mine)

Obviously, there were individuals in this local church, as in most every local church, who weren't saved or born again. When God calls some of them "blind" and "naked," he is speaking to the lost within the local called-out assembly. However, when addressing the born-again believers or "overcomers" in the same local church assembly of Laodicea, the Lord says in Revelation 3:21:

"To him that overcometh will I grant to sit with me in my throne, even as I also overcame, and am set down with my Father in his throne" (Rev. 3:21).

An overcomer being a born-again or "born of God" believer in Jesus Christ.

"For whatsoever is born of God overcometh the world: and this is the victory that overcometh the world, even our faith. Who is he that overcometh the world, but he that believeth that Jesus is the Son of God?" (1 John 5:4–5).

The obvious conclusion is that the churches of Revelation were local churches comprised of both saved and lost individuals, which we will call professing churches.

An example of the church definition 7: The called-out assembly of the body and bride of Christ consisting of born-again believers only.

"For the husband is the head of the wife, even as *Christ* is *the head* of *the church*: and he is the saviour of the body" (Eph. 5:23; emphasis mine).

We acknowledge that Christ should be the head of every local church, but this verse is not speaking to that. This verse declares that Christ is the head of the church; a singular church. Christ may or may not be the head of some churches, but there is a single church body of which Christ is the head. The believer is placed into this church body by the Spirit of God at the moment of salvation and not by water baptism.

"For by *one Spirit* are we all baptized into *one body*, whether we be Jews or Gentiles, whether we be bond or free; and have been all made to drink into *one Spirit*" (1 Cor. 12:13; emphasis mine).

Unlike a local church which may contain lost souls, this church body is comprised of born-again believers only and will be assembled in toto at the Lord's coming in 1 Thessalonians 4:13–18. For those who may have been taught that the word "church" always denotes a local church, this subject will be considered in more detail in a later chapter.

"And I say also unto thee, That thou art Peter, and upon this rock I will build my church; and the gates of hell shall not prevail against it" (Matt. 16:18).

This is an example of an exception to the rule, because the Lord Jesus is not referring to any existing called-out assembly, but rather a *future* assembly. You may ask, "How do we know this?" Notice the language, the Lord doesn't say, "…upon this rock I am building my church…," but "…upon this rock *I will build* my church…," alluding to a future church body. We know this today as the born-again church or the possessing church. Our Lord would begin this church on the day of Pentecost when the Holy Ghost began sealing individuals after his resurrection and ascension. All recipients of the Holy Ghost are part of the born-again possessing church.

An example of multiple references: Both 6 and 7.

"Praising God, and having favour with all the people. And the Lord added to the church daily such as should be saved" (Acts 2:47).

In this verse, the Lord added to the local assembly daily, but more importantly to the body of born-again believers in Christ. The Lord added to the professing church as well as the possessing church.

Another example of multiple references: Both 5 and 6.

"For this cause have I sent unto you Timotheus, who is my beloved son, and faithful in the Lord, who shall bring you into remembrance of my ways which be in Christ, as I teach every where in every church" (1 Cor. 4:17).

Now we have a clearer understanding of how the text defines the word church.

6. Draw your conclusions from logic not emotionalism.

One person speaking with me about Calvinism came to the conclusion that since many famous preachers held Calvinistic doctrine that Calvinism must be correct. This is a nonlogical emotional argument. God often blesses us not because we're sinful, but in spite of the fact that we're sinful. Did God bless Jacob because he was a deceiver or in spite of the fact that Jacob was a deceiver? Isn't it more likely that God blessed these famous men because of their personal sacrifice to preach the gospel, to pray faithfully and go where they were sent, rather than because they held to Calvinistic doctrine? History has recorded the fact that God used many famous Arminian preachers as well. Most likely, God blessed them because of their personal sacrifice to preach the gospel, pray faithfully, and go where they were sent and not because they held to Arminian doctrine. Other emotional arguments include positions such as "My dad and grandpa were the holiest people I ever knew, therefore their theological position must be correct!" or "I was raised in this belief system and I'm not going to change!" Dear reader, it's not my intent to "change" anyone, but rather to ask you to "consider" that upon which you base your theology. A person isn't correct in their theology because they have written many books, had large followings, or lived holy lives. The great apostle Paul wrote the following: "Be ye followers of me, even as I also am of Christ" (1 Cor. 11:1).

Even though the apostle Paul was a great man, he was still a man. Paul knew that he wasn't sinless; therefore, he admonished those who knew him, as well as believers today, to only follow him "as" he followed Christ. Where Paul may have fallen short of living the perfect teachings of Christ, Paul has wisely advised us to not follow him, but Christ. Let's apply this same principle to the doctrine of eternal life. Where the teachings of Calvin and Arminius may stray from what the Bible actually says, let us follow Christ.

7. Don't forget to pray.

So far, we have considered six rules used to help determine truth. Let's consider one more. Study and critical thinking are indispensable when searching for truth, but without the guidance of the Holy Spirit, Bible truth will elude us. As we pray and apply our hearts to seek sincere truth and learning, these verses speak for themselves.

"Ye lust, and have not: ye kill, and desire to have, and cannot obtain: ye fight and war, yet ye have not, because ye ask not" (James 4:2).

"He taketh the wise in their own craftiness: and the counsel of the froward is carried headlong" (Job 5:13).

"For the wisdom of this world is foolishness with God. For it is written, He taketh the wise in their own craftiness" (1 Cor. 3:19).

"Professing themselves to be wise, they became fools" (Rom. 1:22).

"I am the vine, ye are the branches: He that abideth in me, and I in him, the same bringeth forth much fruit: for without me ye can do nothing" (John 15:5).

"Ask, and it shall be given you; seek, and ye shall find; knock, and it shall be opened unto you" (Matt. 7:7).

"And I say unto you, Ask, and it shall be given you; seek, and ye shall find; knock, and it shall be opened unto you" (Luke 11:9).

"Howbeit when he, the Spirit of truth, is come, he will guide you into all truth: for he shall not speak of himself; but whatsoever he shall hear, that shall he speak: and he will shew you things to come" (John 16:13).

"For rebellion is as the sin of witchcraft, and stubbornness is as iniquity and idolatry" (1 Sam. 15:23).

A word about terms:

While it is best to use authentic Bible words and terms whenever possible, sometimes we use man-made or synthetic terms to clarify our point. Using such terms and words is fine when they are well defined and understood. For example, most Christians use the term "rapture" for the coming of the Lord for born-again believers, which is perfectly fine. Some believers refuse to use the term because it doesn't appear in the Bible, but neither do the words trinity or Bible appear in scripture. These terms are generally understood and are in popular use. We could substitute for trinity the Bible term "Godhead" and the terms "scripture" and "the Word of God" for the Bible. Ultimately, the most important point isn't which terms are used, but which terms are understood. If everyone understood the term "Godhead" or "triune Godhead," this would be best, but the word *trinity*, if properly understood, expresses essentially the same idea. Please note that it isn't pragmatic to define every possible term in this study, but simply know that people use various terms to express the same basic meaning. Many disagreements are simply a matter of semantics.

3

When Did the Church Begin?

In chapter 1, we saw seven rules that can be used in defining Bible words and terms. Before we apply some of those rules to the study of the doctrine of eternal life as understood by Calvin and Arminius, let's apply them to another subject. If someone asked you the question, "When did the church begin?" how would you answer? If your answer is when the Lord Jesus called out his disciples, Acts 2, or any other similar answer, you have missed the entire point of chapter 1. The answer you give is contingent upon what is meant by the word "church." As we have seen, there are no less than seven different definitions for the word "church" based upon each individual Bible context. The answer then to "when did the church begin?" is contextual and contingent upon how we define the word "church." My intention is not to make a full study of the word church in the Bible, but to do a quick study and apply those results to our larger study of eternal life. Indeed, if we fail to understand how a single word such as "church" can have multiple meanings in the Bible, we will also fail to see where the teachings of Calvin and Arminius can differ with what the Bible actually teaches. What then is the answer to the question, "When did the church begin?" The proper answer is, "What do you mean by the word church?" or "Please define the word church."

We have seen that the word church has no less than seven different Bible meanings depending on the context in which it is used. If the reader is in doubt as to the multiple meanings of the word church, I invite you to look up *all* references of the words "church" and "churches" and study them in their contexts as I have done. The following is a quick reference of the various definitions of the word church.

1. The general definition: Any called-out assembly.
2. Specifically: Moses's called-out assembly in the wilderness (mixed multitude of saved and lost).
3. Specifically: The called-out assembly of John Baptist's disciples separate and distinct from the Lord's disciples (Matt. 9:14, Matt. 11:2, Mark

2:18, Luke 5:33, Luke 7:18, Luke 7:19, Luke 11:1, John 1:35, John 3:25, John 4:1).

Note: Although the Bible does not specifically refer to John's disciples as a "church," the same could be argued regarding Jesus' called-out assembly. In Matthew 16:18, the Lord was referring to a future church, which he had not started while in Matthew 18:17, it could be argued that the Lord was citing the established church assembly or synagogue. The word "church" can be used in a generic way meaning any called-out assembly (potentially saved and lost).

4. Specifically: the called-out assembly of Jesus' disciples (saved and lost).
5. Specifically: The assembly point, gathering place or building (saved and lost).
6. Specifically: The called-out assembly of professing New Testament believers (saved and lost).
7. Specifically: The body of born-again believers only, to be ultimately assembled in heaven (saved only).

So then, if someone asks, "When did the church begin?" and they are reading Acts 7:37–38, the answer will be different than if they are reading Matthew 18:17.

> This is that *Moses*, which said unto the children of Israel, A prophet shall the Lord your God raise up unto you of your brethren, like unto me; him shall ye hear. This is he, that was in the *church* in the wilderness with the angel which spake to him in the mount Sina, and with our fathers: who received the lively oracles to give unto us. (Acts 7:37–38; emphasis mine)
>
> "And if he shall neglect to hear them, tell it unto the *church*: but if he neglect to hear the church, let him be unto thee as an heathen man and a publican" (Matt. 18:17; emphasis mine).

The church of Moses was generally the same type as John Baptist's and the church of the Lord's disciples in Matthew 18:17 in that they were all called-out assemblies, consisting potentially of both redeemed and non-redeemed persons. Concerning the church of Moses, we read in Exodus 12:38:

"And a *mixed multitude* went up also with them; and flocks, and herds, even very much cattle" (Exod. 12:38; emphasis mine).

In like manner, the church mentioned in Matthew 18:17 (whether we identify it as the Lord's disciples or the local synagogue) was a called-out assembly of both redeemed and non-redeemed persons. If this doesn't set well with the reader, let me remind you what the Lord Jesus said about his own called-out assembly of handpicked disciples.

"Jesus answered them, Have not I chosen you twelve, and *one of you is a devil?*" (John 6:70; emphasis mine).

This was the Lord's handpicked "church," which included Judas Iscariot or as my grandson once called him

"Judas the scary it." Judas was also sent out into the world to do miracles.

> And when he had called unto him *his twelve disciples*, he gave them power against unclean spirits, to cast them out, and to heal all manner of sickness and all manner of disease. Now the names of the twelve apostles are these; The first, Simon, who is called Peter, and Andrew his brother; James the son of Zebedee, and John his brother; Philip, and Bartholomew; Thomas, and Matthew the publican; James the son of Alphaeus, and Lebbaeus, whose surname was Thaddaeus; Simon the Canaanite, and *Judas Iscariot*, who also betrayed him. These twelve Jesus sent forth, and commanded them, saying, Go not into the way of the Gentiles, and into any city of the Samaritans enter ye not: But go rather to the lost sheep of the house of Israel. And as ye go, *preach*, saying, *The kingdom*

of heaven is at hand. *Heal* the sick, *cleanse* the lepers, *raise the dead, cast out devils*: freely ye have received, freely give. (Matt. 10:1–8; emphasis mine)

Yes, Judas Iscariot was a part of the pre-Pentecost church or assembly of Jesus Christ. So, we realize that the Old Testament church of Moses was similar in some ways to the Lord's called-out assembly of handpicked disciples, yet they were not exactly the same. These assemblies were, of course, distinguished by two different leaders; Moses being one and Christ being another, and the time factor differentiates them as well. This one factor of time more than anything else causes us to render two different answers to the question, "When did the church begin?" Without going into further detail here, let's agree that the church of Moses and the church of Jesus' disciples before Pentecost were the same in some ways yet different in others.

Now we have two different answers to the "When did the church begin?" question, depending upon the context of scripture and the definition of the word church. Using this method, we can list six different answers to the same question, "When did the church begin?"

1. "When did the church begin?"

    Church: Any called-out assembly.

    Answer: We must specify which one.

2. "When did the church begin?"

    Church: Acts 7:37–38. The called-out assembly of Moses in the wilderness (saved and lost).

    Answer: The church or assembly of Moses began when Moses led them out of Egypt.

3. "When did the church begin?"

    Church: The called-out assembly of John Baptist's disciples (potentially both saved and lost).

    Answer: Before the Lord Jesus began calling out his disciples.

4. "When did the church begin?"

    Church: The called-out assembly of Jesus' disciples before Pentecost (saved and lost).

    Answer: Shortly after the Lord Jesus began his earthly ministry and before the beheading of John the Baptist.

5. The assembly point, gathering place or building (potentially populated by both saved and lost).

   Answer: We must specify which one.

6. The local church or the professing church body. Specifically: The called-out assembly of professing New Testament believers (potentially populated by both saved and lost).

   Answer: On the day of Pentecost.

We have seen how the word "church" in the Bible can refer to called-out assemblies of various types such as the Old Testament church of Moses or the church of Jesus' disciples before Pentecost. The word "church" in the Bible also refers to local assemblies potentially made up of saved and lost persons. The term local church is not to be confused with the bride and body of Christ, which is a body consisting of born-again believers only. So then, the *local* New Testament church may be referred to as the *professing* church, while the body consisting of only born-again believers may be called the *possessing* church. The local or professing church can be defined as any local assembly gathered in the name of Christ, being comprised potentially of both redeemed and non-redeemed individuals.

Here is an important observation.

A. Moses had a professing church consisting of both saved and lost or redeemed and non-redeemed.

"And a *mixed multitude* went up also with them…" (Exod. 12:38a; emphasis mine).

B. The Lord Jesus had a professing church consisting of both saved and lost or redeemed and non-redeemed.

"Jesus answered them, Have not I chosen you twelve, and one of you is a devil?" (John 6:70).

C. The local churches or assemblies today are professing churches made up of both saved and lost or redeemed and non-redeemed individuals. Believers, of course, can trust the Saviour to know the difference.

"Nevertheless the foundation of God standeth sure, having this seal, *The Lord knoweth them that are his.* And, Let every one that nameth the name of Christ depart from iniquity" (2 Tim. 2:19; emphasis mine).

The Bible distinguishes unsaved church members from members in the body of Christ by the Spirit of Christ.

"But ye are not in the flesh, but in the Spirit, if so be that the Spirit of God dwell in you. Now *if any man have not the Spirit of Christ, he is none of his*" (Rom. 8:9; emphasis mine).

So then, an unsaved person may be a part of a local church body or professing church, but not part of the possessing church or body of Christ, whereas a born-again believer may be part of both. Failure to make this distinction results in not rightly dividing the word of truth. The local church is not the same as the body of all born-again believers. Although local churches are called by name in the Bible, the term "local church" is never used in scripture. Many doctrinal issues arise when believers fail to differentiate between the varied uses of the word church, especially these three.

a. The church of Jesus' *professing* disciples before Pentecost.

b. The local, *professing* church from Pentecost on.

c. The *possessing* church of born-again, sealed believers only since Pentecost.

It's absolutely necessary to recognize the differences between these three distinct types of churches if we are to rightly divide the word of truth.

Example 1: Context: The church of Jesus' disciples *before* Pentecost and before the Lord's death, burial, and resurrection. In Matthew 16, the Lord spoke of a *future church* in addition to the one he himself had already begun before Matthew 5. This is why Christ used such unusual language when he said, "I will build my church" not "I am building," "I will continue to build," or "I am adding to my church," but "I will build my church."

> "And I say also unto thee, That thou art Peter, and upon this rock *I will build* my church; and the gates of hell shall not prevail against it" (Matt. 16:18; emphasis mine).

If I say, "I will change the oil in my car," I'm referring to an event yet future. This is the exact language of our Saviour, not "I am building…"

and not "I am adding to my church…," but I will build my church. When the Lord Jesus said in Matthew 16:18, "I will build my church," he was referring to a yet future church very different from all preciously mentioned churches. We will look deeper into this truth later in this chapter.

Let's now consider one final definition of the word church.

7. "When did the church begin?"

Church: A single body comprised of born-again believers only, sealed with the Holy Ghost regardless of any local church affiliation. We will refer to this group as the born-again or possessing church, as opposed to the professing church, which is the local church.

Answer: On the day of Pentecost in Acts 2 after the beheading of John the Baptist and after the death, burial, resurrection, and ascension of our Lord and Saviour Jesus Christ.

For your consideration, concerning the born-again church:

If the church existed before the cross, she had a *physical* head.

If the church existed after the cross, but before the resurrection, she had a *mortal* head.

If the church existed before the ascension, she had an *earthly* head.

If the church came into existence after the ascension on the day of Pentecost, she has a *heavenly, exalted* head! Also, she began her existence with the promised coming of the Holy Ghost, and she will continue her growth until the promised extraction of the Holy Ghost.

What are some of the characteristics of the possessing church?

A. Is the possessing church denominational?
   Is the possessing church made up of all members of all denominations?
   Is the possessing church made up of only denominational members?
   Is the possessing church made up of only born-again denominational church members?

B. Is the possessing church singular?

C. Is the possessing church physical or spiritual?

D. Is the possessing church eternal or temporal?

E. Is the possessing church visible or invisible?

Is the possessing church denominational?

Is the possessing church made up of all members of all denominations? No. Not all church members are born-again. In fact, some denominations don't believe in being born-again! There are, of course, false brethren.

> In journeyings often, in perils of waters, in perils of robbers, in perils by mine own countrymen, in perils by the heathen, in perils in the city, in perils in the wilderness, in perils in the sea, in perils among *false brethren.* (2 Cor. 11:26; emphasis mine)
>
> And that because of *false brethren* unawares brought in, who came in privily to spy out our liberty which we have in

Christ Jesus, that they might bring us into bondage: (Gal. 2:4; emphasis mine)

Whereas some denominations have a greater percentage of born-again believers than others, we are not attempting to determine which denomination is the oldest, largest, best or most important. Please draw your own conclusions there. Neither am I promoting ecumenism, but the necessity of Christ's born-again church to cross denominational lines. My main point here is that every born-again person has the same gift of eternal life regardless of their affiliation or lack thereof, with any denomination. It should be obvious to any thinking Christian that salvation is not in a denomination, but in the person Christ Jesus. I give here a note of caution not to add to or take away from what the Bible says. While the Lord Jesus said to Nicodemus, "Ye must be born again," he didn't say ye *must* join a local, denominational church. Neither did any apostle equate written church membership with salvation. There is great danger in thinking that there is only one "true" denomination or sect and that denomination or sect is "our church." Historically, the Catholics have believed that somehow, they are the Church. Some Baptists also think that they are the church and/or the bride of Christ. While people are free to believe what they will, no earthly group, sect, or denomination can legitimately claim to be "the church" or "the bride" of Christ. First, one has to wonder how God managed to get along before they showed up! Second, no group, sect, or denomination can bestow eternal life to anyone; only Christ can do that and eternal life is given as a gift, not as a payment for doing good works.

"For the wages of sin is death; but the *gift* of God is *eternal life* through Jesus Christ our Lord" (Rom. 6:23; emphasis mine).

"For by grace are ye saved through faith; and that not of yourselves: it is the *gift* of God: Not of works, lest any man should boast" (Eph. 2:8; emphasis mine).

"And they of the circumcision which believed were astonished, as many as came with Peter, because that on the Gentiles also was poured out the *gift* of the Holy Ghost" (Acts 10:45; emphasis mine).

Salvation from hell and eternal life are not payments for joining a denomination but are in fact gifts given to a repentant and believing heart.

> "That if thou shalt confess with thy mouth the Lord Jesus, and shalt *believe* in thine heart that God hath raised him from the dead, thou shalt be saved" (Rom. 10:9; emphasis mine).

Furthermore, people can beat their own denominational drum until the Lord comes and they can build their church buildings wide, but the born-again church body which Christ himself calls "my church" is not a church that *we* build at all, but one that Christ builds!

> "And I say also unto thee, That thou art Peter, and upon this rock *I will build my church*; and the gates of hell shall not prevail against it" (Matt. 16:18; emphasis mine).

You may say, but I'm helping Christ build his church. Yes, we may be the tools our Lord uses to build his house, but the tools don't build the house; the carpenter, the Lord Jesus, does!

There is a teaching that all occurrences of the word church refer to a local church. While this is most often true, it's not true in every case. Please, before you take the stand that all occurrences of the word church refer to a local church, do yourself a favor. Chances are you are parroting what you heard someone else say. Do yourself a favor and look up all references of the word church, read and study every context. Then do the same thing for associated words, e.g., body, believers, saints, overcomer et. al., and terms such as the body of Christ, his body, the bride. If you do, you will save yourself some embarrassment and will keep yourself from the common trap of repeating others without doing the research yourself. When I was young and dumb, an "older and wiser" gentleman once taught me that the word "thoroughly" does not appear in the King James Bible, only the word "throughly." I repeated this for years before I was corrected. The word *throughly* appears twelve times in eleven verses, but the word *thoroughly* does appear in Exodus 21:19 and 2 Kings 11:18. My point is that I took someone's word for it without doing my own research, and my teacher was wrong. This same person later told me that people's souls don't get saved, only their spirits. This time, I made the effort to look up every reference of the word soul and souls in the Bible and found the definitive verse.

> "But we are not of them who draw back unto perdition; but of them that believe to *the saving of the soul*" (Heb. 10:39; emphasis mine).

I believe unto the saving of the soul; not to believe unto the saving of the soul is perdition, a damnable heresy. Yes, a person's spirit is also saved or preserved unto God after it is regenerated.

> "And the very God of peace sanctify you wholly; and I pray God your whole *spirit* and *soul* and body be *preserved* blameless unto the coming of our Lord Jesus Christ" (1 Thess. 5:23; emphasis mine).

With this in mind, does every occurrence of the word church refer to a local church?

> And so terrible was the sight, that Moses said, I exceedingly fear and quake:) But ye are come unto mount Sion, and unto the city of the living God, the heavenly Jerusalem, and to an innumerable company of angels, To the general assembly and *church of the firstborn*, which are written in *heaven*, and to God the Judge of all, and to the spirits of just men made perfect, And to Jesus the mediator of the new covenant, and to the blood of sprinkling, that speaketh better things than that of Abel. (Heb. 12:21–24; emphasis mine)

To which local church does this refer?

> "That he might present it to himself a glorious church, not having spot, or wrin-

kle, or any such thing; but that *it* should
be holy and without blemish" (Eph. 5:27).

Which local church will Christ present to himself?
Everyone likes to belong to a group or club and everyone
likes to have truth and be "right," but the highest truth is to
know Christ and the greatest group is the heavenly assembly of born-again believers. Is the possessing church made
up of only denominational members? No. A person who
belongs to no denomination can lead someone to Christ
just as well as someone steeped in denominationalism. This
born-again person may or may not join a denomination,
yet he still possesses the exact same salvation as any other
born-again person. Is the possessing church made up of
only born-again denominational church members? No.
The possessing church is made up of only born-again persons regardless of their denominational slant. A born-again
Methodist has the same salvation as a born-again Baptist,
which has the same salvation as a born-again non-denom-
inational person. Christ's church ultimately is not a sect or
a collection of denominations or a group of local churches
made up of some saved and some lost souls but is a sin-

gle body of only saved souls both within and outside of organized religion. For example, a missionary may lead a person to Christ who never heard the gospel before, and that newly born-again person has the same salvation as the apostle Paul and as any other saved person. If the missionary dies or leaves and the new convert never learns another thing about Christ from organized religion, he still and forever remains part of the saved born-again body of believers. One thing is for certain, Christ Jesus knows the possessors of the Holy Ghost from the mere professors.

"Nevertheless the foundation of God standeth sure, having this seal, *The Lord knoweth them that are his*. And, Let every one that nameth the name of Christ depart from iniquity" (2 Tim. 2:19; emphasis mine).

Is the possessing church singular?

There are many local churches and denominations, but a single body in Christ. The Bible uses the terms churches,

churches of Christ, and churches of God to address local assemblies as we have covered under definition six. The Bible, however, never uses the terms bodies of Christ or brides of Christ because there is in fact a single unified body, which is the singular bride of Christ. If the reader is unfamiliar with the idea of a single church assembly or gathering of all born-again believers, we need to look no further than the epistles to the Thessalonians.

"Now we beseech you, *brethren*, by the *coming of our Lord Jesus Christ*, and by *our gathering together* unto him" (2 Thess. 2:1; emphasis mine).

All born-again believers or brethren will be gathered, i.e., assembled together unto Christ. This future gathering is for *all* the brethren both dead (asleep in Christ) and living at the time of Christ's return.

But I would not have you to be ignorant, *brethren*, concerning them *which are asleep*, that ye sorrow not, even as others which have no hope. For if we believe that Jesus died and rose again, even so them also which sleep in Jesus *will God bring with him.* For this we say unto you by the word of the Lord, that we which are alive and remain unto the coming of the Lord shall not prevent them which are asleep. For the Lord himself shall descend from heaven with a shout, with the voice of the archangel, and with the trump of God: and the dead in Christ shall rise first: Then *we which are alive and remain* shall be caught up *together with them* in the clouds, to meet the Lord in the air: and so shall we ever be with the Lord. (18) Wherefore comfort one another with these words. (1 Thess. 4:13–18; emphasis mine)

This is not a gathering of local churches or of old carnal physical bodies, but of resurrected and glorified spiritual bodies and redeemed souls. Notice that the living and departed born-again believers in Christ will be put *together* as a *single body* and as a single collective body we will meet the Lord in the air. Dealing with the same subject matter, Paul to the Corinthians writes:

> Now this I say, brethren, that flesh and blood cannot inherit the kingdom of God; neither doth corruption inherit incorruption. Behold, I shew you a mystery; We shall not all sleep, but *we* shall *all* be changed, In a moment, in the twinkling of an eye, at the last trump: for the trumpet shall sound, and the dead shall be raised incorruptible, and we shall be changed. (1 Cor. 15:50–52; emphasis mine)

Notice again that *all* the brethren will be changed into glorified beings. The word "all" refers to every saved person in Paul's day as well as all the saved since Paul's day or all born-again believers from Acts 2 until the Lord's coming for his bride. This event is commonly known as the rapture; however, some prefer other terms to describe this event. The Holy Bible clearly teaches a single unified body of born-again believers possessing the Spirit of Christ in the rapture event.

> "For as we have many members in *one body*, and all members have not the same office" (Rom. 12:4; emphasis mine).

> "So we, being many, are *one body* in Christ, and every one members one of another" (Rom. 12:5; emphasis mine).

> "For we being many are one bread, and *one body*: for we are all partakers of that one bread" (1 Cor. 10:17).

> "For as the body is one, and hath many members, and all the members of that one body, being many, are *one body*: so also is Christ" (1 Cor. 12:12; emphasis mine).

> "For by one Spirit are we all baptized into *one body*, whether we be Jews or Gentiles, whether we be bond or free; and have been all made to drink into one Spirit" (1 Cor. 12:13; emphasis mine).

But now are they many members, yet but *one body*. (1 Cor. 12:20; emphasis mine).

"And that he might reconcile both unto God in *one body* by the cross, having slain the enmity thereby" (Eph. 2:16; emphasis mine).

"There is *one body*, and one Spirit, even as ye are called in one hope of your calling" (Eph. 4:4; emphasis mine).

"And let the peace of God rule in your hearts, to the which also ye are called in *one body*; and be ye thankful" (Col. 3:15).

"That the Gentiles should be fellow heirs, and of *the same body*, and partakers of his promise in Christ by the gospel" (Eph. 3:6; emphasis mine).

"Who now rejoice in my sufferings for you, and fill up that which is behind of the afflictions of Christ in my flesh for *his body*'s sake, which is *the church*" (Col. 1:24; emphasis mine).

"And he is the head of *the body, the church*: who is the beginning, the first-born from the dead; that in all things he might have the preeminence" (Col. 1:18; emphasis mine).

"And hath put all things under his feet, and gave him to be *the* head over all things to *the church*" (Eph. 1:22; emphasis mine).

Of course, Christ is, or at least he should be, the head of the local churches, but that's not what the Bible is teaching in these verses. The Bible is teaching that Christ is a single head of a single church body.

"For the husband is the head of the wife, even as Christ is *the* head of *the church*: and he is the saviour of the body" (Eph. 5:23; emphasis mine).

"Husbands, love your wives, even as Christ also loved the church, and gave himself for *it*" (Eph. 5:25).

"That he might sanctify and cleanse *it* with the washing of water by the word" (Eph. 5:26).

"That he might present *it* to himself *a* glorious *church*, not having spot, or wrinkle, or any such thing; but that *it* should be holy and without blemish" (Eph. 5:27; emphasis mine).

Yes, there are many local churches and denominations, yet all born-again persons together comprise a single body which will be gathered unto Christ and presented to him.

Is the possessing church physical or spiritual?

The answer is both. Today, Christ's physical body is now glorified and the professing local churches act as "his body." Please bear with me through this next section as we must never over simplify the Holy Bible or restrict it in order to make it fit our limited thinking. With this in mind, let's do some mental gymnastics to warm up our thought processes.

THE DOCTRINE OF ETERNAL LIFE

a. Are you in Christ or is Christ in you? Pause to consider. The correct answer is, "Yes!"

Yes, we are in Christ.

"Therefore if any man be in Christ, he is a new creature: old things are passed away; behold, all things are become new" (2 Cor. 5:17).

Yes, Christ is in us.

"To whom God would make known what is the riches of the glory of this mystery among the Gentiles; which is Christ in you, the hope of glory" (Col. 1:27).

Often, the Bible answer to a question is more complex than a simple yes or no answer and may very well be a yes and no answer.

b. Is a person a physical or a spiritual being? I submit that a person is both physical and spiritual, or if you would rather, a person possesses both a physical and a spiritual component. Obviously, the body of a man is the physical component while the soul and spirit of a person are spiritual aspects, which we cannot see with the physical eye. We will see more on the composition of man in chapter 4. Suffice it to say that a person is both physical and spiritual.

c. Was the Lord Jesus physical or spiritual? Obviously, he was both, or more correctly, a spiritual being who manifested himself in a physical body.

d. Is the word of God physical or spiritual? In one way, Jesus Christ is the Word and we know that he is both physical and spiritual. Beyond this, we know that the Holy Bible is both physical and spiritual. We can hold God's words in our hand and read it, copy it, and speak it from a physical book, yet no believer would say that God's word is purely physical. What does the Bible say about itself?

The Lord Jesus said, "It is the spirit that quickeneth; the flesh profiteth nothing: *the words that I speak unto you, they are spirit,* and they are life" (John 6:63; emphasis mine).

We also know that flesh and blood cannot inherit the kingdom of God, (1 Cor. 15:50) because they are physical things and heaven is a spiritual place. Since God's word is forever settled in heaven, then God's word must also have a spiritual component.

"For ever, O LORD, thy word is settled in heaven" (Ps. 119:89).

e. So then, if we agree that mankind is both physical and spiritual as well as the Lord Jesus and the word of God, should the possessing church then, which consists of only born-again believers, be any less? Please, before you say, "I don't believe in a spiritual church, no way no how!" remember that I'm not suggesting that the born-again church is *only* spiritual, neither am I saying that it is *only* physical. As Christ was both, the scriptures teach that Christ's church, made up of people, is manifest in both physical and spiritual forms. First, let's consider the physical aspect of the born-again church.

The physical component of the possessing church:

Most of the times when the word church is used in the Bible, it's referring to a local assembly of professed believers as we saw under point six. The physical church on earth is made up of physical persons who meet in physical locations, preach from physical Bibles, and sing with physical voices to God. We give our offerings and tithes so that the physical needs of the human body can be met. Those who minister the word need food, housing, transportation, etc., and we all need a worship building to keep us dry, etc. We, as the church, are not a nebulous disembodied mass, but neither are we strictly physical.

The spiritual aspect of the possessing church:

What does the Bible say about the spiritual side, component or aspect of the Church of Jesus Christ? Once again, before you say, "I don't believe in a spiritual church, no way no how!" please consider Romans 7:4.

"Wherefore, my brethren, ye also are become dead to the law by the body of Christ; that *ye should be married to another, even to him who is raised from the dead*, that we should bring forth fruit unto God" (Rom. 7:4; emphasis mine).

If we refuse to consider the spiritual aspect of the Church of Christ, we are confronted with a very awkward situation! The marriage of the church of born-again believers to Christ cannot be a physical one, it must be spiritual. The doctrine of believers being married to Christ is not an isolated teaching.

"For I am jealous over *you* with godly jealousy: for I have *espoused* you to one husband, that I may present you as a chaste virgin to Christ" (2 Cor. 11:2; emphasis mine).

Here again, we are confronted with the doctrine of a single body, "as *a* chaste virgin" being joined to Christ. The collective "you" addressed to the Corinthian believers is, by extension, applicable to any and all saved believers.

"Wherefore, my brethren, ye also are become dead to the law by the body of Christ; that *ye* should be *married* to another, even *to him* who is raised from the dead, that we should bring forth fruit unto God" (Rom. 7:4; emphasis mine).

Honestly, I'm not trying to confuse anyone, but if we are to appreciate the depth of the Scriptures, we must be specific and as the old-time teachers would say "put on our thinking caps." Before we go deeper into the spiritual aspect of the born-again body of Christ, which is the possessing church, let's consider Christ the Rock. We all know that Christ is the "Rock" of scripture. The question is, was (or is) Christ a spiritual rock or a physical rock? Please take a little time to consider this question in light of the following verse.

THE DOCTRINE OF ETERNAL LIFE

"And Moses lifted up his hand, and with his rod he smote the rock twice: and the water came out abundantly, and the congregation drank, and their beasts also" (Num. 20:11).

Did Moses strike a physical rock or a spiritual rock? Did Moses carry a physical rod or a spiritual rod? Certainly, Moses struck a physical rock with a physical rod and physical water flowed sustaining physical life. How could Moses strike a spiritual rock with a physical rod? Now then, was this physical rock *only* physical and in no way spiritual? What saith the scriptures?

"And did all drink the same spiritual drink: for they drank of that *spiritual Rock* that followed them: and that Rock was *Christ*" (1 Cor. 10:4; emphasis mine).

Okay then, was the rock physical or spiritual? The answer is yes, both physical and spiritual! The rock was the Lord Jesus Christ, a spiritual being, *manifest* in a physical form. We call this a Christophany.

When we compare the physical and spiritual aspects of Christ to his body the church the same truth applies. Christ's church is made of spiritual beings (people made in the image of God) who are manifested physically, i.e., in physical bodies and physical locations. Man seems to have little problem understanding physical concepts but labors to understand the spiritual. In fact, as a side note, if you do a study of all the times where our Lord was misunderstood, you will find that most of the time, Christ was speaking about spiritual things, e.g., spiritual bread, while others were thinking on a purely physical plane. Let us not be guilty of neglecting the spiritual aspect of Christ's body the church.

In addition, if we would reexamine all of the verses under the question, "Is the possessing church singular?" we would see a clear point. That is, it would be clear that when Paul was speaking to the Romans, Corinthians, Ephesians, and the

Colossians of "one body" that it would of necessity be a spiritual one. Indeed, any body consisting of departed saved souls in heaven, e.g., Paul and living saved souls on earth, must by necessity be a spiritual body.

Is the church of Jesus Christ temporal or eternal?

As we have considered, Christ's physical body is now glorified and the professing local churches act as "his body." We of the professing church, profess Christ with our mouths and also do his work with our God-given hands and feet. As we have seen, the church of Christ today has both physical and spiritual aspects; our physical bodies are temporal while our souls and spirits are eternal. The *physical* aspects of the body of Christ are *temporal* while the *spiritual* aspects are *eternal.*

"Now this I say, brethren, that *flesh and blood cannot inherit the kingdom of God*; neither doth corruption inherit incorruption" (1 Cor. 15:50; emphasis mine).

The kingdom of God cited here is a reference to the eternal kingdom of God, which will be populated by eternal bodies that are both heavenly and spiritual.

One day, every redeemed person will receive a spiritual body, thank the Lord!

> "It is sown a natural body; it is raised *a spiritual body*. There is a natural body, and *there is a spiritual body*" (1 Cor. 15:44; emphasis mine).
>
> "And as we have borne the image of the earthy, *we shall* also bear the image of the *heavenly*" (1 Cor. 15:49; emphasis mine).

It's demonstrable in scripture that even after the physical body is dead and decayed that the soul, which is a spiritual component of man, continues on. Our Lord said it simply:

> "And whosoever liveth and believeth in me shall *never die*. Believest thou this?" (John 11:26; emphasis mine).

And the great apostle Paul wrote:

> "We are confident, I say, and willing
> rather to be absent from the body, and to
> be present with the Lord" (2 Cor. 5:8).

Therefore, it makes complete sense that there is a spiritual, eternal body for each and every redeemed soul as a living stone in a spiritual house or a cell in a grand spiritual body.

The church of born-again believers sealed with the Holy Ghost, which began on the day of Pentecost, is a spiritual body comprised of all born-again believers in Christ transcending time and space. This church is ultimately referred to as Christ's bride, the Lamb's wife in Revelation 21:9. Let's illustrate the distinction between a local, physical, temporal, church and the heavenly, spiritual, eternal church, consisting of all born-again believers throughout the present dispensation, by asking another question. Is Paul a part of a local church? Notice I did not ask, "Was Paul a part of a local church," but *is* Paul right now, today, a part of a local church? The answer is no, yet Paul is a part of another "church" that transcends space and time called

Christ's bride! This is why we see the language of a spiritual church body used in 1 Corinthians 12:13.

> "For by *one Spirit* are we all baptized into *one body*, whether we be Jews or Gentiles, whether we be bond or free; and have been all made to drink into *one Spirit*" (1 Cor. 12:13; emphasis mine).

It would be indefensible to argue that the *one body* in 1 Corinthians 12:13 refers to one local church. Although a believer may be baptized with *water* into a *local* church body by a pastor, a believer is never said to be baptized into a single *local* church by the Holy Spirit. Neither does the Holy Spirit baptize *all born-again believers* into *one local* church. Please notice the Bible wording again.

> "For by *one Spirit* are we all baptized into *one body*, whether we be Jews or Gentiles, whether we be bond or free; and have been all made to drink into *one Spirit*" (1 Cor. 12:13; emphasis mine).

Back in Paul's day (as well as today), a person in prison may receive Christ as Saviour never setting foot in any local church, his name never appearing on any membership roll or baptismal certificate. Yet through the work of the Spirit of God, he is baptized (immersed) into the spiritual part of the body of Christ at the moment of salvation and given the Spirit to drink. This action is by necessity a spiritual action into a spiritual body. Let's recall that water baptism is an outward representation and demonstration of previously completed actions.

- Water baptism is representative of the gospel, i.e., of the death, burial, and resurrection of the Lord Jesus; these events having already taken place previously in time.

- Water baptism is representative of the believer's death and burial of the old man (Rom. 6:6) and the resurrection of the new man (Rom. 6:4). These events having already taken place previously in time.

- Water baptism is representative of the believer being baptized by the Holy Spirit as well as the believer's emersion into the body of Christ by the Holy Spirit at the moment of salvation. These events having already taken place previously in time.

One ongoing problem we, as Bible students, have is the tendency to lump all baptisms together just as we tend to lump all references to the word church together. This lumping problem will be addressed in its own chapter.

To answer the question, "Is the church of Jesus Christ temporal or eternal?" directly, the physical aspects of the church such as our buildings, budgets, and bodies are temporal while the spiritual aspects, such as our souls, our new glorified bodies, and our rewards given at the judgment seat of Christ, are eternal.

Is the church of Jesus Christ visible or invisible?

The answer is both because the Church of Christ is made up of people with physical bodies and eternal souls. We see the physical body but not the eternal soul, which leaves the body at the moment of death. More on this fact in the next chapter. When discussing the invisible aspect of the Church of Christ, one person said, "I have never seen an invisible church!" Ha! Of course not, that's what makes it invisible! Seriously though, while we can see the physical bodies of individuals, we don't see their eternal and invisible souls. Indeed, we may be very surprised in heaven to find who is there and who is not there!

Since the possessing or born-again church of Christ has both physical and spiritual components, to dismiss either is wrong. Today, the born-again church is both physical and spiritual, but in eternity, of course, she will only possess a celestial, glorified, incorruptible, honorable, heavenly, spiritual body.

> There are also celestial bodies, and bodies terrestrial: but the glory of the celestial is one, and the glory of the terrestrial is another. There is one glory of the sun, and another glory of the moon, and another glory of the stars: for one star differeth from another star in glory. So also is the resurrection of the dead. It is sown in corruption; it is raised in incorruption: It is sown in dishonour; it is raised in

glory: it is sown in weakness; it is raised in power: It is sown a natural body; it is raised a spiritual body. There is a natural body, and there is a spiritual body. And so it is written, The first man Adam was made a living soul; the last Adam was made a quickening spirit. Howbeit that was not first which is spiritual, but that which is natural; and afterward that which is spiritual. The first man is of the earth, earthy: the second man is the Lord from heaven. As is the earthy, such are they also that are earthy: and as is the heavenly, such are they also that are heavenly. And as we have borne the image of the earthy, we shall also bear the image of the heavenly. Now this I say, brethren, that flesh and blood cannot inherit the kingdom of God; neither doth corruption inherit incorruption. Behold, I shew you a mystery; We shall not all sleep, but we shall all be changed. In a moment, in the twinkling of an eye, at the last trump: for the trumpet shall sound, and the dead shall be raised incorruptible, and we shall be changed. For this corruptible must put on incorruption, and this mortal must put on immortality. So when this corruptible shall have put on incorruption, and this mortal shall have put on immortality, then shall be brought to pass the saying that is written, Death is swallowed up in victory. O death, where is thy sting? O grave, where is thy victory? (1 Cor. 15:40–55)

We may also consider the matter of the term church in this way.

1. Any called-out assembly can be "a" church.
2. Moses had "a" church…
3. John the Baptist had "a" church…
4. The Lord Jesus before Acts 2 had "a" church…
5. The assembly point or building can be called "a" church…

6. Today we, along with other professing believers, are "a" church...

7. But the born-again, sealed and spiritually unified body as Christ said is "my church."

Now that we have seen how very different the born-again possessing church is from all other types of churches, we can begin to see other scriptures more clearly. When the Lord Jesus said in Matthew 16:18, "I will build my church," he was referring to a yet future church, very different from the first six church definitions which we have examined. So, what exactly did the Lord mean in Matthew 16:18 when he said "upon this rock?" We all realize that the Lord Jesus himself was and is "this rock;" with this in mind, let's ask these questions:

1. Do we build a physical church building upon Jesus' physical body? No.

2. Do we build a physical church building upon his gospel? No.

3. Did the Lord say here that we as believers were to build anything upon the rock? No.

4. Did the Lord say, "I will build…?" Yes.

5. Did Christ say, "I will build my churches," plural? No.

6. Does Christ himself build a physical building upon his body? No.

7. Did Christ mean he would build a physical building upon his gospel? No.

8. Did Christ mean that he as a *spiritual* Rock would build a *spiritual* church? Yes!

9. Is Christ himself building a *spiritual* church (not made with hands) upon himself the *spiritual* Rock? Yes! Christ is a spiritual Rock, and he is building a spiritual church, upon himself, which is different from all other forms of churches. While it is true that Christ's church manifests itself physically today, it is equally true that Christ's church possesses a spiritual component.

"Praising God, and having favour with all the people. And the Lord added to the church daily such as should be saved" (Acts 2:47).

Notice that this scripture doesn't read "the Lord added to the local church or churches, such as should be members." While it's true that the local church or churches grew, the emphasis is on *spiritual* salvation by faith not local church membership. We should correctly understand Acts 2:47 to imply that the Lord was not only building or adding to his *physical* "church," but to his *spiritual* "church" as well, both during and after Pentecost fulfilling the promise of Matthew 16:18 and John 10:15–16.

> As the Father knoweth me, even so know I the Father: and I lay down my life for the sheep. And other sheep I have, which are not of this fold: them also I must bring, and they shall hear my voice; and *there shall be one fold*, and one shepherd. (John 10:15–16; emphasis mine).

Obviously, the Lord didn't mean that there should be only one local church. The Lord Jesus was looking beyond Pentecost to a single fold or body of believers consisting of both Jews and Gentiles. This body we know today as the born-again body of Christ, his bride, the church or the possessing church. Yes, Acts 2:47 is a fulfilment of prophesy, fulfilling both Matthew 16:18 and John 10:15–16!

The astute reader may wonder why the Lord Jesus told Nicodemus in John 3 that he must be born again, before Acts 2 and before the subsequent day of Pentecost? John 3 is written in the same spirit as Matthew 16:18, where in both portions of scripture the Saviour is *looking forward* in anticipation to the day of Pentecost which was at that time, in the very near future. Another scripture to be placed into this category is Luke 22:32, dealing with Peter's conversion.

> "But I have prayed for thee, that thy faith fail not: and *when thou art converted*, strengthen thy brethren" (Luke 22:32; emphasis mine).

If you, the reader, find it unlikely that our Lord told Nicodemus that he must be born again in anticipation of the day of Pentecost, let me ask this question. How many of Christ's disciples preached "ye must be born again?" Did the Lord Jesus ever publicly preach "ye must be born again?" No, he only told one person, Nicodemus, that he must be born again and that, in anticipation of the day of Pentecost in a private setting. I invite you to find any other reference to being born again in the synoptic gospels. Christ himself did not preach "ye must be born again," but only told Nicodemus in private, knowing he would understand this message on the day of Pentecost! Again, Peter, who had been Christ's disciple for some time, was told in private by the Lord that he needed to be converted. Peter's conversion also saw its completion on the day of Pentecost, praise God!

The difference between the spiritual church, which is the eternal body and bride of Christ, and the church of Jesus' disciples before Pentecost can be made clear by one fact. We have seen earlier in Matthew 10:1–8 that Judas Iscariot was in fact a part of the "church" of Jesus' disciples before Pentecost (see also John 6:70). However, we would all agree that Judas Iscariot is not a part of the body and bride of Christ, which is his church. The point being that any local physical assembly can have a devil in the midst, including the church of Moses, the church of Jesus' disciples before Pentecost, and the local church after Pentecost today, but the *spiritual* church (or spiritual component of the church), which is the spiritual "body of Christ" is made up of only born-again believers and has no devil. Yeah!

It's very easy to blur the lines between the assembly of Jesus' disciples and the New Testament born-again church. Please remember that just because most of the "church" of Jesus' disciples before Pentecost *became* part of the spiritual born-again "church" at Pentecost, does not make these two churches the same. If you are still unclear, please review the examples in this section.

Even as we must make a distinction between Jesus' non-born-again assembly before Pentecost and the born-again sealed church after Pentecost, it is imperative that we also differentiate between the local church or churches consisting of both saved and lost souls and Christ's single "church" body, which is eternal and completely redeemed.

The bride of Christ and the spiritual side of the church.

1. The spiritual component of Christ's church after Pentecost is singular extending beyond the physical.

For by one *Spirit* are we all baptized into *one body*, whether we be Jews or Gentiles, whether we be bond or free; and have been all made to drink into *one Spirit.* (1 Cor. 12:13; emphasis mine)

Which he wrought in *Christ*, when he raised him from the dead, and set him at his own right hand in the heavenly places, Far above all principality, and power, and might, and dominion, and every name that is named, not only in this world, but also in that which is to come: And hath put all things under his feet, and gave him to be the head over all things to *the church*, Which is *his body*, the fulness of him that filleth all in all. (Eph. 1:20-23; emphasis mine)

Who now rejoice in my sufferings for you, and fill up that which is behind of the afflictions of *Christ* in my flesh for *his body*'s sake, which is *the church*. (Col. 1:24; emphasis mine)

2. Christ's body is his wife, the spiritual side of the church.

> For *we are members of his body*, of his flesh, and of his bones. For this cause shall *a man* leave his father and mother, *and* shall be joined unto *his wife*, and they two shall be one flesh. This is a great mystery: but I speak concerning *Christ* and *the church*. (Eph. 5:30–32; emphasis mine)

It should be obvious that Christ will not join himself in a physical way to any local church. Also, if we were to turn "the church" into a purely physical thing and claim, as some do, that the word "church" always means local church, we get confusion. Is every member of a local church going to heaven? Must written church membership be added to the born-again command for salvation?

3. The Lamb's wife is his bride.

"And there came unto me one of the seven angels which had the seven vials full of the seven last plagues, and talked with me, saying, Come hither, I will shew thee *the bride, the Lamb's wife*" (Rev. 21:9; emphasis mine).

Please remember that this reference, chronologically speaking, is after sin has been put away and all believers are dwelling in glorified spiritual bodies.

4. The Lamb is Jesus the Christ.

"The next day John seeth *Jesus* coming unto him, and saith, Behold *the Lamb* of God, which taketh away the sin of the world" (John 1:29; emphasis mine).

5. The spiritual component of the church is Christ's bride.

    "And the Spirit and the *bride* say, Come" (Rev. 22:17; emphasis mine).

    Who invites people to come to Christ, except those persons who have the Spirit of God? The bride being born-again persons, the spiritual component of the church, or the wife and body of Christ. Christ Jesus, therefore, is the Lamb of God and the spiritual component of the church is made up of only born-again souls. Christ's spiritual church is his body and bride. This is why The Lord Jesus said in Matthew 16:18, "I will build *my* church" when he already had *a* church made up of his non-born-again disciples. Our Lord was looking forward to a new type of church, that being a spiritual, unified body with no devils allowed!

    Please consider Matthew 16:18 from a historical view.

"And I say also unto thee, That thou art Peter, and upon this rock *I will build my church*; and *the gates of hell shall not prevail* against it" (Matt. 16:18; emphasis mine).

History records how that at many times the gates of hell have prevailed against local churches, but never against the spiritual body of Christ to subtract one member! Devils have overrun local churches before, but no devil has ever or will ever crash the gates of the spiritual church, which is Christ's bride. In other words, no evil being will enter the eternal new heaven or the New Jerusalem, and no devil can cause any member of the spiritual body of Christ to be lost.

Let's look a little deeper at the spiritual side of the possessing church, which transcends time and space from another angle. We know that the word disciple means follower. The Lord Jesus had disciples on the earth who followed him literally, but does Christ have disciples on earth today? Yes, but do they follow him around literally? No. Is Christ even on earth literally so that we might follow him? No. Is Christ here in spirit form that we might follow him in a spiritual way? Yes. The Holy Spirit is Christ's Spirit and it is having Christ's Spirit, which distinguishes the possessing believer from the merely professing or would-be, wannabe, someday, hope-so, believer.

> "But ye are not in the flesh, but in the Spirit, if so be that the Spirit of God dwell in you. Now if any man have not *the Spirit of Christ*, he is none of his" (Rom. 8:9; emphasis mine).

Today, we follow Christ spiritually because we are part of his *spiritual body, the church*. The Lord Jesus having ascended to heaven before Acts chapter two and *before* the Holy Spirit sealed any believer. The sealing of every believer by the holy Ghost is the primary difference between the spiritual body of Christ, his church, and the called-out assembly of Jesus' disciples before Pentecost. Of course, many actions of the spiritual church manifest themselves in the physical world, i.e., we have bodies, attend a local church, read our Bible and witness. Perhaps it would be wise to clarify that the multiple meanings of the word church are not necessarily mutually exclusive. Allow me to explain.

For example, consider the time before the Lord Jesus started his earthly ministry. A person may have been a disciple of John the Baptist and have been part of his local church assembly. Later, after John was beheaded and the Lord was teaching his disciples, a follower of John's assembly could very easily have become a part of Jesus' called-out assembly before Pentecost. Still later, after the death, burial, resurrection, ascension, and outpouring of the Holy Ghost, that same person who was once John's disciple could have become part of the spiritual body of sealed born-again believers in Christ on the day of Pentecost. Still later, the same believer could very well have joined himself to a distinct local church group. The events mentioned only cover a period of a few years making this scenario very possible. Reading Acts 19 will help our understanding here. We do know that eleven of the disciples in Jesus' called-out assembly became part of the body of Christ on the day of Pentecost and also became affiliated with local churches. Those of us living today were never a part of John Baptist's church nor Jesus' assembly before Pentecost, but we can be a part of the *spiritual* body of Christ as well as a *local* church. Let's also appreciate the fact that a person may never be a part of any local church assembly yet still may be part of the body of Christ. One example would be a man I knew named Kyle, who lived with severe birth defects. Kyle's legs were folded up flat to his chest, and he had very limited use of his clawlike left hand and no use of his right. This man spent his life on his back in a nursing home and as far as I know, never became a member of or even entered into any local church. My pastor friend and I would drive some distance to visit Kyle and one day, he received the Lord as his Saviour and became a part of the spiritual body of Christ. Another example used to distinguish the difference between the spiritual body of Christ and the local church is if children in a heathen family read or hear the gospel through tracts and receive Christ as Saviour. These children may not be allowed to attend any local church, but they are still part of the spiritual body of Christ and will be received into heaven.

Let's splash some cold water on our faces and consider one final practical and important proof that the called-out assembly or "church" that The Lord Jesus started with his disciples, including Judas Iscariot, was not and is not, the same as the Lord's "church" which began on the day of Pentecost.

> "And as I began to speak, the Holy
> Ghost fell on them, as on us *at the beginning*.
> Then remembered I the word of the Lord,
> how that he said, John indeed baptized with
> water; but ye shall be baptized with the Holy
> Ghost" (Acts 11:15–16; emphasis mine).

What did Peter mean by "at the beginning?" At the beginning of what? Well, the church! But which church? The Holy Ghost did not fall on anyone as he did at Pentecost, i.e., permanently sealing them, before the death, burial and resurrection of Christ. Some may remember the account of John 20 and make the point that at least some of Christ's disciples had the Holy Ghost before Pentecost.

> "And when he had said this, he
> breathed on them, and saith unto them,
> *Receive* ye the *Holy Ghost*" (John 20:22;
> emphasis mine).

If we contend that some of Christ's disciples already had the Holy Ghost, how then do we reconcile John 20:22 with what the Lord Jesus said shortly before his ascension in Acts 1:8?

> "But *ye shall receive* power, *after* that the Holy Ghost is come upon you: and ye shall be witnesses unto me both in Jerusalem, and in all Judaea, and in Samaria, and unto the uttermost part of the earth" (Acts 1:8; emphasis mine).

The answer is that although some of the disciples did receive the Holy Ghost in John 20:22, before Acts 2, no one was permanently sealed by God's Spirit until the day of Pentecost. It is this sealing by the Spirit of God that marks all born-again believers as part of the possessing body Christ.

> "Who hath also *sealed* us, and given the earnest of the *Spirit* in our hearts" (2 Cor. 1:22; emphasis mine).

"In whom ye also trusted, after that ye heard the word of truth, the gospel of your salvation: in whom also after that ye believed, ye were *sealed* with that holy *Spirit* of promise" (Eph. 1:13; emphasis mine)

"And grieve not the holy *Spirit* of God, whereby ye are *sealed* unto the day of redemption" (Eph. 4:30; emphasis mine).

With this understanding, Acts 11:15–16 makes perfect sense.

And as I began to speak, the Holy Ghost fell on them, as on us *at the beginning.* Then remembered I the word of the Lord, how that he said, John indeed baptized with water; but ye *shall be* baptized with the Holy Ghost. (Acts 11:15–16; emphasis mine)

The phrase *at the beginning* refers back to Acts 2 and marks the beginning of sealed believers as opposed to the "church" of Jesus' disciples before Acts 2. It's necessary to know that the coming of the promised Spirit was fulfilled in Acts 2 in order that we might understand scriptures such as Matthew 16:28.

> "Verily I say unto you, There be some standing here, which shall not taste of death, till they see the Son of man coming in his kingdom" (Matt. 16:28).

Remember, Christ Jesus in Matthew's gospel was speaking to a Jewish called-out assembly who possessed no knowledge of the sealing of the holy Spirit. With this in mind, when did any of the apostles or Jewish disciples ever see the Lord "coming in his kingdom?" The answer is no, they never did. If this is referring to a yet future event then there must still be "some" individual disciples still alive today who literally heard the Lord speak these words. You don't believe that there are persons yet living on earth who heard these words from the mouth of Jesus Christ, do you? Nor do I, so *when* was Christ seen "coming in his Kingdom?" Yes, of course, this scripture and others like it were fulfilled in Act 2, when Christ came in the person of the Holy Spirit and established "his kingdom"—a spiritual kingdom of Spirit-sealed believers and not the Jewish kingdom, which is yet future.

Why is it so important to know that the church of born-again believers is separate and distinct from any and all local churches and also when it began? Some readers may think this to be an insignificant truth, but it is a monumental truth which many old-time believers understood clearly and I dare say, most modern scholars overlook completely. Knowing *when* the New Testament church of born-again believers began, gives us *context* and allows the scholar to rightly divide the word of truth. There are many other doctrines very pertinent to our time that are complicated beyond reconciliation because the scriptures are inappropriately applied to the born-again church of Christ. I will briefly touch on one such very pertinent doctrine, i.e., the pre-tribulational rapture of the church. My goal here is not to cause anyone to change their doctrinal view on anything, including the timing of the rapture of born-again believers in relation to the coming tribulation. However, my goal today is to cause the reader to think and utilize a *proper method* of arriving at truth. My point is this, to date, virtually every person not taking a pre-tribulational rapture position of born-again believers, resorts to using Matthew 24. Do you see the problem? The Lord Jesus wasn't even crucified until Matthew chapter 27, and his resurrection wasn't recorded until Matthew 28. Matthew 24, while physically located in the New Testament, was written on Old Testament ground, i.e., before the death, burial, and resurrection and the sealing of believers in Acts 2. In Matthew 24, the Lord was speaking to a called-out assembly of Jewish disciples, not born-again New Testament believers! A simple cursory view of the context of Matthew 24 should cause any honest scholar to realize that chapter 24 has nothing whatsoever to do with the yet future church of Christ. In summary...

Matthew 23 records the rejection of the Lord Jesus *by* the Jewish nation.

Matthew 24 records the return of the Lord Jesus *to* the Jewish nation.

Matthew 25 records the subsequent restoration *of* the Jewish nation or "kingdom of heaven."

The context of Matthew 24 is not that of Christ coming *for* his bride before the tribulation, but the Jewish Messiah coming *to* the nation of Israel *after* the tribulation!

> Immediately *after the tribulation* of those days shall the sun be darkened, and the moon shall not give her light, and the stars shall fall from heaven, and the powers of the heavens shall be shaken: And then shall appear the sign of the Son of man in heaven: and then shall *all* the tribes of the earth mourn, and they shall see the *Son of man coming* in the clouds of heaven with power and great glory. (Matt. 24:29–30; emphasis mine)

Furthermore, the tribulation is Jacob's trouble, not the church's trouble or the bride's trouble. The term "the Son of man" is a strictly Jewish title and is never attributed to Christ in any New Testament "church" epistle. Volumes could be written to put the book of Matthew in its proper context and show that it is not a New Testament church epistle and cannot be applied as such. Simply put, if we know that the body of born-again believers didn't begin until Acts 2, then we know that Matthew 24 cannot be applied to born-again believers in Christ to prove anything, but I digress. The most important doctrine relating to when the New Testament church began isn't the rapture, but the doctrine of eternal life, as we will see.

Lastly, in regards to all of the non-Bible terms in general, even though these terms—e.g., "local church" and "new testament church"—do not appear in the Bible, they serve a useful function. Also, some may use the terms universal church, invisible church, collective church, et. al. I'm not endeavoring to promote a new doctrine, but only to express characteristics of the church of Christ. In other words, you may say, "I don't believe in a universal church!" That's fine, as long as you believe the Bible which teaches that Christ's church includes all born-again believers worldwide. Again, you may say, "I don't believe in an invisible church!" and that's fine, as long as you understand that those souls who have died in Christ are in heaven and are just as much a part of Christ's church as we. Also, while we're on earth, we can't always be certain who is possessed by the Spirt of God and who isn't; this is part of the invisible aspect. When God looks down from heaven, he sees two major groups or bodies. Those who are sealed with the Spirit of Christ and those who are not. Those who are sealed are part of Christ's church regardless of any denominational name, while those who lack God's spirit are not part of Christ's church regardless of any denominational name or position. We may explain our individual beliefs using different terms as long as we understand the full scope and character of the body of Christ is both physical and spiritual in nature. The physical expressing itself in a visible way and spiritual in an invisible. The physical is manifest in a temporal way and the spiritual in an eternal. The physical is seen in many bodies, with some attending local churches and the spiritual a singular unified body, ultimately appearing in heaven as the bride of Christ.

No Lumps Please!

Things that are not the same are different. We must not lump together things which have dissimilar distinguishing characteristics. If I have learned nothing else during my pilgrimage with the Lord, I have learned to make a distinction between terms that are different.

> "And that ye may put difference between holy and unholy, and between unclean and clean" (Lev. 10:10).

Below are some common Bible terms which are usually lumped together. These terms have multiple meanings or definitions and cannot be lumped together without causing confusion.

1. church
2. disciples

3. resurrection

4. judgment

5. coming

6. gather, gathering

7. tribulation

8. gospel

9. saint

10. kingdom

11. heaven

12. Elect, chosen

It's not my intention to do an exhaustive study on any of these terms, but to give a brief explanation so that the reader may clearly understand that each term possesses multiple meanings or definitions.

1. church

We have already seen that the word "church" has no less than seven different meanings in the previous chapters.

2. disciples

- Old Testament Jewish followers: "Bind up the testimony, seal the law among my disciples" (Isa. 8:16).
- The followers of John the Baptist: "And the disciples of John shewed him of all these things" (Luke 7:180.
- The followers of Christ before Acts 2: "And Jesus arose, and followed him, and so did his disciples" (Matt. 9:19).
- The followers of Christ after Acts 2: "And Saul, yet breathing out threatenings and slaughter against the disciples of the Lord, went unto the high priest" (Acts 9:1).

3. resurrection

If someone asks our thoughts on the resurrection, before we answer we must ask, which resurrection? There are several resurrections in the Bible; among them are:

- The bodily resurrection of our Lord Jesus: "And with great power gave the apostles witness of the resurrection of the Lord Jesus: and great grace was upon them all" (Acts 4:33).

- The resurrection of the saints at the time of Christ's crucifixion: "And the graves were opened; and many bodies of the saints which slept arose, And came out of the graves after his resurrection, and went into the holy city, and appeared unto many" (Matt. 27:52–53).

- The bodily resurrection of born again believers in Christ: "For the Lord himself shall descend from heaven with a shout, with the voice of the archangel, and with the trump of God: and the dead in Christ shall rise first: Then we which are alive and remain shall be caught up together with them in the clouds, to meet the Lord in the air: and so shall we ever be with the Lord" (1 Thess. 4:16–17).

- The final resurrection: "But the rest of the dead lived not again until the thousand years were finished. This is the first resurrection" (Rev. 20:5).

4. judgment

There are many judgments in the Bible; the top three being placed in chronological order are:

a. The judgment seat of Christ for all the believers in Christ who lived during the church age: The believer's salvation is not in question here, but his rewards only. "For we must all appear before the judgment seat of Christ; that every one may receive the things done in his body, according to that he hath done, whether it be good or bad" (2 Cor. 5:10).

b. The sheep and goat judgment (to separate the believers from the nonbelievers at the end of the tribulation period, before the kingdom of heaven which is the Millennial reign of Christ): "And before him shall be gathered all nations: and he shall separate them one from another, as a shepherd divideth his sheep from the goats: And he shall set the sheep on his right hand, but the goats on the left" (Matt. 25:32–33).

c. The Great White Throne Judgment: (this judgment is for all the unsaved throughout time. All are judged according to their works and all receive the lake of fire because salvation is not by works.

And I saw a great white throne, and him that sat on it, from whose face the earth and the heaven fled away; and there was found no place for them. And I saw the dead, small and great, stand before God; and the books were opened: and another book was opened, which is the book of life: and the dead were *judged* out of those things which were written in the books, according to their works.

And the sea gave up the dead which were in it; and death and hell delivered up the dead which were in them: and they were *judged* every man according to their works. And death and hell were cast into the lake of fire. This is the second death. And whosoever was not found written in the book of life was cast into the lake of fire. (Rev. 20:11–15; emphasis mine)

d. Just a quick observation; notice that these three judgments are in chronological order and the first one (the next future judgment) is for believers only. This is fitting and apropos. "For the time is come that *judgment* must begin at the house of God: and if it *first* begin at *us*, what shall the end be of them that obey not the gospel of God?" (1 Pet. 4:17; emphasis mine). Wow!

5. coming

There are yet two future comings of the Lord Jesus Christ. First, in the rapture (coming in the air 1 Thessalonians) when born again believers are "caught up" (1 Thess. 4:13–18) before the tribulation, and second, when the Lord comes to the Jews and stands on the earth literally at the end of the tribulation to set up the Jewish kingdom. If we force these two separate and distinct comings together, we violate the scriptures in the same way as lumping all the varied meanings of the word "church" together.

A. The Lord's coming for born-again believers before the tribulation. This Bible teaching is worthy of an entire book (which I hope to complete before my death) for two reasons:

1) Because belief determines behavior: In other words, if you believe that born-again believers will enter into the worldwide tribulation period, then you had

better have lots of food, water, shelter et. al. to try to save yourself. Conversely, if you believe that the Antichrist cannot be revealed and the tribulation cannot start until after the Holy Ghost is taken out (2 Thess. 2:7–8), then you can spend your time in peace serving, knowing that the Lord will save your hide and you don't have to save yourself.

2) Christians often muddy-up the clear water of truth by lumping Bible terms together that need to be separated. We will consider a list of twelve terms that people take out of context to argue against the pre-trib-ulational rapture of born-again believers. Invariably opponents to the pre-tribula-tional position turn to Matthew 24 and say, "See, the Bible says…elect, kingdom, gather, coming, gospel, disciples…" First, ask yourself, "What is the context of the book of Matthew?" The answer is, it was written before Acts 2, before the death,

burial, and resurrection of the Lord Jesus. Matthew was not written to the "church" of born-again believers, so to make a direct application is to take scripture out of context. Please allow me one simple example.

B. The Lord's coming to the Jews after the tribulation on the earth:

Immediately *after the tribulation* of those days shall the sun be darkened, and the moon shall not give her light, and the stars shall fall from heaven, and the powers of the heavens shall be shaken: And then shall appear the sign of the Son of man in heaven: and then shall all the tribes of the earth mourn, and they shall see the *Son of man coming* in the clouds of heaven with power and great glory. (Matt. 24:29–30; emphasis mine)

Then shall *the LORD* go forth, and fight against those nations, as when he fought in the day of battle. And *his feet shall stand in that day upon the mount of Olives*, which is before Jerusalem on the east, and the mount of Olives shall cleave in the midst thereof toward the east and toward the west, and there shall be a very great valley; and half of the mountain shall remove toward the north, and half of it toward the south. (Zech. 14:3–4; emphasis mine)

Citing Matthew 24:29–30, one Christian emphatically stated that "Obviously the Lord can't return until after the tribulation." With this I agree, but what is the context or which return is being cited? The context of the book of Matthew and especially chapter 24 is the Lord's return for the believing *Jews*—not for born-again "church" believers. Matthew doesn't teach that the Lord can't return for born-again believers until after the tribulation, but only teaches that the Lord can't return for Israel until after the tribulation. Remember, there are two future comings of the Lord. Matthew is referring to the Lord's coming to the Jews specifically at the end of the tribulation. Still not convinced that there are two different and yet future returns or comings of Christ? Please answer this question, "At the Lord's coming, will it be a time of comfort or mourning?" If you say the Lord's return for born-again believers is to be a time of comfort and not of trouble, you're right!

> Now we beseech you, brethren,
> by *the coming of our Lord Jesus Christ,*
> and by our gathering together unto
> him, That ye *be not* soon shaken in
> mind, or be *troubled,* neither by spirit,
> nor by word, nor by letter as from us,
> as that the day of Christ is at hand. (2
> Thess. 2:1–2; emphasis mine)

For *the Lord himself shall descend from heaven* with a shout, with the voice of the archangel, and with the trump of God: and the dead in Christ shall rise first: Then we which are alive and remain shall be *caught up* together with them in the clouds, to meet the Lord in the air: and so shall we ever be with the Lord. Wherefore *comfort* one another with these words. (1 Thess. 4:16–18; emphasis mine)

If you say the Lord's coming triggers a time of wailing and mourning, you are also right!

"Behold, *he cometh* with clouds; and every eye shall see him, and they also which pierced him: and *all* kindreds of the earth *shall wail* because of him. Even so, Amen" (Rev. 1:7; emphasis mine).

"And then shall appear the sign of the Son of man in heaven: and then shall *all* the tribes of the earth *mourn*, and they shall see the *Son of man coming* in the clouds of heaven with power and great glory" (Matt. 24:30; emphasis mine).

So, does the Lord's coming trigger a time of comfort or a time of mourning. I'm sure you realize that it depends to which "coming" of the Lord we are referring. My main point, whether you agree with the pre-tribulational rapture of born-again believers or not, is that there are two future comings of Christ. So, before we can answer the question, "When the Lord comes, will it be a time of comfort or mourning?" we must ask ourselves, "To which coming of the Lord are you referring, his coming in the rapture in the air or at the end of the tribulation to the earth?" The Bible has several references concerning the Lord's coming, worded in various ways, but the context tells us which coming it is. Misunderstanding Bible terms is nothing new. In the Old Testament, Christ was prophesied as coming in two ways; one as a meek lowly servant, riding upon a colt and also as a ruling and reigning King. Obviously, the Jews in Christ's day preferred to see a delivering king, rather than a suffering servant. Perhaps the preachers in the synagogues in Christ's day neglected to preach on Messiah coming as a suffering servant. The point is that the Old Testament described Christ as coming in two ways foreshadowing two separate comings. This is the same reason the Bible shows a drastic contrast between the Lord's coming for born-again believers in the air and his coming to the Jews and to the earth.

A special note to the reader. Before you take a stand on the basic timing of the rapture of born-again believers in respect to the tribulation, I encourage you to look up all associated terms. Yes, all of them! In your study, realize that each term has several meanings, so we must allow the context to define each term. For example, when we find the word "disciple", is it a disciple of Moses, John the Baptist, the Lord Jesus before Acts 2, or a disciple of Christ after Acts 2? When we find the word "saint," is it an Old Testament saint or a New Testament saint? Is it a saint before Acts 2 or after Acts 2? Is it a tribulation saint or a kingdom-age saint? To be sure, these twelve terms listed below are not the only terms we must define to have a clear understanding of the rapture in relation to the tribulation, but these are key. Amazingly, people will argue their position on when the rapture of the church will take place in relation to the tribulation without defining the word church. Eager Bible teachers will rush to Matthew 24 because it uses terms such as disciples, the Lord's coming, gather, tribulation, gospel, kingdom, heaven, and elect. The problem is that all these terms in their proper context have no relationship to the born-again church. The Lord is speaking to Jewish "disciples" before Acts 2, not born-again disciples. The Lord's "coming" mentioned there is his coming at the end of the tribulation to the earth and to the

Jews, not for the born-again church in the air, as in 2 Thessalonians 2. The terms "gather" and "elect" are used in the context of the nation of Israel and not in relation to born-again believers who didn't exist at the time. The tribulation is Jacob's trouble and not the church's trouble. The gospel mentioned is the gospel of the kingdom and not the gospel of Christ. A faithful student of the Bible will follow truth wherever it leads and will not grab a term out of context to bolster his point simply because it's convenient to do so. Once more, all of the following terms have multiple meanings.

1) church
2) disciple, disciples
3) resurrection
4) judgment
5) come, coming, cometh
6) gather, gathering
7) tribulation
8) gospel
9) saint

10) kingdom

11) heaven

12) elect, elect's, chosen

6. gather/gathering

Even as there are two future comings of Christ, there are also two future gatherings; one gathering at each coming.

A. The gathering of born-again believers at his coming in the air before the tribulation.

"Now we beseech you, brethren, by the coming of our Lord Jesus Christ, and by our gathering together unto him" (2 Thess. 2:1).

B. The gathering of Israel on the earth after the tribulation. "And he shall send his angels with a great sound of a trumpet, and they shall gather together his elect from the four winds, from one end of heaven to the other" (Matt. 24:31).

7. tribulation—any trouble, not always "the" tribulation.

  A. Any trouble: "Who comforteth us in all our tribulation, that we may be able to comfort them which are in any trouble, by the comfort wherewith we ourselves are comforted of God" (2 Cor. 1:4).

  B. General trouble: "Confirming the souls of the disciples, and exhorting them to continue in the faith, and that we must through much tribulation enter into the kingdom of God" (Acts 14:22).

  The previous verse does not teach that born-again believers will go through "the tribulation," but that all Christians in all generations will have trouble in this present evil world before we reach heaven.

  C. The tribulation proper: "Immediately after the tribulation of those days shall the sun be darkened, and the moon shall not give her light, and the stars shall fall from heaven, and

the powers of the heavens shall be shaken"
(Matt. 24:29).

8. gospel—the good message or good news.

    A. "The gospel of the kingdom" a.k.a. "the king-
dom of heaven" or the thousand year/ millennial reign of Christ.

    B. "The gospel of Christ"—salvation by grace
through faith via the death, burial, and resurrection of Christ given to the dispensation of
the church age from Acts 2 to the rapture only.

    C. "The gospel of God"—used seven times and
is synonymous with the gospel of Christ.

    D. "The everlasting gospel"—preached during
the tribulational period.

    E. There are several other gospels mentioned in
scripture which I will leave for the reader to
discover for himself. Our main concern is that
when we see a term such as "the gospel" that
we don't automatically assume that we know
the context. When we assume we know a

Bible term without considering the context, we are setting ourselves up to make doctrinal blunders.

9. saint, saints—a sacred or holy one. Can be Old Testament, New Testament, tribulation or other.

   A. Old Testament saints: "They envied Moses also in the camp, and Aaron the saint of the LORD" (Ps. 106:16).
   B. Born-again Christian saints: "Salute every saint in Christ Jesus. The brethren which are with me greet you" (Phil. 4:21).
   C. Tribulation saints: "And it was given unto him to make war with the saints, and to overcome them: and power was given him over all kindreds, and tongues, and nations" (Rev. 13:7).
   D. Other saints: For the reader to discover.

10. kingdom—can mean the realm over which a ruler reigns, the subjects of the ruler, or the reign of the ruler or ruler himself.

A. The kingdom of heaven: The thousand-year Jewish earthly kingdom used exclusively in Matthew.

B. The kingdom of God: For the reader's discovery, not equivalent to any other kingdom.

C. The kingdom of David: "Blessed be the kingdom of our father David, that cometh in the name of the Lord: Hosanna in the highest" (Mark 11:10).

D. several more: Again, the point is not to define each and every kingdom in the Bible, but to make us aware that the term "the kingdom" may refer to born-again believers or it may have absolutely no application at all.

11. heaven—Paul says there are three. "I knew a man in Christ above fourteen years ago, (whether in the body, I cannot tell; or whether out of the body, I cannot tell: God knoweth;) such an one caught up to the third heaven" (2 Cor. 12:2).

A. sky

B. sun, moon stars, outer space

C. The abode of God

D. Also, we are promised a new heaven!

12. Elect, chosen—God choosing individuals or things for his service.

A. Christ: "Behold my servant, whom I uphold; mine elect, in whom my soul delighteth; I have put my spirit upon him: he shall bring forth judgment to the Gentiles" (Isa. 42:1).

B. The nation of Israel: "For Jacob my servant's sake, and Israel mine elect, I have even called thee by thy name: I have surnamed thee, though thou hast not known me" (Isa. 45:4).

C. Jerusalem: "And the LORD said unto Satan, The LORD rebuke thee, O Satan; even the LORD that hath chosen Jerusalem rebuke thee: is not this a brand plucked out of the fire?" (Zech. 3:2).

D. Angels: "I charge thee before God, and the Lord Jesus Christ, and the elect angels, that thou observe these things without preferring

one before another, doing nothing by partiality" (1 Tim. 5:21).

E. All of the original disciples including Judas
Iscariot: "Jesus answered them, Have not I
chosen you twelve, and one of you is a devil?"
(John 6:70).

F. Paul: "But the Lord said unto him, Go thy
way: for he is a chosen vessel unto me, to bear
my name before the Gentiles, and kings, and
the children of Israel" (Acts 9:15).

G. Many more: A cursory view of all variations
of the terms elect and chosen shows that these
terms most often apply to Israel, but sometimes they refer to born-again believers and
even tribulation saints. It is never correct to
automatically assume that any variation of
the word elect or chosen always applies to
any group, whether it be born-again believers,
Israel or other.

Let's consider one last simple Bible illustration of a
single term, which demonstrates how important it is to

understand the proper meaning of a term in its context. When someone uses the word "temple," do you automatically think of a man-made structure? Most often we do, but if we ask for clarification, we can avoid the pitfall into which some of Christ's detractors fell. Our Lord was often misunderstood, because people assumed they knew the meanings of his terms. Case in point:

> Jesus answered and said unto them, Destroy this temple, and in three days I will raise it up. Then said the Jews, Forty and six years was this temple in building, and wilt thou rear it up in three days? But he spake of the temple of his body. (John 2:19–21)
>
> What? know ye not that your body is the temple of the Holy Ghost which is in you, which ye have of God, and ye are not your own? (1 Cor. 6:19)

Our Lord makes a distinction between a man-made temple building and the God-made temple building, which is the body. The first temple is made by man with hands and the second is by God without hands. Without clarifying terms such as these, we will never understand deeper Bible truths. When we study any Bible doctrine, we must always remember to clarify Bible terms and not to lump terms together. I pray that you appreciate the fact that my intention is not to teach you what to think, but how to think. I'm not attempting to teach you how to think like myself, but how to think for yourself.

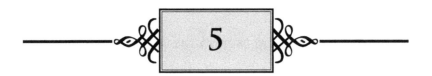

5

The Three Parts of Man

I trust you will agree with the simple statement that conflicts often arise from simple misunderstandings. I say with humility and respect for Calvin's intellectual prowess that an entire system of human reason has been built upon a single misunderstanding of a basic Bible truth. The teaching that man has no free will to believe the gospel is a belief that is founded upon an incorrect assumption. It is assumed that a spiritually dead person can't believe, repent, or have his own will. The Bible truth, which is overlooked, is that of the divine structure and the threefold nature of man. We will later consider the threefold nature of man, including man's will, in greater specificity, but for now, let's understand that the Bible makes a distinction between the spirit and soul of man.

For the word of God is quick, and
powerful, and sharper than any twoedged

sword, piercing even to the *dividing* asunder of *soul* and *spirit*, and of the joints and marrow, and is a discerner of the thoughts and intents of the heart. (Heb. 4:12; emphasis mine)

And the very God of peace sanctify you wholly; and I pray God your whole *spirit and soul* and body be preserved blameless unto the coming of our Lord Jesus Christ. (1 Thess. 5:23; emphasis mine)

Why is it important to understand the Bible distinction between soul and spirit? The reason is because a dead spirit is not a dead soul, neither is a dead spirit a dead mind or body. Calvinists reason that since man is spiritually dead and a dead man can't repent or believe anything, including the gospel, that man therefore has no free will to choose.

Calvinism's basic reasoning

1. Man is spiritually dead.
2. A dead man has no will.

3. A man with no will cannot repent or believe anything.

4. Therefore, God must believe the gospel for man.

The Bible answer to this reasoning is that while man before being regenerated by God is indeed spiritually dead and cut off from God and heaven, he is still a living, thinking, feeling, decision-making being. Even an un-regenerated person with a dead spirit can laugh, cry, reproduce, think, and communicate. The reason a spiritually dead person is able to do these things is because God made man a *living soul*, and it is man's *soul* which encompasses his emotions, appetites, desires, and longings, including his reasoning mind. Un-regenerated persons buy, sell, reason, accept, reject, and function in a busy world in spite of being spiritually dead unto God. The key point to acknowledge is that man repents and believes not with his *spirit* which is *dead*, but with his *soul* which is *alive!* After man *believes* the gospel in his *soul* and repents in his heart, God in the person of the Holy Ghost comes into man's heart. Again, the Holy Ghost comes in only *after* man asks God to do so. This divine order is clearly taught in scripture and will be examined in a later chapter. The action of God entering man in the person of the Holy Spirit makes him spiritually alive or "quickens" the believer's spirit and seals him unto the day of redemption.

> "And grieve not the holy Spirit of
> God, whereby ye are sealed unto the day
> of redemption" (Eph. 4:30).

This, of course, is what the Bible refers to as being saved, born again, redeemed and being made spiritually *whole*.

We will consider Bible verses showing that man reasons, longs after, desires, etc., with his soul later in this chapter, but for now, let's understand clearly that a dead spirit isn't a dead soul, a dead mind, or a dead will. Please consider a common Bible account of two individuals who were spiritually dead yet they believed and accepted God's atonement or gospel and one person who was spiritually dead who didn't believe or accept God's atonement. Ask yourself the question, "Why are all babies born spiritually dead and need to be regenerated?" You probably know that the answer is because of the fall of our parents, Adam and Eve. God told Adam and Eve that they would die the same day that they ate of the tree of knowledge. Adam and Eve ate of the tree of knowledge. They didn't die physically that same day, but they did die spiritually that same day. This is the reason we must be born again and have our spirit, which is the part of man that is conscious of God, renewed unto God. The point should be obvious to the reader that even though Adam and Eve were spiritually dead in Genesis 3:6, they were still able to reason, repent, believe and accept God's atonement for their sin in Genesis 3:21! God provides and offers the atonement to man and man either rejects and refuses it or accepts and receives it; this is the Bible pattern.

> "And not only so, but we also joy in God through our Lord Jesus Christ, by whom *we* have now *received the atonement*" (Rom. 5:11; emphasis mine).
>
> "But as many as *received him*, to them gave he power to become the sons of God, even to them that believe on his name" (John 1:12; emphasis mine).

Moreover, Adam and Eve could have chosen to reject God's plan of salvation through the blood atonement. Later in the next chapter of Genesis, we read how their son Cain did reject the blood sacrifice, condemning his own soul. Now we understand clearly that mankind is able to make soul saving decisions with his living and conscious soul in spite of his dead spirit. There is no need for God to believe anything for man or to force anything onto man. Simply put, man is *not* able to save his own soul, but he is able to *call* upon the one God who is able. Let's take a brief look at the three parts of man.

> "So God created man in his own image, in the image of God created he him; male and female created he them" (Gen. 1:27).

God is a triune God consisting of Father, Son and Holy Spirit, these three being one eternal God. What does it mean when the Bible states that man was made in the image of God? It means many things, but for our study we'll consider two points.

1. Like God his creator, man is immortal. Man will exist forever either in heaven above or in the lake of fire.

2. Like God his creator, man has three parts or aspects. The Bible identifies the three parts of man in 1 Thessalonians 5:23 as spirit, soul, and body.

> "And the very God of peace sanctify you wholly; and I pray God your whole *spirit* and *soul* and *body* be preserved blameless unto the coming of our Lord Jesus Christ" (1 Thess. 5:23; emphasis mine).

Briefly stated:

1. The body = is aware of its surroundings, hot, cold, hunger, etc. The body is the temporary physical part of man which houses the soul and spirit.

2. The soul = a spiritual and eternal component of man including man's individuality, emotions, appetites, desires, longings, and reasoning mind. The soul is aware of self, "I think, therefore I am."

3. The spirit = a spiritual component of man which is aware of God after salvation.

We must understand that the soul of man is eternal and that the soul of an un-regenerated man is also a living, spiritual component, not a physical component. As we have seen with Adam and Eve, even in an unsaved state, the soul of man is completely capable of thinking, reasoning, repenting, and believing. There are hundreds of references containing the words soul or souls, and it's important to look up every one and examine its context. Only after finishing this exhaustive task will we understand the soul of man in a clear and useful way. Here are some Bible facts relating to the soul of man.

Bible facts relating to the soul of man.

Fact 1: God is a triune God existing as God the Father, God the Son and God the Holy Spirit/Ghost. These three being distinct while remaining one.

"Hear, O Israel: The LORD our God is one LORD" (Deut. 6:4).

"And Jesus answered him, The first of all the commandments is, Hear, O Israel; The Lord our God is one Lord" (Mark 12:29).

Fact 2: A triune God made man in his own image.

"And God said, Let *us* make man in *our* image, after our likeness" (Gen. 1:26a; emphasis mine).

There is a plethora of truth here which time and space disallows, but the most relevant Bible doctrine is that of the threefold nature of man. This verse, along with several others, teaches that man exists in three parts while remaining one person. The apostle Paul to the Thessalonians explained the three parts of a whole man this way:

"And the very God of peace sanctify you wholly; and I pray God your whole *spirit* and *soul* and *body* be preserved blameless unto the coming of our Lord Jesus Christ" (1 Thess. 5:23; emphasis mine).

Does it make any sense at all for God to create man in his own image, i.e., a three in one tri-unity of body soul and spirit only to let one-third perish? Born-again believers will be preserved whole as God intended.

> "Beloved, now are we the sons of God, and it doth not yet appear what we shall be: but we know that, when he shall appear, *we shall be like him*; for we shall see him as he is" (1 John 3:2; emphasis mine).

For example, we will be a complete triune being like God.

Fact 3: God has a soul.

A. "Behold my servant, whom I have chosen; my beloved, in whom *my soul* is well pleased: I will put *my spirit* upon him, and he shall shew judgment to the Gentiles" (Matt. 12:18; emphasis mine).

Note: God also mentions his spirit in the same verse revealing the triune nature of God, i.e., Father, Son, and Holy Spirit.

B. God's soul experiences delight. "Behold my servant, whom I uphold; mine elect, in whom *my soul delighteth*; I have put my spirit upon him: he shall bring forth judgment to the Gentiles" (Isa. 42:1; emphasis mine).

Fact 4: The soul of man desires, has longings, feels delight and anguish.

A. "When the LORD thy God shall enlarge thy border, as he hath promised thee, and thou shalt say, I will eat flesh, because thy *soul longeth* to eat flesh; thou mayest eat flesh, whatsoever thy soul lusteth after" (Deut. 12:20; emphasis mine).

B. "In the multitude of my thoughts within me thy comforts *delight* my *soul*" (Ps. 94:19; emphasis mine).

C. "And they said one to another, We are verily guilty concerning our brother, in that we saw the *anguish* of his *soul*, when he besought us, and we would not hear; therefore is this distress come upon us" (Gen. 42:21; emphasis mine).

D. "Men do not despise a thief, if he steal to satisfy his *soul* when he is *hungry*" (Prov. 6:30; emphasis mine).

E. "He shall see of the *travail* of his *soul*, and shall be satisfied: by his knowledge shall my righteous servant justify many; for he shall bear their iniquities" (Isa. 53:11; emphasis mine).

Fact 5: A human soul is precious.

"None of them can by any means redeem his brother, nor give to God a ransom for him: (For *the redemption of their soul is precious*, and it ceaseth for ever:)" (Ps. 49:7–8; emphasis mine).

The phrase "it ceaseth for ever" means that if earthly treasures were given for the ransom of one soul, the ransom payment could never cease coming or in other words, it would never be enough. Here, again, a single soul is compared to the riches of the world.

> "For what shall it profit a man, if he shall gain the whole world, and lose his own soul? Or *what shall a man give in exchange for his soul?*" (Mark 8:36–37; emphasis mine).

The answer to the question of course is that nothing that man can offer can purchase his soul, only the blood of the only begotten Son of God can purchase man's soul.

Fact 6: Death takes place when the soul and spirit of life depart from the body. The context here is Elijah resurrecting the widow woman's son.

> And he stretched himself upon the child three times, and cried unto the Lord, and said, O Lord my God, I pray thee, let this child's *soul* come *into* him again. And the Lord heard the voice of Elijah; and the

soul of the child came *into* him again, and he
revived. (1 Kings 17:21–22; emphasis mine)

Here is another scripture pertaining to death and the
departing soul of Jacob's wife, Rachel.

"And it came to pass, as her *soul* was
in departing, (for she died) that she called
his name Benoni: but his father called him
Benjamin" (Gen. 35:18; emphasis mine).

Fact 7: The soul of man is immortal.

The Lord Jesus said: "And fear not them which kill the
body, but are not able to kill the soul: but rather fear him
which is able to destroy both soul and body in hell" (Matt.
10:28).

The destroying of a soul in hell is never-ending,
ever-dying, and never being dead.

Man is a trichotomy (three-part being), not a dichotomy (two-part being) or more accurately, man is a triune
being like God. The soul of man exists separately from the
body and spirit and is not as E. W. Bullinger suggested.

Bullinger maintained that the soul of man was simply the result of the combining of the spirit and body and at the point of death the soul ceases to exist. This is a gross error. The book of Revelation clearly teaches that martyred souls were seen in heaven by John after their death and before their bodily resurrection.

> "And I saw thrones, and they sat upon them, and judgment was given unto them: and *I saw the souls* of them that were *beheaded* for the witness of Jesus, and for the word of God, and which had not worshipped the beast, neither his image, neither had received his mark upon their foreheads, or in their hands; and they lived and reigned with Christ a thousand years" (Rev. 20:4; emphasis mine).

Christ's soul existed after his death.

> "He seeing this before spake of the resurrection of *Christ*, that his *soul* was

not left in hell, neither his flesh did see corruption" (Acts 2:31; emphasis mine).

Note: Before the resurrection of Christ, hell (shol/sheh-ole') had two main divisions; paradise or Abraham's bosom and the torment area. Our Lord Jesus descended into the paradise part of hell. After the resurrection of Christ, the Old Testament saints were taken to heaven and today hell contains only the damned. "Wherefore he saith, When he ascended up on high, he led captivity captive, and gave gifts unto men" (Eph. 4:8).

Fact 8: The spirit and soul of man are saved at the moment of conversion. Yes, the spirit of man is regenerated and saved.

"To deliver such an one unto Satan for the destruction of the flesh, that the *spirit* may be *saved* in the day of the Lord Jesus" (1 Cor. 5:5; emphasis mine).

Bullinger believed that the spirit of man is that which is saved and not the soul. The Bible teaches that both are saved.

> "But we are not of them who draw back unto perdition; but of them that believe to the *saving* of the *soul*" (Heb. 10:39; emphasis mine).

Not only does the Bible clearly teach that the soul of man is that which is saved in Hebrews 10:39, it also declares that not believing in the saving of one's soul is perdition, which is a damnable heresy. The psalmist believed in the salvation or redemption of his soul.

> "My lips shall greatly rejoice when I sing unto thee; and my soul, which thou hast redeemed" (Ps. 71:23). Note: Here the action is past tense denoting a completed action!

There may be those who believe that man is a dichotomy or two-part being who becomes a trichotomy or three-part being at the moment of salvation. This is not the case. Even as there is a great difference between a dead horse and no horse at all, there is a difference between a person with a dead un-regenerated spirit and a person with no spirit. In other words, an unsaved person does have a spirit, albeit a dead one.

Fact 9: The word of God is powerful enough to save our souls.

> "Wherefore lay apart all filthiness and superfluity of naughtiness, and receive with meekness the engrafted *word*, which is able to *save* your *souls*" (James 1:21; emphasis mine).

The word of God contains the gospel message concerning the cleansing power of the blood of Christ. When we receive God's word, we are receiving the atonement. It's also not surprising that the same mighty word of God that framed the worlds is also able to save our souls.

> "Through faith we understand that *the worlds were framed by the word of God,* so that things which are seen were not made of things which do appear" (Heb. 11:3; emphasis mine).

Fact 10: Salvation of the soul is the end result of our faith.

> "Receiving the end of your faith, even the salvation of your souls" (1 Pet. 1:9).

Fact 11: The eternal anguish of the unsaved soul.

> And he spake a parable unto them, saying, The ground of a certain rich man brought forth plentifully: And he thought within himself, saying, What shall I do, because I have no room where to bestow

PASTOR KEVIN KLINE

my fruits? And he said, This will I do: I will pull down my barns, and build greater; and there will I bestow all my fruits and my goods. And I will say to my soul, Soul, thou hast much goods laid up for many years; take thine ease, eat, drink, and be merry. But God said unto him, Thou fool, this night thy *soul* shall be *required* of thee: then whose shall those things be, which thou hast provided? (Luke 12:16–20; emphasis mine)

There was a certain rich man, which was clothed in purple and fine linen, and fared sumptuously every day: And there was a certain beggar named Lazarus, which was laid at his gate, full of sores, And desiring to be fed with the crumbs which fell from the rich man's table: moreover the dogs came and licked his sores. And it came to pass, that the beggar died, and was carried by the angels into Abraham's bosom: the rich man also died, and was buried; And in hell he lift up his eyes, *being in torments*, and seeth Abraham afar off, and Lazarus in his bosom. And he cried and said, Father Abraham, have mercy on me, and send Lazarus, that he may dip the tip of his finger in water, and *cool my tongue*; for I am *tormented* in this flame. (Luke 16:19–24; emphasis mine)

There are many things to learn here. Let's consider a few.

1. It, by necessity, was the rich man's soul that was tormented because he was spiritually dead and according to verse 22 his body was dead, leaving only his conscious soul.
2. Both the soul of the rich man and Lazarus existed after death.
3. The rich man's soul was in torments, plural.
4. Even though this man was physically and spiritually dead, his soul was thirsty and felt torment.

Fact 12: Believing God's Bible genders personal confidence and assurance in the soul!

A. "But *God will* redeem *my soul* from the power of the grave: for he shall receive me. Selah" (Ps. 49:15; emphasis mine).

B. "And though after *my* skin worms destroy this body, yet in *my* flesh shall *I* see God: Whom *I* shall see for *myself*, and *mine* eyes shall behold, and not another" (Job 19:26–27a; emphasis mine).

C. "Beloved, now are *we* the sons of God, and it doth not yet appear what *we shall* be: but *we know* that, when he *shall* appear, *we shall* be like him; for *we shall* see him as he is" (1 John 3:2; emphasis mine).

Fact 13: You may remember that in chapter one we saw the Bible definition of the soul. You may ask, "What does it matter if my soul is saved as long as my spirit is saved?" One part cannot be saved without the other and a little more study reveals how important the soul of man ("your soul") really is. Let's reconsider a Bible definition for the soul of man, seen in chapter 1.

A. "For what is a man profited, if he shall gain the whole world, and lose *his* own *soul*? or what shall a man give in exchange for *his soul*?" (Matt. 16:26; emphasis mine).

B. "For what shall it profit a man, if he shall gain the whole world, and lose *his* own *soul*?" (Mark 8:36; emphasis mine).

C. "For what is a man advantaged, if he gain the whole world, and lose *himself*, or be cast away?" (Luke 9:25; emphasis mine).

Answer: Your soul is your true self, that which makes you distinct.

Some readers may be helped by looking at the important subject of the three parts of man in another way. If we were to apply simple reason to the composition of man, we could make these general observations.

1. Man being composed of a spirit, a soul, and a body is two-thirds or mostly a spiritual being.

2. Even an unsaved person with a dead spirit, a living soul, and a living body must be looked upon as being half of a spiritual being at least.

3. It is in fact an unsaved man's spiritual half, i.e., his living soul that decides and chooses to accept or reject the gospel.

Review: The most important points to remember from this chapter are that even an unsaved spiritually dead person has a mind and a will (more on this topic later) and is able to repent and believe. This is made possible by man possessing a living soul in spite of his having a dead spirit. Some may find it easier to review the subject like this:

1. The spirit in an unsaved man is dead.

2. The soul is not the spirit; it is separate and distinct.

3. The soul of man is a living, spiritual component of an unsaved man.

4. The soul of man is the living, spiritual component of mankind that makes decisions.

6

The God-Given Free Will of Man

Let's first define the will of man as: Man's desire with an intention to be expressed in the future. To believe that mankind, saved or lost, has no will to choose Christ, is to fly in the face of common sense as well as a mountain of Bible evidence. The common-sense person knows that even two and three-year-olds have a will. This will is sometimes positive and often negative, but it is blatantly obvious. Why do some theologians deny that man has a free will? As we have seen in the previous chapter on the three parts of man, the doctrine disallowing the free will of man stems from the premise that man is spiritually dead and therefore has no will. However, we have seen from the Bible that a dead spirit is not a dead soul; neither is a dead spirit a dead mind or body. Man's free will and ability to make choices stems from his God-given, living soul, not his dead spirit. Since God made man in his image and God has a free will, it naturally follows that man must have a free will also. But what does the Holy Bible actually teach; does man have a free will?

We will examine these topics in this order of reasoning in light of scripture.

1. God has a will.
2. Mankind in general has a will to make choices.
3. God expects man to make choices with his will.
4. Unsaved man in particular has a will and can make choices.
5. Does having a will to make conscious choices mean that a person wills himself to be saved?
6. What is God's will for man pertaining to salvation?
7. God's will is sometimes contingent upon man's will.

God has a will.

And the LORD God said, It is not good that the man should be alone; *I will* make him an help meet for him. (Gen. 2:18; emphasis mine)

And the LORD smelled a sweet savour; and the LORD said in his heart, *I will not* again curse the ground any more for man's sake; for the imagination of man's heart is evil from his youth; neither will I again smite any more every thing living, as I have done. (Gen. 8:21; emphasis mine)

God in the person of Christ

"And Jesus put forth his hand, and touched him, saying, *I will*; be thou clean. And immediately his leprosy was cleansed" (Matt. 8:3; emphasis mine).

Clearly God has a will and makes choices.

Mankind in general has a will to make choices.

God's instructions to Israel:

"And when *ye will* offer a sacrifice of thanksgiving unto the LORD, offer it at *your own will*" (Lev. 22:29; emphasis mine).

General New Testament verses:

"For the prophecy came not in old time by *the will of man*: but holy men of God spake as they were moved by the Holy Ghost" (2 Pet. 1:21; emphasis mine).

"Nevertheless he that standeth stedfast in his heart, having no necessity, but hath power over *his own will*, and hath so decreed in his heart that *he will* keep his virgin, doeth well" (1 Cor. 7:37; emphasis mine).

"Then said Jesus unto his disciples, *If any man will* come after me, let him deny himself, and take up his cross, and follow me" (Matt. 16:24; emphasis mine).

"So that we may boldly say, The Lord is my helper, and *I will not* fear what man shall do unto me" (Heb. 13:6; emphasis mine).

"Wherefore (as the Holy Ghost saith, To day *if ye will* hear his voice, Harden not your hearts, as in the provocation, in the day of temptation in the wilderness" (Heb. 3:7–8; emphasis mine).

"While it is said, To day *if ye will* hear his voice, harden not your hearts, as in the provocation" (Heb. 3:5; emphasis mine).

"Again, he limiteth a certain day, saying in David, To day, after so long a time; as it is said, To day *if ye will* hear his voice, harden not your hearts" (Heb. 4:7; emphasis mine).

"Yea, and *all that will* live godly in Christ Jesus shall suffer persecution" (2 Tim. 3:12; emphasis mine).

The Bible teaches that everyone has a will:

"For *whosoever will* save his life shall lose it: and *whosoever will* lose his life for my sake shall find it" (Matt. 16:25; emphasis mine).

"But it shall not be so among you: but *whosoever will* be great among you, let him be your minister" (Matt. 20:26; emphasis mine).

"And *whosoever will* be chief among you, let him be your servant" (Matt. 20:27; emphasis mine).

"And when he had called the people unto him with his disciples also, he said unto them, *Whosoever will* come after me, let him deny himself, and take up his cross, and follow me" (Mark 8:34; emphasis mine).

"For *whosoever will* save his life shall lose it; but whosoever shall lose his life for my sake and the gospel's, the same shall save it" (Mark 8:35; emphasis mine).

"But so shall it not be among you: but *whosoever will* be great among you, shall be your minister" (Mark 10:43; emphasis mine).

"And *whosoever will* not receive you, when ye go out of that city, shake off the very dust from your feet for a testimony against them" (Luke 9:5; emphasis mine).

"For *whosoever will* save his life shall lose it: but whosoever will lose his life for my sake, the same shall save it" (Luke 9:24; emphasis mine).

God expects man to make choices with his will.

"I call heaven and earth to record this day against you, that I have set before you life and death, blessing and cursing: therefore *choose* life, that both thou and thy seed may live" (Deut. 30:19; emphasis mine)

Some of these people made the right choice and some did not.

> And if it seem evil unto you to serve the LORD, *choose you* this day whom ye will serve; whether the gods which your fathers served that were on the other side of the flood, or the gods of the Amorites, in whose land ye dwell: but as for me and my house, *we will* serve the LORD. (Joshua 24:15; emphasis mine).
>
> But if I live in the flesh, this is the fruit of my labour: yet what *I shall choose* I wot not. (Phil. 1:22; emphasis mine).

The two tribulation witnesses:

> "These have power to shut heaven, that it rain not in the days of their prophecy: and have power over waters to turn them to blood, and to smite the earth

with all plagues, as often *as they will*" (Rev. 11:6; emphasis mine).

Man's will is also seen in the negative.

"And it shall come to pass, that *whosoever will not* hearken unto my words which he shall speak in my name, I will require it of him" (Deut. 18:19).

"And *whosoever will not* do the law of thy God, and the law of the king, let judgment be executed speedily upon him, whether it be unto death, or to banishment, or to confiscation of goods, or to imprisonment" (Ezra 7:26).

The phrase "if ye will not" is used eighteen times in scripture. The Bible clearly teaches that man has a will and he is free to choose.

Unsaved man in particular has a will and can make choices.

Someone may be thinking that all of the verses presented above are verses relating to saved individuals, as though a saved person possesses a will, but an unsaved person does not. Fair enough; let's now consider Bible verses relating to the *unsaved* individual and his will to make choices.

> "And the Spirit and the bride say,
> Come. And let him that heareth say,
> Come. And let him that is athirst come.
> And *whosoever will,* let him take the water
> of life freely" (Rev. 22:17; emphasis mine).

This verse offers a clear invitation to all unsaved individuals outside the bride of Christ to be saved today.

> O Jerusalem, Jerusalem, thou that
> killest the prophets, and stonest them
> which are sent unto thee, how often would

THE DOCTRINE OF ETERNAL LIFE

I have gathered thy children together, even as a hen gathereth her chickens under her wings, and *ye would not*! (Matt. 23:37; emphasis mine)

The past tense of will is would. Please notice that the Bible does not say that "ye could not," but rather ye "would not!" Here the Lord offered to gather the people of Jerusalem, but *their own will* prevented it. This verse is proof that an unsaved person has a free will and can make choices.

The parallel account of Matthew 23:37 says:

"O Jerusalem, Jerusalem, which killest the prophets, and stonest them that are sent unto thee; how often would I have gathered thy children together, as a hen doth gather her brood under her wings, and *ye would not*!" (Luke 13:34)

Matthew 23:37 and Luke 13:34 prove that an unsaved person has a free will and can make choices.

God giving man choices is consistent throughout scripture. God gave man a choice whether or not to eat of the tree of knowledge and man, as we know, made the wrong choice. On the day of Jesus' crucifixion, the Jerusalem crowd was given a choice, Barabbas or Christ, and the majority chose Barabbas. Further, the mixed multitude that came out of Egypt consisting of redeemed and non-redeemed persons was given a choice.

> "I call heaven and earth to record this day against you, that I have set before you life and death, blessing and cursing: therefore *choose life*, that both thou and thy seed may live" (Deut. 30:19; emphasis mine).

The Lord Jesus also gave mankind the life or death choice in a spiritual way:

> "Verily, verily, I say unto you, He that heareth my word, and believeth on him that sent me, hath everlasting life, and

shall not come into condemnation; but is passed from death unto life" (John 5:24).

"For the wages of sin is death; but the gift of God is eternal life through Jesus Christ our Lord" (Rom. 6:23).

Eternal life is a gift which must be received as such, requiring the free will of man to choose to receive it. God did not create automatons or robots, God created beings in his image; each one with a free will to choose. The fact that man has a free will to choose in no way suggests that man enters heaven because he chooses to, but that he enters heaven because he chose to receive Christ!

"But as many as *received him*, to them gave he power to become the sons of God, even to them that believe on his name" (John 1:12; emphasis mine).

Remember the reasoning that man has no will is based on the misunderstanding of the composition of man. This was covered extensively in chapter 5, but to summarize: It is believed that since an unsaved man is spiritually dead and a dead man can't reason or believe anything, he also has no will to choose Christ. The Bible answer to this line of reasoning again, is that, although unsaved man has a dead spirit, man's soul is alive and able to reason and believe the gospel. The living soul of an unsaved person contains his identity, reasoning power, and his will. The clear teaching of the Bible declares that man does have a free will and to deny this fact is to directly contradict the Bible. Man's decision to believe or not to believe in Christ is a free will choice.

> The other disciples therefore said unto him, We have seen the Lord. But he said unto them, Except I shall see in his hands the print of the nails, and put my finger into the print of the nails, and thrust my hand into his side, *I will not* believe. (John 20:25; emphasis mine)

Please notice that Thomas said *I will not* believe, not I cannot believe, in other words, Thomas was saying, I choose not to believe until I put my finger...

If anyone maintains that an unsaved person has no free will to choose because he is spiritually dead, then let us ask "what does the Bible say?" Without any twisting of scripture or any theological gymnastics, does the Bible plainly teach that unsaved man has a will? The answer is yes. If unsaved man has a will, then it follows that God doesn't need to believe the gospel for him. Can you answer this Bible question? What are the first two reasons given by the Christ Jesus for casting individuals into the lake of fire?

> But the *fearful*, and *unbelieving*, and the abominable, and murderers, and whoremongers, and sorcerers, and idolaters, and all liars, shall have their part in the lake which burneth with fire and brimstone: which is the second death. (Rev. 21:8; emphasis mine)

These unsaved, spiritually dead individuals who will be cast into the lake of fire are those who in life were too fearful to come to Christ. This proves that a spiritually dead person is conscious and can be fearful. The second reason

Christ gives for casting spiritually dead persons into the lake of fire is unbelief. God would not be just in punishing anyone in the lake of fire for their unbelief if they were not able to believe. Arguably, the clearest verse stating that man indeed has a free will comes from the Saviour. Consider carefully what the Lord himself said on the subject of man's will as it relates to the doctrine of salvation and eternal life.

"And *ye will not* come to me, that ye might have life" (John 5:40; emphasis mine).

Please notice that the Saviour did not say, ye cannot come to me, but rather "*ye will not* come to me."

The Holy Bible clearly teaches that man has a free will to choose. This is why God is justified in punishing those who chose not to *obey* the gospel.

"For the time is come that judgment must begin at the house of God: and if it first begin at us, what shall the end be of them that *obey not* the gospel of God?" (1 Pet. 4:17; emphasis mine).

Obedience to the gospel expresses a free will choice! And again, we read:

> And to you who are troubled rest with us, when the Lord Jesus shall be revealed from heaven with his mighty angels, In flaming fire taking vengeance on them that know not God, and that *obey not* the gospel of our Lord Jesus Christ. (2 Thess. 1:7–8; emphasis mine)

God would be unjust if he punished man for not obeying the gospel if man had no ability or choice to obey.

And to those who are willing to obey the gospel the Bible says:

> "Seeing *ye have* purified your souls *in obeying* the truth through the Spirit unto unfeigned love of the brethren, see that ye love one another with a pure heart fervently" (1 Pet. 1:22; emphasis mine).

Does having a will to make conscious choices
mean that a person wills himself to be saved?

No, of course not.

> He came unto his own, and his own
> received him not. But as many as received
> him, to them gave he power to become the
> sons of God, even to them that believe on his
> name: Which were *born*, not of blood, nor
> of the will of the flesh, *nor of the will of man*,
> but of God. (John 1:11–13; emphasis mine)

The distinguishing point here is that man does not will himself to be saved, but man does make a conscious choice to either accept or reject Christ as Saviour. So, it's not the person saving themselves by his will, but the Saviour saving him because the Saviour said "I will."

> "Behold, I stand at the door, and
> knock: *if any man* hear my voice, and
> *open the door, I will* come in to him, and

will sup with him, and he with me" (Rev. 3:20; emphasis mine).

The teaching that man, at times, willingly seeks God is consistent throughout scripture; Old Testament and New.

"And ye shall *seek me*, and *find me*, when ye shall search for me with all your heart" (Jer. 29:13; emphasis mine).

"For *every one* that asketh receiveth; and he *that seeketh findeth*; and to him that knocketh it shall be opened" (Luke 11:10; emphasis mine).

What does the Bible say is God's will for man pertaining to salvation?

We can be helped to find what the will of God is by eliminating that which is not God's will.

"The Lord is not slack concerning his promise, as some men count slackness; but is longsuffering to us-ward, not willing that any should perish, but that all should come to repentance" (2 Pet. 3:9).

The word "perish" in its context refers to those who die and go to hell. If we hand a Bible to an average person and ask him to read this verse and then ask, "according to this verse does God want anyone to perish?" The answer would be, "No, God doesn't want anyone to perish." If we then had him read John 3:16:

> "For God so loved the world, that he gave his only begotten Son, that whosoever believeth in him should not perish, but have *everlasting life*" (John 3:16).

And ask, "For whom did the Son of God die according to this verse?" The plain answer would be "for the world" and not for a certain few.

If someone maintains that the word "any" in 2 Peter 3:9 really means "any elect person" and the word "world" in John 3:16 really means "the elect," then we are reading into God's holy word. Another person could just as easily say the word "any" in 2 Peter 3:9 really means "purple unicorns" and have just as much authority as the person who says it means "any elect person." We cannot add to or take away from God's word with impunity.

The plain truth of the Bible declares that the will of God is for all to come to him and be saved.

> "For this is good and acceptable in the sight of God our Saviour; Who will have all men to be saved, and to come unto the knowledge of the truth" (1 Tim. 2:3–4).

The Bible declares without reservation that God, because of the sacrifice of his Son, is the Saviour of all men.

> "For therefore we both labour and suffer reproach, because we trust in the living God, who is the Saviour of all men, specially of those that believe" (1 Tim. 4:10).

You may be wondering how God could be the Saviour of all men when all men obviously won't be in heaven. Simply put, God is the Creator of all men yet some reject that truth. But the fact that some men reject the truth that God created them doesn't change that fact that God is still their Creator. The same reasoning applies to God being the Saviour of all men. Just because some men reject the fact that God is the Saviour of all men (i.e., they reject that Christ died for all mankind) in no way changes the fact that God is their Saviour. Some people may reject the truth that God is their Saviour and their Creator, but the truth that he is still remains. For those who reject God as their Saviour and refuse to receive Christ, no salvation is given; even though God is still their Saviour in that God provided a way for them to be saved. However, without receiving the Son of God, no benefits of salvation or eternal life from God can flow. Furthermore, for those who do accept God's sacrifice on Calvary, God is their Saviour in a special way or as the Bible states in 1 Timothy 4:10:

"For therefore we both labour and suffer reproach, because we trust in the living God, who is the Saviour of all men, specially of those that believe" (1 Tim. 4:10).

The two most important doctrines to understand here are that: God can be called the Saviour of all men because he has provided salvation for all men, and to those who accept God's salvation, God is special. This doctrine is a universal Bible concept.

"And he is the propitiation for our sins: and not for ours only, but also for the sins of the whole world" (1 John 2:2).

Again, the atonement or propitiation has been provided by the Father through the Son for the whole. Some folks may have been taught that Jesus didn't die for all, because somehow his blood would be wasted on nonbelievers. This misunderstanding will be covered in the chapter covering the doctrine of limited atonement. Ask yourself if these verses are true.

"For the Son of man is come to save that which was lost" (Matt. 18:11).

"For the Son of man is come to seek and to save that which was lost" (Luke 19:10).

If you believe that these verses are true, then ask yourself, whom did the Son of man come to seek and save? If your answer is that which was lost. Who then was lost? Was not the whole world lost and not just a certain few? Yes, the whole world was lost, not just some.

"And we know that we are of God, and the whole world lieth in wickedness" (1 John 5:19).

Consequently, the Lord commanded the gospel to be preached throughout the whole world providing an opportunity of salvation to all.

"Verily I say unto you, Wheresoever this gospel shall be preached in the whole world, there shall also this, that this woman hath done, be told for a memorial of her" (Matt. 26:13).

The truth that God wants every person to be saved is clearly seen in these two verses of scripture:

> "The Lord is not slack concerning his promise, as some men count slackness; but is longsuffering to us-ward, not willing that any should perish, but that all should come to repentance" (2 Pet. 3:9).
>
> "And he is the propitiation for our sins: and not for ours only, but also for the sins of the whole world" (1 John 2:2).

The teaching that man has no free will creates an insurmountable problem; that being that it reverses the onus, obligation, and burden which God Almighty has placed upon man and places it on God! This will be examined in the chapter on unconditional election. The pure teaching that God wants all mankind to be saved is clearly seen in the plain teaching of scripture.

God's will is sometimes contingent upon man's will.

God's choice offered to the church at Pergamos:

> "Repent; or else I will come unto thee
> quickly, and will fight against them with
> the sword of my mouth" (Rev. 2:16).

God is indicating if you will not repent, I will come and I will fight against you, but if you will repent, then I will not come and fight. God is simply giving man a warning and a choice to do the right thing. Here is another example of God giving man a choice while encouraging man to do the right thing:

> "Draw nigh to God, and he will draw
> nigh to you. Cleanse your hands, ye sin-
> ners; and purify your hearts, ye double
> minded" (James 4:8).

God places the burden upon man to draw nigh first and then God promises to draw nigh to the individual. Put simply, the Lord indicates if we will draw near to him, he will draw near to us. Let's reconsider some recently examined scripture.

> "For this is good and acceptable in the sight of God our Saviour; Who will have all men to be saved, and to come unto the knowledge of the truth" (1 Tim. 2:3–4).

God's method of dealing with man for salvation in 1 Timothy 2:3–4 is exactly the same as it is in Revelation 2:16, and James 4:8, that being that God's will (or the action he takes) is contingent upon man's will. God's will is for all men to be saved, but all men will not (refuse to) be saved. Those persons who will not be saved are faced with the consequences of hell and the lake of fire.

While it's true that God's will is greater than man's will and God does most things regardless of man's will, God does some things contingent upon man's will. In other words, God indicates in scripture that if man will do some things then God will respond accordingly. This is simply God giving man choices and consequences based upon those choices. Adam and Eve were given choices such as whether or not to eat of the tree of knowledge of good and evil. God told Adam that he would suffer the consequence of death for eating; still God allowed Adam to make his choice. The story of Adam and Eve illustrates the difference between the primary will of God and God's alternate will, or if you would rather, the perfect will of God and the permissive will of God. In simple terms, God's primary and perfect will for Adam was to not eat of the tree of knowledge, but God allowed Adam and Eve to make their own choices. Even though God didn't want Adam and Eve to disobey his perfect will, their choice was allowed within the boundaries of God's permissive will. When Adam and Eve chose God's permissive will over God's perfect will, they were faced with the consequences of being physically banished from paradise, working much harder, and eventual death. After man was fallen and disallowed to return to Eden, God's new perfect will for Adam and Eve became the acceptance of the blood atonement. The best that Adam and Eve could do was to repent of their wrongdoing and accept God's blood sacrifice. Does this sound familiar? God's perfect will for fallen man today is to repent and believe the gospel. When man rejects the gospel, he is choosing God's alternate or permissive will and like Adam and Eve he must suffer the consequences. When man receives God's perfect will by accepting Christ, then God's perfect will becomes that of service. Some born-again believers choose God's perfect will and serve Christ fully; others choose God's permissive will and serve less than fully. When we choose not to serve in God's perfect will of full service and choose rather God's permissive will of lesser or no service, we suffer the consequences as always. A simple way to look at this subject is to realize that God always has two general categories from which man can choose. God's perfect will, which yields positive benefits, and God's permissive will within God's allowable boundaries. God's permissive will always has some negative consequences, including possible death. One example is 1 Corinthians 11:30: God will allow people to abuse the Lord's supper, but there are consequences.

"For he that eateth and drinketh unworthily, eateth and drinketh damnation to himself, not discerning the Lord's body. For this cause many are weak and sickly among you, and many sleep" (1 Cor. 11:29–30).

Because God has given man a free will to make choices, God places the onus and responsibility upon man to seek him, draw near to him, choose his life, and open up to him.

"And ye shall seek me, and find me, when ye shall search for me with all your heart" (Jer. 29:13).

"Draw nigh to God, and he will draw nigh to you. Cleanse your hands, ye sinners; and purify your hearts, ye double minded" (James 4:8).

"I call heaven and earth to record this day against you, that I have set before you life and death, blessing and cursing: therefore choose life, that both thou and thy seed may live" (Deut. 30:19).

"Behold, I stand at the door, and knock: if any man hear my voice, and open the door, I will come in to him, and will sup with him, and he with me" (Rev. 3:20).

I will repeat that while it's true that God's will is ultimately greater than man's will and God does many things independent of man's will, God does some things contingent upon man's will. Yes, God's will is sometimes contingent upon man's will. God will have all men to be saved; that is God offers the gift of eternal life to all mankind, but because some men will not open salvation's door when God knocks, God will not force the heart door open and save them, and that person must suffer loss.

One last example: The prodigal son is among the most famous of Bible stories. In this example offered by the Lord Jesus, the lost person chooses to return to his Father. Please notice the Bible language.

And when he had spent all, there arose a mighty famine in that land; and he began to be in want. And he went and joined himself to a citizen of that country; and he sent him into his fields to feed swine. And he would fain have filled his belly with the husks that the swine did eat: and no man gave unto him. And when he came to himself, he said, How many hired servants of my father's have bread enough and to spare, and I perish with hunger! I will arise and go to my father, and will say unto him, Father, I have sinned against heaven, and before thee, And am no more worthy to be called thy son: make me as one of thy hired servants. And he arose, and came to his father. But when he was yet a great way off, his father saw him, and had compassion, and ran, and fell on his neck, and kissed him. (Luke 15:14–20)

The obvious point is that the Bible declares that the son made a conscious choice to return to the father by using the words "I will." Yes, the Bible clearly teaches that both saved and unsaved persons have a free will given to them by God Almighty and he expects us to use it!

7

The Name Game and the Doctrine of Eternal Life

"Knowing this first, that no prophecy of the scripture is of any private interpretation" (2 Pet. 1:20).

This same principle of not holding any private interpretation in prophesy can be applied to Bible doctrines as well. The words of God need not be altered by any man to render its doctrines understandable. If anyone feels the need to alter the scriptures in any way, in order to bolster a doctrine, then that doctrine is not a clear Bible doctrine, but rather a private doctrine. Please allow me to ask a simple, sincere question, "Can you prove your doctrine without adding to, taking away, or replacing any Bible words; or do you play the name game?" What is the name game? The name game is the illegal practice of changing, exchanging, adding or subtracting Bible words in order to promote a close held doctrine. This practice could also be called the word game or the shell game because words and terms are shuffled around at will in order to reinforce a private interpretation of scripture or doctrine. The Bible text itself isn't always physically altered, but the expositor teaches what the Bible "should say," thus changing the words of God. The word "illegal" is used with authority to express God's protection of his holy words. Please consider the following scriptures from God's point of view:

> For I testify unto every man that heareth the *words* of the prophecy of this book, If any man shall *add* unto these things, God shall add unto him the plagues that are written in this book: And if any man shall *take away* from the *words* of the book of this prophecy, God shall take away his part out of the book of life, and out of the holy city, and from the things which are written in this book. (Rev. 22:18–19; emphasis mine)

Ye shall not *add* unto the *word* which I command you, neither shall ye *diminish* ought from it, that ye may keep the commandments of the LORD your God which I command you. (Deut. 4:2; emphasis mine)

Did an all-wise God inspire *words*, or thoughts and concepts? What does the Bible say?

"All *scripture* is given by inspiration of God, and is profitable for doctrine, for reproof, for correction, for instruction in righteousness" (2 Tim. 3:16; emphasis mine).

Scripture consists of written words; God's words. Please notice that God didn't inspire some of his words or most of his words, but "all" of his words. This Bible fact makes all of God's words pure.

"*Every word* of God is pure: he is a shield unto them that put their trust in him" (Prov. 30:5; emphasis mine).

How pure are the words of God?

"The words of the LORD are *pure words*: as silver tried in a furnace of earth, *purified seven times*" (Ps. 12:6; emphasis mine).

Back at this time when this scripture was written, the metal silver was heated, purified and cooled seven times, making it as pure as possible.

Did God inspire his words just to let them pass away? The Lord Jesus declared on the subject of Bible preservation:

"Heaven and earth shall pass away, but my *words* shall not pass away" (Matt. 24:35; emphasis mine).

"Heaven and earth shall pass away: but my *words* shall not pass away" (Mark 13:31; emphasis mine).

"Heaven and earth shall pass away: but my *words* shall not pass away" (Luke 21:33; emphasis mine).

Was man ultimately responsible for preserving God's words? No!

"*Thou* shalt keep them, O LORD, *thou shalt* preserve them from this generation *for ever*" (Ps. 12:7; emphasis mine).

Please note that the LORD is the one who is keeping his words and not man. God, however, is well able to use man, as a tool, to pen down and preserve his words. Remember, God did not promise to preserve his concepts, ideas or thoughts, but his words, because words gender and convey thoughts, concepts, and ideas. When we change God's words, we change the concepts, ideas, and meanings God intends to convey. Why is it so very important that we have confidence in the ability of God to keep and preserve his words? The answer is because our eternal life is based upon our faith and our soul-saving faith is based upon the very word of God.

"So then faith cometh by hearing, and hearing by the word of God" (Rom. 10:17).

"Wherefore lay apart all filthiness and superfluity of naughtiness, and *receive* with meekness *the* engrafted *word, which is able to save your souls*" (James 1:21; emphasis mine).

Let's consider something very basic.

"For God so loved the world, that he gave his only begotten Son, that whosoever believeth in him should not perish, but have everlasting life" (John 3:16).

If we ask a hundred people of average intelligence, with no church background, to read this verse and then ask, "According to this verse, whom did God love so much that he gave them his Son?" The answer would be, "The world," "The people of the world," or something similar. However, a traditional Calvinist may very well say the word "world" really means elect. I know one man who went to a Calvinistic church where he was made to cross out the word "world" in his Bible and write "elect!" No kidding! This is a flagrant and illegal abuse of God's word. No Bible word should ever be changed, exchanged, added to, or removed from the text to promote a belief or a doctrine no matter how beloved the doctrine may be.

"Knowing this first, that no prophecy of the scripture is of any private interpretation" (2 Pet. 1:20).

Imagine if we compare the practice of changing Bible words to mathematics, where the values of X and Y could be intentionally changed so that the equation could balance to a desired value! Or more simply put, if a seven were changed to an eight to produce the desired answer, especially since seven is so close to eight anyway. Changing number values would be an illegal mathematical function and changing God's words is disallowed by the Almighty Himself.

Another example of illegally changing God's word would be if a person of Muslim faith decided to remove every reference of the word "God" in the Bible and replace it with the word "Allah" because he believes that Allah is

God, would this be acceptable to you? By the very same token, it's never acceptable for anyone promoting any doctrine, no matter how strongly or sincerely held, to change, substitute, replace or remove any Bible word. Here are some very common word substitutions and additions used to promote a Calvinistic belief system. Some have the idea that God only sent his Son to save a chosen few from hell, hence the alteration of John 3:16.

Example 1

> "For God so loved the *world*, that he gave his only begotten Son, that whosoever believeth in him should not perish, but have everlasting life" (John 3:16; emphasis mine).

The belief is that this verse really means God so loved the "elect." So, the Bible word "world" is removed and the word "elect" inserted. Again, the teacher may not literally substitute the word, but the result in the student's mind is the same as if he had.

THE DOCTRINE OF ETERNAL LIFE

Example 2

> "That they all may be one; as thou,
> Father, art in me, and I in thee, that they
> also may be one in us: that the *world* may
> believe that thou hast sent me" (John
> 17:21; emphasis mine).

The explanation of this verse would again be that "world" really means "elect," but this word substitution violates scripture. Let's take this verse for what it says, the world is not the elect and the elect are not the world.

> "That they all may be one; as thou,
> Father, art in me, and I in thee, that they
> also may be one in us: that the world (not
> the elect, but all the people of the world)
> may believe that thou hast sent me" (John
> 17:21).

The concept that God loves the world, i.e., all the people of the world is expressed in other scriptures.

Example 3

> "For this is good and acceptable in the sight of God our Saviour; Who will have *all men* to be saved, and to come unto the knowledge of the truth" (1 Tim. 2:3–4; emphasis mine).

The obvious truth here is that God's will is for all men to be saved. Some would contend that this verse really means all "elect" men. Inserting the word "elect" to bolster their belief system is an illegal practice.

Example 4

> "And ye *will not* come to me, that ye might have life" (John 5:40; emphasis mine).

A Calvinistic belief system promotes the idea that God chose individuals for heaven and hell; therefore, only the elect can possibly come to God for salvation and the non-elect cannot. The Lord Jesus teaching in John 5:40 said that these individuals, as some folks today, "will not" come to him. Some Calvinists say that this verse really means "can" not come, removing the Bible word "will" and inserting the word "can." There is a great difference between will not and cannot! Let's consider another verse with the will not concept, as opposed to the cannot concept.

Example 5

"For even when we were with you, this we commanded you, that if any *would not* work, neither should he eat" (2 Thess. 3:10; emphasis mine).

The word *would* is the past tense of will. "I will not work today." "I would not work yesterday." This verse teaches that if someone can work and chooses not to work that he should not eat. However, a person who cannot work may be fed. The difference between "will not" and "cannot" here determines whether or not a person gets food. If we replace the phrase "will not" with "cannot" we cause havoc to the scriptures every time. Can you imagine not feeding someone who cannot work? The point is clear; in the Bible there is a profound difference between will not and cannot and we must never exchange the two. If you've been taught that man has no free will, it would be to your benefit to re-read chapter six.

Example 6

"This is a faithful saying, and worthy of all acceptation, that Christ Jesus came into the world *to save sinners*; of whom I am chief" (1 Tim. 1:15; emphasis mine).

Some believe this verse really means that Christ Jesus came into the world to save only "elect" sinners; inserting the word "elect" and changing the truth that God will have all men to be saved.

Again, the word "sinners" in chapter 1 is defined in chapter 2 as "all men," which makes perfect sense since all have sinned and come short of the glory of God (Rom. 3:23).

"For this is good and acceptable in the sight of *God* our Saviour; Who *will have all men to be saved,* and to come unto the knowledge of the truth" (1 Tim. 2:3–4; emphasis mine).

If at this point the reader would say, "God means all *elect* men...," then my point is well made; the point being that a person who never heard of Calvinism would need someone to virtually rewrite the Bible in order that he might understand Calvin's interpretation of it.

Example 7

"And the times of this ignorance God winked at; but now commandeth *all men every where* to repent" (Acts 17:30; emphasis mine).

No adult on earth is excluded in the phrase "all men every where." Some mistakenly believe this verse really means all "elect" men everywhere, inserting the word "elect." It would be unjust of God to command all persons to repent for salvation and then punish them for not complying if they never possessed the ability to repent. God knows that all men everywhere can repent.

Before we consider the next example, please consider the question, "Whom did the Lord Jesus come to seek and save?" What did Christ Jesus himself say concerning whom he came to seek and save?

Example 8

> "For the Son of man is come to seek and to save *that which was lost*" (Luke 19:10; emphasis mine).

This verse cannot possibly mean, "For the Son of man is come to seek and to save the elect." Why not? Were the elect the only ones who were lost? Were non-elect persons already saved? No, that would be ridiculous. The whole world was lost through the fall of Adam; not just some. The common-sense teaching of the Bible is that all men were lost and since the Son of man is come to seek and to save that which was lost, he therefore sought all men for salvation. Along these same lines, we know that the mission of the Holy Ghost, who is the Comforter, matches the ministry of Christ perfectly.

> Nevertheless I tell you the truth; It is expedient for you that I go away: for if I go not away, the *Comforter* will not come unto you; but if I depart, I will send him unto you. And when he is come, he will reprove the *world* of sin, and of righteousness, and of judgment. (John 16:7–8; emphasis mine)

According to John 3:16, the Son of God was given for the world and according to John 16:7–8, the Comforter's mission on earth is also to the *world*. Thank the Lord! The plain teaching of scripture is that the Holy Ghost, who is the Comforter, came to reprove the *world* of sin! Even so, some readers may still feel justified in adding, subtracting and/or exchanging Bible words in these examples in order to justify their beliefs. If the Calvinist reader would still feel justified in saying that the word "world" should be "elect,"

PASTOR KEVIN KLINE

please consider the following. Would you allow a person with Arminian doctrine, for example, to have equal liberty to do the same thing that you yourself are doing? I invite you to carefully consider the next example.

Example 9

"For the wages of sin is death; but the *gift* of God is eternal life through Jesus Christ our Lord" (Rom. 6:23; emphasis mine).

Would the reader be upset if the word "gift" in this verse were replaced with "payment?" Think about it; not all Arminians believe the same things, but there are some Arminians who absolutely believe that they earn heaven by performing good works. So, do these individuals have the right to change the word "gift" to "payment" to make the Bible align with their private interpretation? No, absolutely not, and by the same token, no one has the authority to change, replace, take away or add to any Bible words, either literally, or in their explanation of the scriptures. If the reader truly believes that he is justified in changing the word "world" in John 3:16 to "elect," he is setting up himself as the final authority instead of the Word of God.

Example 10

"For *whosoever* shall call upon the name of the Lord shall be saved" (Rom. 10:13; emphasis mine).

Does "whosoever" mean whosoever, i.e., whoever, or does it mean "whosoever of the elect group…?" The point should be clear that if it's necessary to change the Bible in any way, no matter how subtle, to prove your belief system or to make your belief system understandable, then your belief system isn't biblical. Anyone who is allowed to change the Bible could build any religious system he chooses.

"But I fear, lest by any means, as the serpent beguiled Eve through his subtilty, so your minds should be corrupted from the *simplicity* that is in Christ" (2 Cor. 11:3; emphasis mine).

There is simplicity in Christ. The gospel is simple. All have sinned (Rom. 3:23) and all need a Saviour. The Saviour died for all, was buried for all, and rose from the dead for all, and all are offered the free gift of eternal life. Calvinism confuses the simplicity of salvation by misapplying election and choosing. The Bible doctrine of election or choosing is a great Bible doctrine mentioned many times in scripture. The author has no difficulty with the Bible doctrine of election, but only with Calvin's interpretation and misapplication of this great Bible doctrine. Election and choosing will be covered in chapter 10.

The main point here is that if Calvin's interpretation of election were true, then all of these Bible verses, examples, and dozens of other Bible verses would need to be altered in order to line up with Calvin's interpretation of the Bible. Changing Bible words to prop up any doctrine is intellectually dishonest and disallowed by God's decree because every Bible word is God's word. The name game isn't exclusive to any particular belief system. Intellectual dishonesty is also apparent in Arminian doctrine.

The name game and Arminian doctrine.

Please allow me to reiterate that I have friends in both Arminian and Calvinist camps. We can certainly disagree in doctrine and love the person. With that said, let's use some of the same verses we used for Calvinism and apply them to Arminian doctrine.

Example 1

> "For God so loved the world, that he gave his only begotten Son, that whosoever believeth in him should not perish, but have *everlasting life*" (John 3:16; emphasis mine).

I submit that my Arminian friends change what the Bible actually says as do my Calvinist friends and would qualify this verse with something like this:

> "For God so loved the world, that he gave his only begotten Son, that whoso-

ever believeth (and continues to believe) in him might not perish, but (might) have eternal life" (John 3:16).

Or more specifically:

> For God so loved the world, that he gave his only begotten Son, that whosoever believeth in him (and continues to do sufficient good works and not too many bad works) should not perish, but (might) have everlasting life. (John 3:16)

If the reader imagines that I'm being unfair, I invite him to give me a Bible definition of eternal life. What is your definition of eternal life? Not one from theology class, grandpa, your preacher or from your own mind, but from the Bible itself. What then is your definition of eternal life from the Bible?

The Bible definition of eternal life is synonymous with everlasting life.

That whosoever believeth in him should not perish, but have *eternal life*. For God so loved the world, that he gave his only begotten Son, that whosoever believeth in him should not perish, but have *everlasting life*. (John 3:15–16; emphasis mine)

The Bible definition of eternal life is to have everlasting life or to never perish.

"And I give unto them *eternal life*; and they shall *never perish*, neither shall any man pluck them out of my hand" (John 10:28; emphasis mine).

The point should be self-evident that the Bible definition of eternal life is to have everlasting life or to never perish. By definition, life that can be lost is *not* eternal; it is temporal life, conditional life, or something else. The definition of eternal life is a fundamental biblical point and is far too important to gloss over. *Anyone who believes he can have eternal life (as stated in Joh 10:28) and still somehow perish, does not believe in the doctrine of eternal life.* That person believes in something called temporal (temporary) life or conditional life or some other kind of life foreign to the Bible.

What is conditional life? The belief that someone must earn, add to, complete or somehow maintain eternal life. This concept is contrary to Bible truth. Please consider a hypothetical point. If eternal life were obtained by man's good works, logic would dictate that he could lose eternal life by doing bad works. However, the Holy Bible declares that eternal life is not earned by works but is in fact a gift given by God through his Son.

> "For the wages of sin is death; but the *gift* of God *is eternal life* through Jesus Christ our Lord" (Rom. 6:23; emphasis mine).

If the reader has the idea that God only gives the gift of eternal life to faithful, deserving, philanthropic, obedient or otherwise good people, then please allow me to reiterate, if eternal life is given in exchange for preforming good works, that makes eternal life a *payment* and not a *gift*. Someone who believes that he must do something to earn, complete, and/or keep salvation does not believe in eternal life, but rather in conditional life. Does the Bible teach that we earn eternal life or that it's a free gift?

> "For the wages of sin is death; but the *gift* of God *is eternal life* through Jesus Christ our Lord" (Rom. 6:23; emphasis mine).

In Romans 6:23, God is promising eternal life as a gift. Let's compare this verse to 1 John 2:25.

> "And this is the promise that he hath promised us, even eternal life" (1 John 2:25).

God's promise of eternal life is without added conditions or works. Furthermore, if works were involved, the verse would, by necessity, read something like this:

> "And this is the *payoff* that he hath promised us *for doing good works*, even eternal life" (1 John 2:25; emphasis mine).

No; eternal life is not conditional life, neither is it temporary life, but it is life everlasting. What is temporary life? Temporary life is life that has an end, e.g., every man's physical life will have an end, so God offers eternal life as a gift to every man. Once a person has received the gift of eternal life, he will never perish, even when his physical, temporary life has ceased.

> "Jesus said unto her, I am the resurrection, and the life: he that believeth in me, though he were dead, yet shall he live: And whosoever liveth and believeth in me *shall never die*. Believest thou this?" (John 11:25–26).

God's physical gift of temporal life will cease, but God's spiritual gift of eternal life will never cease.

Author's note: When we study the verses in scripture where individuals didn't understand what the Lord Jesus was talking about, usually the Lord was referring to spiritual things while the individuals were considering physical things. This was the case in John 11 where the Lord was speaking of spiritual life that never dies or ends versus physical life, which has an end.

Someone may believe that through exceptional circumstances, a person who has received eternal life as a gift may still somehow lose it. I apologize for being redundant, but in salvation, God only promises to give eternal life, not conditional life or temporary life. These other non-eternal forms of life are foreign to the God of the Bible and are inventions of man. There can be no exceptions. That which can be lost is not eternal. In my experience, proponents of Arminian theology usually dismiss logic at this point and concoct some bizarre scenario that begins with the phrase, "You mean to tell me...?" One example might be, "You mean to tell me that if a Christian kills someone and then kills himself, that that person is going to heaven?" The point is that if a person has been born again, they have received that gift of eternal life and they will never perish but will enter heaven, and if a person has not been born again, he will not enter heaven. The more pertinent question is, would a truly born-again person act out such a scenario? Isn't it more likely that such a person was never born-again in the first place regardless of their profession? My Arminian friends always agree that this explanation makes more sense.

We must neither diminish or over exalt the importance of good works, but rather understand their proper biblical position and balance. It is wrong to exalt our good works to the level of a savior, for our good works could never take away our sin as Christ did. It is equally wrong to exalt good works to the level of keeping or maintaining eternal life. This is true for two reasons: (1) eternal life needs no maintenance from us because it is eternal by nature and cannot cease, and (2) only God and his eternal power can keep that which he has promised us.

Blessed be the God and Father of our
Lord Jesus Christ, which according to his
abundant mercy hath begotten us again
unto a lively hope by the resurrection of

THE DOCTRINE OF ETERNAL LIFE

Jesus Christ from the dead, To an inheritance incorruptible, and undefiled, and
that fadeth not away, reserved in heaven
for you, Who are *kept by the power of God*
through faith unto salvation ready to be
revealed in the last time. (1 Pet. 1:3–5;
emphasis mine)

The Bible undeniably teaches that we are kept by God's
power and not by our own efforts. Still, some may have
been taught that 1 Peter 1:5 says that we are kept through
faith and that if we lose our faith, we'll lose our eternal life.
Once again, *eternal life cannot be lost* because that would
make it temporal and conditional life. I never ran into a
Christian who was worried that he would somehow stop
"believing" in Jesus Christ. However, if you believe that
eternal life is somehow contingent upon individuals maintaining their faith, then how would you answer this verse?

"*If we believe not*, yet he abideth faithful: he cannot deny himself" (2 Tim. 2:13;
emphasis mine).

I've heard defenders of Arminian doctrine say things such as, "If I totally denounce God and give up my faith, then I'll lose my salvation." First, I can't imagine a truly born-again believer doing such a thing. Second, God says the exact opposite in the previous verse! God, through Paul, says that even if we believe not, God will keep his promise, God *cannot* deny himself.

Also, along the lines of holding onto our faith, we don't finish our faith; the Lord Jesus does!

"Looking unto Jesus the author and finisher of our faith" (Heb. 12:2a).

The Lord has promised that "I will never leave thee, nor forsake thee."

"Let your conversation be without covetousness; and be content with such things as ye have: for he hath said, *I will never leave thee*, nor forsake thee" (Heb. 13:5; emphasis mine).

The Lord Jesus doesn't say, I will never leave thee unless you leave me first, but simply, I will *never* leave you, period. This is possible in part because of the sealing of every born-again believer.

"And grieve not the holy Spirit of
God, whereby ye are *sealed* unto the day of
redemption" (Eph. 4:30; emphasis mine).

Every born-again believer is sealed with the Holy Ghost at the moment of salvation until we appear in the very presence of God. Once a person is born again and has received the gift of eternal life, a contract is finalized with God and God himself keeps his promise regardless of our shortcomings.

"And *I give* unto them *eternal life*; and
they shall never perish, neither shall any
man pluck them out of my hand" (John
10:28; emphasis mine).

Two very important points are noteworthy here. First, never perish means never perish, and second, those who believe that they can do something to undo God's promise of eternal life are faced with a problem. Not only has God declared that the recipient of eternal life can never perish, but God also declares "neither shall *any man* pluck them out of my hand," i.e., that no man can pluck any born-again soul out of God's hand. This means that not only can I not pluck you out of God's hand, but you can't pluck me out of God's hand either. Furthermore, I can't pluck myself out of God's hand, neither can *you* pluck yourself out. You, the reader, may have been taught that you can pluck yourself out of God's almighty hand, but wait, are you not a man? Christ said, "Neither shall *any man* pluck them out of my hand." No, dear friend, once you have become a truly born-again child of God, your soul can never perish. This isn't a doctrine from Calvin, but a doctrine from God. At the moment of salvation, our soul becomes God's possession, and eternal life becomes our possession without our feeble works!

> "He that hath the Son *hath life*; and
> he that hath not the Son of God hath not
> life" (1 John 5:12; emphasis mine).

Please notice the tense of the verb, hath (or has in modern English) is present tense. This means that the moment we receive the Son we have eternal life. Let's consider the context of 1 Peter 1:3–5 again, going a little deeper.

> Blessed be the God and Father of our Lord Jesus Christ, which according to his abundant mercy hath begotten us again unto a lively hope by the resurrection of Jesus Christ from the dead, To an inheritance incorruptible, and undefiled, and that fadeth not away, reserved in heaven for you, Who are *kept by the power of God* through faith unto salvation ready to be revealed in the last time. (1 Pet. 1:3–5; emphasis mine)

Here is a very important point. When the Bible declares that the child of God is "...kept by the power of God through *faith*...," it's referring to the faith that was exhibited at the moment we believed and not some nebulous, uncertain, hypothetical, future faith. Plainly stated, we are kept by the power of God through the faith demonstrated at the moment we called upon Christ.

> "That if thou shalt confess with thy
> mouth the Lord Jesus, and shalt believe in
> thine heart that God hath raised him from
> the dead, thou *shalt* be saved" (Rom. 10:9;
> emphasis mine).

The moment we confess the Lord Jesus with a repentant and believing heart the Bible says, "thou shalt be saved." Not thou might be saved or thou might be saved if you do many good works and don't do too many bad works, but "thou shalt be saved." Please trust the simple teaching of the Bible.

As was stated earlier regarding Calvin's interpretation of Bible, if his interpretation were true, then dozens if not hundreds of other Bible verses would need to be altered in order to line up with Calvin's interpretation of the Bible. This is no less true of Arminian doctrine. If God could take eternal life away for any reason, then it wouldn't be eternal life, but conditional, temporary life and not everlasting, eternal life. Those who are given eternal life by God will never perish; thus saith the Lord!

Example 2

"Teaching them to observe all things whatsoever I have commanded you: and, lo, *I am with you alway, even unto the end of the world.* Amen" (Matt. 28:20; emphasis mine).

How can someone hold Arminian doctrine and believe this verse at face value the way it was written? If he were honest, wouldn't an Arminian necessarily say that this verse really means...lo, I am with you always, even unto the end of your good works..., or I am with you until you fail me..., or until you lose faith or totally mess up? Does the Holy Bible need to be changed or reinterpreted in order to accommodate Arminian doctrine? No, the Bible is correct the way it is. God gives eternal life as a gift and he promises to keep us by his power. What could be better?

Example 3

"Beloved, now are we the sons of God, and it doth not yet appear what we shall be: but we know that, when he shall appear, *we shall be like him*; for we shall see him as he is" (1 John 3:2; emphasis mine).

This is one of my favorite Bible verses of all time. Why? I invite you to meditate on it and discover the unlimited riches hidden within. The single point here is simple, how could the believer who penned down this scripture possibly declare to all the children of God, that *we shall* (not only I shall, but we shall) be like him? If there were the slightest possibility of any child of God losing eternal life, this statement would be false. If any child of God could possibly lose their eternal life, then the apostle would have to have written something like, "Beloved, now are we the sons of God, and it doth not yet appear what we shall be: but we know that, when he shall appear, *some of us might be like him if we have maintained sufficient good works and have not done too many bad works*; for *then maybe* we shall see him as he is." No, the apostle writes to all the children of God and boldly declares that we (all of us, each one of us) shall be like him, which means we will see him and be glorified like him. The only way this verse makes sense is when we know the proper understanding of the doctrine of eternal life, which is, God's gift of everlasting spiritual life that God gives to every believer at the moment of salvation, promising his child that he will never perish.

Example 4

> "Verily, verily, I say unto you, *He that* heareth my word, and *believeth* on him that sent me, *hath everlasting life*, and *shall not come into condemnation*; but is passed from death unto life" (John 5:24; emphasis mine).

The Lord himself declared that he that believeth (believes) hath (has) eternal life and *shall not* come into condemnation. This verse does not say anything such as he that continues to believe and do good works. There are no exceptions or qualifiers given. Once we believe, we have eternal life and we shall not come into condemnation. Others may say, "and *might* not come into condemnation," but the Lord said *shall* not. Whom will you believe; the interpretation of man or the promise of God?

Example 5

"And to wait for his Son from heaven, whom he raised from the dead, even Jesus, which *delivered* us from the wrath to come" (1 Thess. 1:10; emphasis mine).

Please notice that the tense of the verb is past tense declaring a finalized transaction, which is nothing less than the promise of God.

Example 6

"For whosoever shall call upon the name of the Lord *shall* be saved" (Rom. 10:13; emphasis mine).

The proper context of this verse refers to someone with repentance and saving faith. Does this verse then teach that whosoever shall call upon the name of the Lord *might* be saved as long as he does many good works and few bad works or does it teach that they *shall* be saved?

Example 7

> "No man can come to me, except the Father which hath sent me draw him: and *I will raise him up at the last day*" (John 6:44; emphasis mine).

Let's begin by looking at the first half of this verse. When the Lord says, "No man can come to me, except the Father which hath sent me draw him," there is no truer statement, but this does not mean that the Father only draws or wants some and not others. I'm sure we all agree that the Father draws people by his Spirit. This brings us to a very fundamental Bible doctrine, which many Christians tend to overlook, that being, whom does God draw? Whom does the Holy Ghost, who is the Comforter, convict or reprove?

Nevertheless I tell you the truth; It is expedient for you that I go away: for if I go not away, the Comforter will not come unto you; but if I depart, I will send him unto you. And when he is come, he *will* reprove the *world* of sin, and of righteousness, and of judgment. (John 16:7–8; emphasis mine)

Yes, the answer is the world, every person of the world and not just a chosen few. The Holy Ghost is totally doing his job by convicting all men everywhere and man's job is to repent. So then, to those who yield to the call or drawing of the Comforter in John 6:44b, the Lord says, "And *I will raise him up at the last day*." Not, I might raise him up, or if he continues to do good works and not too many bad works, I will raise him up, but a blanket declaration, *I will raise him*. The Lord Jesus could only state this as fact if each and every child of God were justified and kept by the blood of Christ and power of God at the moment of salvation and not by individual works.

Example 8

"And though after my skin worms destroy this body, yet in my flesh *shall I see God*" (Job 19:26; emphasis mine).

Even old testament saints carried the assurance of God's promise of eternal life. Job could not make this statement honestly if he were depending on his good works to solidify his salvation. Job was trusting in God's power and not his own when he declared, "shall I see God."

Example 9

"And this is the record, that God *hath given* to us *eternal life*, and this life is in his Son" (1 John 5:11; emphasis mine).

Please notice the tense of the verb, God hath (has) given. This is a past perfect tense, which indicates a condition that has happened in the past and continues into the future; in this case, into eternity.

Example 10

"For *we know* that if our earthly house of this tabernacle were dissolved, we have a building of God, an house not made with hands, *eternal* in the heavens" (2 Cor. 5:1; emphasis mine).

Here, Paul is referring to our *eternal* heavenly bodies (see verse 6), but please notice his confidence. Paul says we know, not just I know, but *we know*…Did Paul know any carnal Christians? Yes, of course, the Corinthian church was loaded with them! The only way Paul could have made this bold statement is if all born-again children of God had eternal life.

If I ask an honest Arminian, "When you die, will you go to heaven?" He will likely answer, "I hope so." Not yes and not no; why is this? Because he has been taught that his eternal life depends on his performance, i.e., good works, either to get eternal life, to keep eternal life or both. Indeed, if we had to keep eternal life by our good works, we would lose it every day! Just examine your wicked thoughts throughout a normal day. Every believer can have Paul's very same confidence if he simply believes the Bible promise of God that he has already given us eternal life at the moment of conversion.

"And this is the promise that he hath promised us, even eternal life" (1 John 2:25).

"For all the promises of God in him are yea, and in him Amen, unto the glory of God by us" (2 Cor. 1:20).

So, when a born-again child of God is asked, "When you die, will you go to heaven?" if they're trusting in their works, they should answer no. If they're trusting in the finished work of Christ, they should answer yes, like Paul and James.

"let your yea be yea" (James 5:12).

Paul also states concerning his immortal soul:

"For the which cause I also suffer these things: nevertheless I am not ashamed: for

I know whom I have believed, and am persuaded that *he is able to keep* that which
I have committed unto him against that
day" (2 Tim. 1:12; emphasis mine).

Clearly, Paul was fully persuaded that his own soul was
kept by the power of God from the moment of his salvation. For some believers, it may be easier to view eternal life
less as a possession which we keep in our hand and more
as a prize possession which our God keeps in his mighty,
eternal hand.

Example 11

"These things have I written unto you
that believe on the name of the Son of God;
that ye may *know* that *ye have eternal life*,
and that ye may believe on the name of the
Son of God" (1 John 5:13; emphasis mine).

Can a person know he's saved? Job did in example 7
and Paul did in example 9, and there are many more exam-

ples in scripture. Perhaps the more pertinent question is, does God want us to guess, hope, feel, or know that we have eternal life. What saith the scriptures? God Almighty gave the scriptures to us that we would not doubt his unspeakable gift of eternal life. Some believers could possibly stumble at the word "may." The word may, in this context, does not mean maybe, but can. If someone asks you if they may go to the store and you reply, "Yes, you may," do you mean maybe or yes you can because you have permission? The latter is true; therefore, God tells us that we are permitted to know and can know that we have eternal life. My personal experience of nearly forty years of leading persons to Christ has shown that the majority of individuals who lack the assurance of their salvation have never been born again. Others lacking assurance often are trusting their own fickle works rather than the finished and unchanging work of Christ on the cross. Those trusting in their own works to obtain, maintain or retain eternal life have every reason to doubt their final end, while those who trust in the finished work of Christ alone have no room for doubt. If you, the reader, have even the slightest doubt concerning your eternal soul, please read chapter 19 on salvation.

Example 12

> "Let your conversation be without
> covetousness; and be content with such
> things as ye have: for he hath said, *I will
> never leave thee,* nor forsake thee" (Heb.
> 13:5; emphasis mine).

This is God's direct promise to every born-again believer without qualification or exception. That is to say, God doesn't say unless... Dear reader, if the Holy Bible needs to be altered in any way to make any doctrine understandable, then that doctrine is not biblical. Arguably, there is no clearer demonstration of "the name game" within Arminian circles then that of the misapplication of James 2.

Understanding James 2.

> Even so faith, if it hath not works,
> is dead, being alone. Yea, a man may say,
> Thou hast faith, and I have works: shew
> me thy faith without thy works, and I will

shew thee my faith by my works. Thou believest that there is one God; thou doest well: the devils also believe, and tremble. But wilt thou know, O vain man, that faith without works is dead? Was not Abraham our father justified by works, when he had offered Isaac his son upon the altar? Seest thou how faith wrought with his works, and by works was faith made perfect? And the scripture was fulfilled which saith, Abraham believed God, and it was imputed unto him for righteousness: and he was called the Friend of God. Ye see then how that by works a man is justified, and not by faith only. (James 2:17–24)

Let me assure you that I believe every word of this text just as it is written. However, what those of Arminian faith are taught James says and what James is actually saying are two very different things. The typical Arminian believes in a formula of faith plus his good works equals salvation based heavily on his misunderstanding of this portion of scripture. Let's examine each verse.

Verse 17. "Even so faith, if it hath not works, is dead, being alone."

We all agree that a person who exhibits no good works has no genuine faith.

Verse 18. "Yea, a man may say, Thou hast faith, and I have works: shew me thy faith without thy works, and I will shew thee my faith by my works."

Hear, hear! Genuine saving faith will always produce good works.

Verse 19. "Thou believest that there is one God; thou doest well: the devils also believe, and tremble."

Monotheistic faith is not sufficient for salvation. The Jews and Muslims have faith in a single Creator God but reject the deity of his Son. The devils believe and have even seen the one true God, but believing in the existence of God is not repentance and faith; neither is it the same as calling out for salvation.

Verse 20. "But wilt thou know, O vain man, that faith without works is dead?"

A person without saving faith can only produce dead works.

Verse 21. "Was not Abraham our father justified by works, when he had offered Isaac his son upon the altar?"

Abraham certainly was completely and totally justified by works!

Verse 22. "Seest thou how faith wrought with his works, and by works was faith made perfect?"

Yes, yes; Abraham's works made his faith perfect, i.e., complete.

Verse 23. "And the scripture was fulfilled which saith, Abraham believed God, and it was imputed unto him for righteousness: and he was called the Friend of God."

Please notice that Abraham's faith or belief was imputed unto him for righteousness with God.

Verse 24. "Ye see then how that by works a man is justified, and not by faith only."

Yes, Abraham was justified by his works and by his faith; with this I wholeheartedly agree! By now, my Arminian friends may be totally confused. Let me assure you that I completely agree with the Holy Bible, but not in the Arminian interpretation of the Bible. What do I mean?

As with Calvinism, Bible words are retranslated or at best misunderstood skewing their meanings and changing Bible doctrines.

Here's what traditional Arminians think verse 24 says:

"Ye see then how that by works a man
is *saved*, and not by faith only."

What the Bible actually says:

Verse 24. "Ye see then how that by works a man is *justified*, and not by faith only."

You may say that saved and justified mean exactly the same thing and that false assumption is the root cause of the problem. Justification has more than one application; therefore, justification is not always synonymous with salvation. There are two major kinds of justification in the Bible. Justification before God and justification before man. To see this more clearly, let's use what I call the Newton's law principle of scripture. Newton's law in the natural world states that, "For every action, there is an equal and opposite reaction." This, of course, is a law of physics, which is the study of God's physical universe. In

God's word, there is a congruent, unstated law which dictates that for every scripture there is an equal and opposite scripture. In other words, if we have trouble understanding one scripture, God has given us another scripture to help balance out our understanding. Such is the case of James 2:24, when God states that Abraham was justified by works. God was not meaning that Abraham was saved by works. How do we know? First, being justified by works in the sight of God violates many scriptures including the clear teaching of Galatians 2:16.

> Knowing that a man is not justified by the works of the law, but by the faith of Jesus Christ, even we have believed in Jesus Christ, that we might be justified by the faith of Christ, and not by the works of the law: for *by* the *works* of the law *shall no flesh be justified.* (Gal. 2:16; emphasis mine)

Second, the balancing scriptures on the very same topic as James 2 are found in Romans 4.

What shall we say then that Abraham
our father, as pertaining to the flesh, hath
found? For if Abraham were justified by
works, he hath whereof to glory; but not
before God. For what saith the scripture?
Abraham believed God, and it was counted
unto him for righteousness. Now to him
that worketh is the reward not reckoned
of grace, but of debt. But to him that worketh not, but believeth on him that justifieth the ungodly, his faith is counted for
righteousness. Even as David also describeth the blessedness of the man, unto
whom God imputeth righteousness without works, Saying, Blessed are they whose
iniquities are forgiven, and whose sins are
covered. Blessed is the man to whom the
Lord will not impute sin. (Rom. 4:1–8)

Here, God wonderfully balances out the eight verses of
James 2 with these eight verses from Romans 4.

Verse 1. "What shall we say then that Abraham our father, as pertaining to the flesh, hath found?"

Notice that our attention is focused on that which pertains to the flesh or human good works.

Verse 2. "For if Abraham were justified by works, he hath whereof to glory; but not before God."

Paul writes in the hypothetical when he says, "For if Abraham were justified by works" and we do agree that Abraham was indeed justified by his works according to James 2:24. However, God, through Paul, goes on to say in Romans 4:2, that Abraham was *not justified* before God by works. Ask yourself this question; did Abraham's works justify him before God? The answer must be no. What did justify Abraham before God? Let's continue.

Verse 3. "For what saith the scripture? Abraham *believed* God, and *it* was counted unto him for righteousness."

Abraham's belief or faith, justified him before God. What happens to any person who tries to use his works to be justified before God? The Bible has the answer.

Verse 5. "Now to him that worketh is the reward not reckoned of grace, but of debt."

Our works will not buy us God's grace nor cancel our sin, but will reckon unto us debt. Let's be perfectly clear, all of our good works combined could never cancel out one lie, or prideful thought! That's why our Saviour came and shed his blood! What can wash away my sin? Nothing, but the blood of Jesus.

Verse 6. "Even as David also describeth the blessedness of the man, unto whom God imputeth righteousness without works."

God always imputes, i.e., places on the account of the believer in Christ, righteousness without works.

Verse 7. "Saying, Blessed are they whose iniquities are forgiven, and whose sins are covered."

The blessed or happy man is one who accepts God's forgiveness as a gift, without trying to, as it were, pay God back for salvation by doing good works.

Verse 8. "Blessed is the man to whom the Lord will not impute sin."

We can be truly blessed when we take God at his word and receive the blood of Christ as the complete payment for our sin and not try to offer our pitiful works as partial payment. Please remember Isaiah 64:6.

> "But we are all as an unclean thing,
> and *all our righteousnesses are as filthy rags*;
> and we all do fade as a leaf; and our iniq-
> uities, like the wind, have taken us away"
> (Isa. 64:6; emphasis mine).

So then, faith and faith alone without works justified Abraham before God, while works and works alone out-wardly justified Abraham before man. This is the proper context of James 2:24.

> "Ye see then how that by *works* a man
> is justified, and not by *faith* only" (James
> 2:24; emphasis mine).

Works are seen outwardly because men cannot see our faith, but they can see our actions. God, however, can see our hearts and does not require or accept works for justification before him, but faith only. This is the doctrine of twofold justification. Justified before God by our faith alone and justified before man by our works alone. The Greek word for justification means to be innocent or righteous. At the moment of salvation, God declares the believer in Christ to be innocent and righteous by faith without the believer's works. Why? Because at the moment of salvation, all of our sins are forgiven, and the Father sees the finished work of Christ as the final and complete payment for our sin. So then, Abraham was made perfect or complete because he had faith before God and works before man.

Is it possible for a person to be justified in one way and not the other? Of course! These two types of justification are not the same and are not mutually exclusive. In other words, a man may have one and not the other, both or neither. Is there further scriptural evidence demonstrating that a person may be justified by works before men, but not before God? Yes.

> "And he said unto them, *Ye are they which justify yourselves before men*; but God knoweth your hearts: for that which is highly esteemed among men is abomination in the sight of God" (Luke 16:15; emphasis mine).

A person may be kind and do many good works, outwardly being justified before men while never being born again. Have you ever heard someone say something like, "If anyone makes it to heaven, it'll be Mrs. Smith. She's not a Christian, but she's the kindest soul…?" Bible believers know that persons are not justified before God by their works, including works of kindness.

> "For if Abraham were justified by works, he hath whereof to glory; but not before God" (Rom. 4:2).
>
> "Not by works of righteousness which we have done, but according to his mercy he saved us, by the washing of regeneration, and renewing of the Holy Ghost" (Titus 3:5).

Mrs. Smith would be an example of a person with dead works having never called upon the Lord, lacking saving faith. The opposite can also be true. That is, a person may be truly born again, but because of his life's circumstances, he may not appear to be a mature, saved Christian because he lacks basic and proper Christian works. An example would be a child of seven years old from a heathen household who was allowed to attend a gospel preaching church one time. The child receives the Lord and with joy goes home and shares his faith with his parents. The parents sharply rebuke that child and never allow the child to ever attend church again. This child stays in a wicked household of cursing, lying, drunkenness, drug abuse and so on, until young adulthood. No one can expect this child to act like a decent, knowledgeable, or moderately obedient Christian. They may not be justified by their works before men, but God knew their heart and sincere prayer of faith the moment they called on Christ for salvation. Deathbed conversions and conversions that were followed soon after by death are other examples of believers who may not appear to men as having saving faith.

Are there any Bible examples explaining the teaching of Romans 4; that a person is not justified by good works before God? Yes, of course. Let's consider a man who thought he was justified by good works before God.

Two men went up into the temple to pray; the one a Pharisee, and the other a publican. The Pharisee stood and prayed thus with himself, God, I thank thee, that I am not as other men are, extortioners, unjust, adulterers, or even as this publican. I fast twice in the week, I give tithes of all that I possess. And the publican, standing afar off, would not lift up so much as his eyes unto heaven, but smote upon his breast, saying, God be merciful to me a sinner. I tell you, this man went down to his house justified rather than the other: for every one that exalteth himself shall be abased; and he that humbleth himself shall be exalted. (Luke 18:10–14)

Please ask yourself, how is it that the person with many good works went away unjustified while the person without any apparent good works went away justified? The answer is manifold; first, the Romans 4 principle is in play here. A man may be justified before other men by his works as seen in James 2, but never before God as seen in Romans 4. Second, the Bible teaches us that a man is not justified before God by works, but by faith. The publican was trusting in his works to be justified in the sight of God and went away unjustified while the publican knew his works were worthless and put his faith in God's mercy. Probably every reader would agree that repentance and faith are the two necessary ingredients for salvation. If not, I invite you to do your own study now of all the verses on this subject. Look up all forms of the words "faith" and "believe" in close proximity to all forms of the word "repent."

For individuals who do have repentance toward God and faith toward Christ, the only thing lacking is to call out to God. This is another reason why the publican went away justified without any works and the Pharisee went away unjustified with many good works. Moreover, the Pharisee never asked God for salvation or mercy, but the publican did.

"And the publican, standing afar off,
would not lift up so much as his eyes unto
heaven, but smote upon his breast, saying,

God be merciful to me a sinner" (Luke 18:13).

"yet ye have not, because ye ask not" (James 4:2b).

"That *if thou shalt confess* with thy mouth the Lord Jesus, and shalt believe in thine heart that God hath raised him from the dead, *thou shalt be saved*" (Rom. 10:9; emphasis mine).

Before we move on, we should be clear on these points.

1. Eternal life is not temporary life which has an end.
2. Eternal life is not conditional life; that which can be lost is not eternal.
3. Eternal life is by definition everlasting life—life which can never end or perish.
4. Eternal life is everlasting life which is given to sinners as a gift and not earned by his feeble works.
5. Eternal life is everlasting life which the believer does not maintain by his feeble works.

6. Eternal life is never-ending life which God himself keeps for all of his children.

7. Eternal life is God keeping his children by God's own power.

Now that we have considered the importance of not elevating good works to the level of a savior, used to obtain, maintain or retain salvation, we can consider the proper balance and importance of good works. But before we leave this chapter, I would like to ask you the question again, "Can you prove your doctrine without adding to, taking away or replacing any Bible words, or must you play the name game?"

8

The Proper Balance and Importance of Good Works

The Bible establishes the fact that no person can be justified before God by works.

> *Not by works* of righteousness which we have done, but according to his mercy he saved us, by the washing of regeneration, and renewing of the Holy Ghost. (Titus 3:5; emphasis mine)

> Knowing that *a man is not justified by the works of the law,* but by the faith of Jesus Christ, even we have believed in Jesus Christ, that we might be justified by the faith of Christ, and *not by the works of the law:* for by the works of the law shall no flesh be justified. (Gal. 2:16; emphasis mine)

For if Abraham were justified by
works, he hath whereof to glory; but *not
before God.* (Rom. 4:2; emphasis mine)

The Bible also establishes the fact that justification
before God for salvation is not a combination of our faith,
plus our good works, but by faith alone without works.

"But to him that worketh not, but
believeth on him that justifieth the ungodly,
his *faith* is counted for righteousness"
(Rom. 4:5; emphasis mine).

"For by *grace* are ye saved through
faith; and that not of yourselves: it is the
gift of God: (9) *Not of works,* lest any man
should boast" (Eph. 2:8–9; emphasis
mine).

"Even as David also describeth the
blessedness of the man, unto whom *God
imputeth righteousness without works*"
(Rom. 4:6; emphasis mine)

Just a quick point, let's not gloss over the first half of this verse. According to David, a man is blessed or happy when he trusts in God without works. How then can our dear brothers be truly happy and blessed if they are trusting their own feeble works of righteousness to obtain, maintain or retain salvation? The answer is, they can't. The following verse applies to believers and not just unbelievers.

> "But we are all as an unclean thing,
> and *all our righteousnesses are as filthy rags*"
> (Isa. 64:6a; emphasis mine)

We will consider the subject of justification in more depth later in this chapter. One quick side point, discipleship and salvation are not the same thing. The Lord said in the gospel of Luke.

> "If any man come to me, and hate
> not his father, and mother, and wife, and
> children, and brethren, and sisters, yea,
> and his own life also, he cannot be my
> disciple" (Luke 14:26).

I have been taught that we can learn much from the Bible by what is doesn't say. Case in point, the Lord did not say, If any man…he cannot be *saved*, but he cannot be my *disciple*. In other words, a person may not follow the Lord as he should, but this does not necessarily mean that he isn't saved. This is a salvation issue as opposed to service issue. That is, a person can be a child of God without being a servant of God. Not convinced? The Lord also said:

> "So likewise, whosoever he be of you that forsaketh not all that he hath, he cannot be my disciple" (Luke 14:33).

Have you forsaken all? Do you know anyone who has? My point here is that no one should believe that only disciples who forsake all to follow the Lord are going to enter heaven, because that would be a works based salvation. May I also say that it would make heaven a very lonely place, hypothetically speaking. There is therefore a marked distinction between obedience to the gospel for salvation and obedience in service for discipleship. Listed are three quick points to assist the Bible student in examining soteriology.

1. The Bible scholar will always be confused if he takes his doctrine of salvation from the gospels only instead of the didactical epistles.

2. The Bible scholar will always be confused if he takes his doctrine of salvation (including losing salvation) from parables and not from the didactical epistles.

3. The Bible scholar will always be confused if he takes his doctrine of salvation, as it pertains to born-again persons, from scriptures relating to other groups, persons or time periods and not from the didactical epistles.

Let's consider one often misused scripture as an example.

"Not every one that saith unto me, Lord, Lord, shall enter into the kingdom of heaven; but he that doeth the will of my Father which is in heaven" (Matt. 7:21).

A brother may say, see you have to do the will of the Father or good works to enter into heaven. Ask yourself, what the context of this verse is. Is it to born-again believers? Well, it's in the New Testament! Yes, but the born-again church didn't exist until Acts 2. What then is the context? The context is to the Jews, notice the subject isn't heaven, but the kingdom of heaven, which is the millennial reign of Christ. Moving on, many of these Jews did have works, "many wonderful works."

> "Many will say to me in that day, Lord, Lord, have we not prophesied in thy name? and in thy name have cast out devils? and in thy name done many wonderful works?" (Matt. 7:22).

Yet these people were rejected, why? Well, not because they didn't do enough good works. What then was the reason? The Lord tells us in the same context.

> "And then will I profess unto them, *I never knew you*: depart from me, ye that work iniquity" (Matt. 7:23; emphasis mine).

Once we understand that these Jews were not rejected because of a lack of good works, we can rethink the situation. We can now go back to verse 21 and ask, what was the Father's will that was lacking in these individuals? We know that doing the Father's will wasn't a "good work" in the normal sense, i.e., a work of man, so what was it? Well, the Lord told us the Father's will, which these Jews failed to perform in verse 23. Do you see it? The Lord said, "I never knew you." The plain teaching is that the Father's will that was not performed was to know his Son Jesus Christ! We could spend a great deal of time expounding on this text and its context, but the simple truth is that these Jews didn't enter in because of unbelief, which caused them not to "know" the Saviour in a personal way. The will of the Father, therefore, is not a work of man, but a *work of God*! If we want to make a comparison to the church age today, we can say, we either know Christ as Saviour and will enter into heaven itself or we don't know him, and we will not. Please understand that believing in Christ through repentance and faith is not a work of man! There is a "new doctrine" of no repentance being promulgated today by persons striving for a following they are described in the book of Acts as.

"Also of your own selves shall men arise, speaking perverse things, to draw away disciples after them" (Acts 20:30).

Their new doctrine teaches that repentance is a work of man and as such potential believers only need faith and *no repentance*. Please do yourself a favor, if you think repentance is not necessary for salvation, look up every occurrence of the word repent along with all of its derivations. You will find that repentance is not a work of man, but a work of God and that repentance is absolutely necessary for salvation. It's impossible to keep up with all of the latest heresies, but this one can be easily thwarted.

"And the times of this ignorance God winked at; but now commandeth all men every where to repent" (Acts 17:30).

"Testifying both to the Jews, and also to the Greeks, repentance toward God, and faith toward our Lord Jesus Christ" (Acts 20:21).

Let's chase a rabbit for a moment, this rabbit is a pet of mine and his name is "Peeve." We have considered in a previous chapter, how that we must not lump things together just to make it convenient. We leaders confuse other Christians, especially new ones, by saying things such as, "You must receive Jesus as your Lord and Saviour to go to heaven." The truth is that many Christians know Christ as their Saviour and consequently will enter heaven; however, they may not have made him Lord of their lives. Salvation is one thing and service is another thing, let's not mix the two. It's wonderful and *preferable* to receive Christ as Saviour and Lord of your life at the moment of salvation, but let's be clear. Receiving Christ as Saviour yields for us eternal life, while receiving Christ as Lord of our lives yields eternal rewards in heaven as well as added blessings on earth. I cringe when preachers say, give your life to Jesus and be saved. I know it may seem too technical to some, but giving your life to Jesus will not produce salvation, giving you heart to Jesus, i.e., being born again, will! Some people receive Christ as Saviour and are saved for years before they make him Lord of their life. Others "think" they are saved because they're "trying" to make Jesus Lord of their life by "doing things for the local church," but they were never born again. They got the cart before the horse, the proper order is salvation first and service second. How do we end the confusion? If you're not certain that when you die you will go to heaven, repent of your sin and ask Christ to save you without offering him your filthy works. After you have done this, thank him for his gift, the salvation of your soul. Whether you have done this recently or years ago, it's time now ask your Saviour, by name, the Lord Jesus Christ, to help you make him Lord of your life. Remember, sometimes, we have not because we ask not! It can be that simple. Another way to look at the same issue is you give your heart to Christ for salvation and then you give your life to him for service. Remember, God knows the heart! There are no magic words and a mute person can have the same salvation as any other person. Volumes could be written on the subjects of salvation and service. A final thought here on this subject is this, once the differences between salvation and service become real to you, you will be able to use this to better understand the Bible. Many passages that refer to salvation people take out of context and apply them to service and vice versa. Knowing whether the context of scripture is that of salivation or service will yield a deeper understanding of the holy Bible.

Back to the importance of good works. Let me assure you that a believer's good works are extremely important even though they have absolutely nothing to do with gaining salvation. How can this be? If good works have nothing to with our obtaining, maintaining or retaining our personal eternal life, then how can they be so important? Let's consider three main reasons for believers to continue in good works.

1. The Saviour said that our good works bring glory to God.

"Let your light so shine before men, that they may see your good works, and glorify your Father which is in heaven" (Matt. 5:16).

There are two very important points here. First, the believer's good works glorify our heavenly Father. This glorification of the Father fulfills a fundamental purpose for which we were created.

"Even every one that is called by my name: for *I have created him for my glory*, I have formed him; yea, I have made him" (Isa. 43:7; emphasis mine).

2. The second major reason for a child of God to possess good works is seen as part of a process.

Matthew 5:16 gives us a clue that our good works do justify us before men. The puzzle pieces fit together perfectly. Our good works can never justify us before God, but can, and indeed do, justify us before other men. God can see our faith without works, but men can only see our faith through our works. Why is it so important for believers to be justified before other men? We have probably heard it said that a Christian's life may be the only Bible some people will ever read. Again, Matthew 5:16 expresses the importance for others to see our lights shine because they who seek truth are drawn to the light.

"And I, if I be lifted up from the earth, will draw all men unto me" (John 12:32).

The whole process in a nutshell is that we lift up Christ by our good works; others see the light and are drawn to it. Men may be drawn to Christ in one of two ways, the unsaved for salvation or the saved for service. When we serve our Lord, other believers may be encouraged to serve him as well. It's more difficult to serve the Lord when no one else seems to be serving him. However, in a group of willing and eager servants, we are much more likely to be motivated. The greatest result though is the salvation of precious souls. Think about it! Didn't you come to Christ because someone lifted up the Saviour? Weren't you told of his love, grace, and power to forgive or perhaps you saw these things in the life of someone else? We mortals very often get things backwards and the Bible teaching concerning good works is often reversed. There is a profound point here, i.e., we as believers do good works not for our salvation, but for the potential salvation of others! I apologize for so many exclamation marks, but this blesses my heart! We don't save anyone by our good works, but the Lord uses our works to draw others to himself, so that He might save them! This principle is consistent throughout scripture.

The doctrine of the child of God walking in good works is so important that God almighty has commanded and ordained it. Please understand that the following scriptures are not suggestions, but commands for disciples of Christ.

"*Let your light so shine before men*, that they may see your good works, and glorify your Father which is in heaven" (Matt. 5:16; emphasis mine).

"For we are his workmanship, created in Christ Jesus unto good works, which

God hath before *ordained* that we should walk in them" (Eph. 2:10).

"Was not *Abraham* our father *justified by works*, when he had offered Isaac his son upon the altar?" (James 2:21; emphasis mine).

Once we understand that a child of God is justified by faith alone before God and that the child of God is justified before other men by works alone, we can appreciate the importance of good works.

3. The third and final major reason for Christian good works is for rewards in heaven.

We have probably heard believers say something like, I don't care if I have any rewards in heaven as long as I'm going there. Dear brother, you may truly think that now, but once you see God's rewards for the faithful, you'll want some! Caleb the Hebrew spy and soldier of the Lord wasn't content with whatever plot of land came his way, but he wanted God's promised land. The plot of land that God promised Caleb was a mountain city with great walls, occupied by giants! The great apostle Paul didn't disdain his rewards, but encouraged others to follow him in obtaining them.

I have fought a good fight, I have finished my course, I have kept the faith: Henceforth there is laid up for me a crown of righteousness, which the Lord, the righteous judge, shall give me at that day: and not to me only, but unto *all them* also that love his appearing. (2 Tim. 4:7–8; emphasis mine)

There are a total of five eternal crowns in which the believer may earn. You are encouraged to do your own study and identify all five in the Bible. We all should desire to be like the twenty-four elders in Revelation 4:10 who cast their crowns at the feet of our Lord. Whatever heavenly reward we receive, we'll acknowledge that without the Lord's help, we could have never earned anything.

This acknowledgment will be made clear by casting our rewards at Christ's feet. Several people over the years have asked why should we earn rewards just to give them back to Christ Jesus. The reality is that we don't give them back, we just momentarily cast them off as a gesture of acknowledgment and appreciation to our Saviour and take them back again. Whatever treasures survive the judgment seat of Christ—see 2 Corinthians 5 and 1 Corinthians 3—will belong to the Christian eternally. The Holy Bible teaches that loss of rewards is not loss of salvation.

> "If any man's work abide which he hath built thereupon, he shall receive a reward. If any man's *work* shall *be burned*, he shall suffer loss: but *he himself shall be saved*; yet so as by fire" (1 Cor. 3:14–15; emphasis mine).

These verses establish that a man's work as a Christian directly translates into rewards. If the work is pure the reward remains, if not the work and reward will perish. Yet, in verse 15, it's abundantly clear that the salvation of the child of God is never in question, "but he himself *shall be saved*; yet so as by fire." The Bible does not say, might be saved, but "shall be saved" because eternal life cannot cease to exist. Conditional and temporary life can be taken away, but not the eternal life, which God gives. The judgment seat of Christ is all about the believer's rewards, not the believers salvation. Furthermore, salvation for the believer was judged on mount Calvary based upon Christ and his finished and unchanging work on the cross. You may want to read the entire chapter of 1 Corinthians 3 to get a fuller picture of the believer's rewards.

Bible rewards and carnal Christians.

Sometimes, it seems as though, some of my born-again friends overlook the very existence of carnal Christians. When a believer with carnal habits or lifestyle doesn't measure up to acceptable standards, the carnal Christians are often written off as unsaved. The Bible makes it perfectly clear that there are carnal Christians.

And I, *brethren*, could not speak unto
you as unto spiritual, but as unto *carnal*,

even as unto babes in Christ. I have fed you with milk, and not with meat: for hitherto ye were not able to bear it, neither yet now are ye able. For *ye are yet carnal*: for whereas there is among you envying, and strife, and divisions, are ye not carnal, and walk as men? (1 Cor. 3:1–3; emphasis mine)

Of course, there are carnal Christians, loads of them, you know it, I know it, and God knows it! Even as a person who has been raised in a strict outwardly moral church may appear to be a Christian, but has never been born again, so too may a carnal Christian not appear to be a child of God. In other words, carnal Christians are not justified in the eyes of other men by their works. Moreover, the physical birth places a child into his earthly family and a spiritual birth places the child of God into the heavenly family. The truth in nature is, once a child is born, he cannot become unborn likewise, the spiritual Bible truth is, once we have been born again, we can't become unborn. A child of God may be a good child, a bad child, or a so-so child, but they are forever God's child. This is the tone of Christ's conversation with Nicodemus in John 3. Please don't misunderstand, even though a carnal Christian is still a Christian, he is walking on very dangerous ground. I have been asked more than once what's to stop a person from doing whatever he wants once he's saved, if they can't lose eternal life? Here is a list of reasons that stop me from doing whatever I want, even though I know that I will still go to heaven if I choose to be carnal. Yes, some of these reasons were already covered before.

1. "*Quench not* the Spirit" (1 Thess. 5:19; emphasis mine).

    "And *grieve not* the holy Spirit of God, whereby ye are sealed unto the day of redemption" (Eph. 4:30; emphasis mine).

    I've learned by experience that I can't grieve or quench the Spirit of God and have peace and joy, so I choose to yield to his leading. It can be fearful to obey the leading of the Holy Spirit knowing that others may misunderstand what we are doing and why we are doing it.

2. If I yield to the flesh, I can bring shame to my Saviour and God or at the least, bring little or no glory to him. Again, the peace and joy will flee.

3. The carnal Christian can't help in leading others to Christ, but rather they become a stumbling block. How grievous it would be to stand before my Lord knowing that some didn't want to come to Christ because they saw me do something sinful. The carnal Christian who takes too much liberty will also cause other weak Christians to stumble and not serve the Lord as they should.

"But take heed lest by any means this liberty of yours become a stumbling block to them that are weak" (1 Cor. 8:9).

Both professing and possessing Christians can be a stumbling block and be guilty of bringing reproach upon the name of Christ by partaking of the leaven of the Pharisees. Take a moment and try to remember what the Lord warned against. What is the leaven of the Pharisees?

In the mean time, when there were gathered together an innumerable multitude of people, insomuch that they trode one upon another, he began to say unto his disciples first of all, Beware ye of the leaven of the Pharisees, which is *hypocrisy.* (Luke 12:1; emphasis mine)

Nothing destroys another person's faith quite like hypocrisy. Millions of would-be Christians have turned from salvation in Christ because of damage caused by hypocrites. Millions of genuine Christians have stopped serving Christ for the same reason. If you have been hurt by hypocrisy or you know someone who has been hurt by it, please understand that it's never God's fault! I beg you not to blame God for the actions of carnal or false Christians. Does it make sense to punish God because a preacher ran off with the church's money or some woman? No, we must not let their disobedience become our disobedience. We must not allow their sinful behavior become our lame excuse not to attend church and serve God. It may be necessary to change worship locations or compromising denominations, but we can't blame God because others, including preachers, hurt our feelings. Please pause to consider this unpleasant illustration. If you're seated at a restaurant counter and the person on the right spits on you, should you slug the person on our left? Of course not, for several reasons! One reason being that you would be taking out your frustration on the wrong person. Dear hurt Christian, if another Christian hurt you, you shouldn't punish God for their actions! I know, I know, you were wronged, you were hurt, but don't let their sin keep you from serving God. Please, don't let that disobedient person keep you from living your life in obedience! You may think that your feelings got so badly hurt that you will never trust another pastor, deacon or church family, but please remember that our Lord went unto his own and his own received him not. Christ was betrayed by his own familiar friend and your Saviour and mine was spat upon by his own nation. Please allow me to say that your feelings are not more special or precious than our Saviour's. I could convey account after account of how I've been hurt, lied about, betrayed, threatened with death and extremely disappointed by fellow Christians and Pastors, but I refuse to give up! Why? Because they didn't die for me on the cross and I don't have to answer to them, I have to answer to Christ! How would it be if at the judgment seat of Christ, I say, "Lord, I stayed home from church for twenty years because a pastor I admired stole the church offering or ran off with a woman?" Or "Lord, I refused to enter the ministry because I met too many dishonest preachers." I wouldn't be honest if I said that I never thought about quitting the pastorate because of discouragement, but the Lord Jesus was never the blame! Why should I throw my peace, joy, and eternal rewards down the drain because some sinful Christians wanted to act like heathens? No, I can't use their disobedience as an excuse for my disobedience not to serve Christ. This reasoning won't work when you stand before the one who was willingly crucified for you. Christians who blame God for the actions of disobedient Christians have misdirected anger. Please remember Romans 12:19.

"Dearly beloved, avenge not yourselves, but rather give place unto wrath: for it is written, Vengeance is mine; *I will repay*, saith the Lord" (Rom. 12:19; emphasis mine).

Yes, God will repay. Let God's judgment be upon them alone instead of being on them and you too for quitting. Also, while we're here in Romans 12:19, let's be reminded who owns vengeance. You may say what do you mean, who owns vengeance? Vengeance is a *possession* which belongs to God; this possession, in principle, is no different than a bicycle or a car that a person may possess. If someone takes our possession without permission, that's stealing and if we take revenge on someone who wronged us, we stole something which belongs exclusively to God! Vengeance is a possession that belongs to God. Let him repay. He spanks harder than you anyway! So dear hurt Christian, I ask you not to take your eyes off the Saviour and sink as Peter did, but get back in the boat (of fellowship) where you belong. As one of my good friend says, "Sometimes, we Christians need to get out the big boy pants and put them on." The Bible says it this way.

"Thou therefore endure hardness, as a good soldier of Jesus Christ" (2 Tim. 2:3).

4. There are few to no rewards in heaven for carnal Christians.

Those who say they don't care about rewards in heaven now, will weep and howl later, but in the mean time they have little peace and joy.

5. God may cut our physical life short for being carnal.

God has promised us eternal life, but not eternal and unconditional physical life. Day to day, I don't fear that God may strike me dead, but sometimes, when I see and hear what some Christians have done, I fear for them. In other words, I would be afraid to do what they've done, knowing the scriptures and the chastening hand of God. Do they forget what happened to Ananias and Sapphira in Acts chapter five? Have they not read the following?

"For he that eateth and drinketh unworthily, eateth and drinketh damnation to himself, not discerning the Lord's body. For this cause many are weak and sickly among you, and *many sleep*" (1 Cor. 11:29–30; emphasis mine)

In the Corinthian church, God killed "many" Christians for being carnal. That's a very good motivator not to be carnal! God killing Christians for being disobedient is neither a new or isolated concept!

> "If any man defile the temple of God, *him shall God destroy*; for the temple of God is holy, which temple ye are" (1 Cor. 3:17; emphasis mine).

This verse in its context teaches that God destroys the believer's body for being carnal. The scary part is not knowing exactly when we have gone past the point of no return. Sometimes God's children will stick their little toe into the pool of sin and pull it out quickly and wait for the rocks of God's judgment to fall. If they don't they may lower their whole foot in the same way and pull it out. Before long they're swimming in the pool of sin, oblivious to the impending judgment of God. Of course, God chastens his children and warns them when they are doing wrong. Christians are warned in the Bible how to conduct themselves, but the carnal Christians may not even read their Bible consistently. God may send a pastor or other Christian to rebuke and lovingly warn the carnal Christians of their dangerous behavior, but the carnal don't heed. The early warning sign of a Christian out of fellowship is the absence of peace and joy. When a Christian lacks abundant peace and joy something is seriously wrong. Although there are many reasons why a Christian may lack joy, disobedience is usually near the top of the list. Carnal Christians quench and grieve the Spirit of God, which suppresses peace and joy. Peace and joy are the canary in the mine, i.e., the early warning sign that something is wrong, but the carnal Christians don't notice. God wants his children to get right and not get dead. Yet, for the stubborn child God warns.

> Say unto them, As I live, saith the Lord GOD, *I have no pleasure in the death of the wicked*; but that the wicked turn from his way and live: turn ye, turn ye from your evil ways; for why will ye die, O house of Israel? (Ezek. 33:11; emphasis mine)

The principle can be applied to both the Old and New Testaments as well as the saved and the lost.

"All unrighteousness is sin: and there is a *sin not unto death*" (1 John 5:17; emphasis mine).

"Be not wise in thine own eyes: *fear the LORD, and depart from evil*" (Prov. 3:7; emphasis mine).

There are two basic ways to serve God. The first is out of love and gratitude because of what God has done for us—namely, the gift of eternal life through the death of his Son. The second way to serve God is out of fear. The former way is preferable to the latter, for if we serve God out of love and gratitude, we will also have peace and joy. When we serve God out of fear, which is better than not serving him at all, we cannot have that close fellowship like Abraham had. Let's consider some odds and ends.

Did you hear the joke about the horse who walked into the pastor's office? The pastor took one look at him and said, "Why the long face?" Ha! Well, I guess all horses have long faces.

At any rate, peace and joy are invaluable tools for drawing the unsaved and wayward Christian into fellowship with the Lord. A thorough study on peace and joy in the scriptures is recommended for your edification. I personally received the Lord after I saw a very carnal man become born again. Mind you, he wasn't a model Christian, but I noticed that he did have genuine peace and joy because he was forgiven. I went to that man and said, "I want what you have." Referring to the peace and joy he had with God.

I have led people to the Lord who were literally on their death beds, but those who do receive the Lord at the eleventh hour, like the thief on the cross, have no extra rewards in heaven. Christ Jesus with his blood purchased our salvation and eternal *destination*, and we through our works determine our rewards and eternal *distinction*. All believers who strive to be more Christlike will all fall short of perfection. The context of the next verse is to Christians.

> "If we say that we have no sin, we deceive ourselves, and the truth is not in us" (1 John 1:8).

Please realize that sometimes, the Holy Ghost may be teaching us something that we have misunderstood all of our lives. Please remember that justification before men is by works and justification before God for salvation is by faith. A person may have many good works, but without genuine repentance and faith in God, he will not enter heaven. By the same token, a person may have no outwardly apparent works or justification before man, yet if he has genuine repentance and faith (which God can see), he will enter heaven. A person with outward works, but no saving faith, is incomplete and will not enter heaven, while a person who has saving faith and no apparent outward works will enter heaven in spite of his lack of works. James admonishes us to be complete or "perfect" by possessing saving faith which yields eternal life in the sight of God and good works in the sight of man. In this way, we cannot only possess eternal life, but also demonstrate our faith to the lost and encourage other people of faith to continue to serve God while drawing the unsaved toward truth by our good works. This is what the Bible calls a perfect man. Believers are not required to be justified before men to enter heaven, but justification by faith before God is required to enter heaven. A believer who is justified before man and God having works before man and faith toward

God is indeed a perfect (mature, complete) man. However, a born-again believer without works has the exact same eternal life as a perfect man. The perfect man has added peace and joy on earth which the carnal man lacks. The perfect man has abundant eternal rewards while the carnal Christian has little to none. If you are still unclear about works and justification before God for salvation, I invite you to reread chapters 8 and 9.

Some deeper truth or unsticking the sticking point.

Let's go a little deeper, for those who have been taught that the correct biblical formula is faith *plus* works equals salvation. If we maintain that eternal life is in any way connected to our works, then we have a problem with the many clear scriptures which teach otherwise, such as.

> Therefore *by the deeds of the law there shall no flesh be justified in his sight*: for by the law is the knowledge of sin. (Rom. 3:20; emphasis mine)
>
> *Being justified freely by his grace* through the redemption that is in Christ Jesus. (Rom. 3:24; emphasis mine)

What shall we say then that Abraham our father, as pertaining to the flesh, hath found? For if Abraham were justified by works, he hath whereof to glory; but *not before God*. For what saith the scripture? *Abraham believed God*, and *it was counted unto him for righteousness*. Now to him that worketh is the reward not reckoned of grace, but of debt. But to him that *worketh not, but believeth* on him that justifieth the ungodly, *his faith is counted for righteousness*. Even as David also describeth the blessedness of the man, unto whom *God imputeth righteousness without works*. (Rom. 4:1–6; emphasis mine)

This only would I learn of you, *Received ye the Spirit by the works of the law, or by the hearing of faith?* (Gal. 3:2; emphasis mine)

For *by grace are ye saved* through faith; and that *not of yourselves*: it is *the gift of God*: *Not of works*, lest any man should boast. (Eph. 2:8–9; emphasis mine)

Not by works of righteousness which we have done, but according to *his mercy he saved us*, by the washing of regeneration, and renewing of the Holy Ghost. (Titus 3:5; emphasis mine)

Knowing that *a man is not justified by the works of the law, but by the faith* of Jesus Christ, even we have believed in Jesus Christ, that we might be *justified by the faith* of Christ, and *not by the works of the law*: for *by the works of the law shall no flesh be justified*. (Gal. 2:16; emphasis mine)

Now let's reconsider James 2:14 and how it harmonizes with the other scriptures.

"What doth it profit, my brethren, though a man say he hath faith, and have not works? can faith save him?" (James 2:14).

If we say that James 2:14 teaches that faith plus works equals salvation, then we create a huge contradiction against the clear and majority passages. Whatever conclusion we come to, an honest Bible student must harmonize *all* the scriptures on any given topic and not disregard any. In plain English, if many scriptures say that justification before God, eternal life or salvation, is a gift based upon faith without works, then James cannot be saying that salvation is based on faith plus works. It's perfectly fine to conclude that *I don't understand* how James relates to the clear and majority scriptures. It's also perfectly fine to say, James *seems* to contradict Romans 4 and other scriptures, so I don't really understand. However, it's not acceptable to say the Bible has contradictions or I believe that James teaches salvation is a combination of faith plus works in defiance of the clear and majority scriptures. This would be intellectually dishonest in God's sight. Let's consider three very helpful technics which assists us in reconciling and understanding all of these scriptures.

1. The easy-to-understand or clear scriptures outweigh the cloudy, harder-to-understand scriptures.
2. The many scripture are to be given more weight rather than the few or the one.
3. Compare scripture with scripture.

When we have many clear, easy-to-understand scriptures which state that a person is justified before God without works and one passage in James which *seems* to contradict those abundant scriptures, then our understanding of James must be inadequate. Remember, that when studying the Holy Bible the complex doctrines must always fit into the simple doctrines. We have already seen that the context of James is justification of men before other men and not justification of men before God as in the majority scriptures. In addition, James is pointing out what should be the obvious, i.e., James isn't saying that we must have faith and works to be saved, but rather if we have genuine saving faith, good works will automatically follow. These good works that naturally follow the gift of salvation may or may not be abundant and apparently visible to men. Please remember Christian that we live in a fallen world, and a new convert may be quashed by the world and never show their works as they should. Yes, our works *should* be apparent to others, but they may not always be, God knows the heart. A paraphrase of James 2:14 would be something like, what good is it if someone *says* he has faith in Christ and never demonstrates it? Is he even saved? Here, James is speaking in the hypothetical tense. He is simply saying that not everyone who *says* he is saved *is* genuinely saved. Or rather, James is saying that, simply saying we're saved, doesn't make us saved. James 2:14 edifies us using a teaching method similar to what our Lord used in Luke 6:46.

"And why call ye me, Lord, Lord, and
do not the things which I say?" (Luke 6:46).

Here, the Lord is indicating that he isn't someone's Lord just because someone calls him Lord. In like manner, James is telling us that just because someone says they have faith in Christ doesn't mean that he genuinely does. There is a subtle truth here in James. It's such a very fine and delicate point that it may be difficult for some to grasp, but it is distinct and extremely profound. The point is that the believer isn't producing works to *be* saved or to *stay* saved, but he's producing good works because he *is* saved. In other words, the automatic works that follow salvation, issue forth from the Lord to man and are the Lord's doing, not simply works from man to the Lord. You may want to ponder this truth for a time. Let's consider Philippians 1:6.

> "Being confident of this very thing, that *he* which hath begun a good work in you *will* perform it until the day of Jesus Christ" (Phil. 1:6; emphasis mine).

To summarize, what the Bible teaches is that eternal life is a gift from God and not a payoff for doing good works. James teaches us that genuine believers are indeed justified by their works in the eyes of other men, while Romans 4 teaches that faith justifies us before God for salvation. James is not teaching us that we must have faith and works to be saved or to stay saved, but that a genuine believer produces good works because he is saved. The good works that follow a genuine conversion in Christ are the result of the Lord working through us. In addition, eternal life is not kept by the believer, but the believer himself is kept unto eternal life by the power of God. Moreover, James is teaching us that as genuine believers we need to be justified by our works in the eyes of other men, so that the Lord will receive the glory.

If we contend that we must produce good works in order to get to heaven, we're saying that the blood of Christ is not sufficient to atone for all our sins. This would be a direct violation of scripture and would be salvation by our works.

> My little children, these things write I unto you, that ye sin not. And if any man sin, we have an advocate with the Father, Jesus Christ the righteous: And he is the propitiation for our sins: and not for ours only, but also for the sins of the whole world. (1 John 2:1–2)

Dear reader, what are you trusting for salvation, your works, your works plus Christ or the finished work of Christ only?

> "Blessed is the man that trusteth in the LORD, and whose hope the LORD is" (Jer. 17:7).

We have seen the twofold understanding of justification before man and God. Now we have the solid understanding that a person is justified by faith and faith alone before God for salvation and by works and works alone for before men. Let's use what we have learned and apply it to a potentially troublesome area. Can a person be justified before God by works? The answer is yes and I offer a verse of proof.

> "For not the hearers of the law are just before God, but the doers of the law shall be justified" (Rom. 2:13).

You may be confused at this point, but let's take it slow and clear up the confusion. Does this verse tell us that a person is justified by doing the works of the law before God or not? Yes, it does. Does Galatians 2:16 tell us that a person is not justified before God by the works of the law or not? Yes, Galatians tells us that we are not justified before God by works. How do we reconcile these two scriptures? As we have already learned that, the answer cannot be faith plus works equals salvation because that violates the clear and majority scriptures. The answer is subtle, but distinct. This is the typical salvation verses service paradigm, which we have identified before. In other words, while Galatians is speaking of justification before God *for salvation*, Romans is speaking of justification before God *for service*. A believer in Christ is justified by his faith alone and receives eternal life as a free gift. However, a believer's rewards are based solely on his works. A believer who claims that he loves God with all his heart, but has few works to back it up, is not justified before God as a true servant and as such will suffer loss of rewards, yet he himself shall be saved.

> "If any man's work shall be burned, he shall suffer loss: but he himself shall be saved; yet so as by fire" (1 Cor. 3:15).

So then, faith and faith alone determines salvation while works and works alone determine rewards. Shall we invent a new term? Three-fold justification? A good and obedient Christian (such as Paul) is justified in three ways.

1. Before other men by his outward works.
2. Before God by faith alone *for salvation*.
3. Before God by works alone *for service* or as a servant.

Simply put, a Christian who says he is a servant of Christ and has no works to back it up is not justified before God as a servant and will not get the rewards of a servant. Here is a brief look at the Bible teaching of three fold sanctification.

"Who delivered us from so great a death, and doth deliver: in whom we trust that he will yet deliver us" (2 Cor. 1:10).

Here, we see that God delivered born-again believers from so great a death, i.e., hell through salvation and does continue to deliver us today from temptations and a meaningless life as we yield to him and will yet deliver us in the future, ultimately unto heaven. To keep it short, God has delivered every child of his from the penalty of sin, delivers them daily from the power of sin, and one day from the very presence of sin. The Bible concept of every believer being justified by faith in Christ from all things, without good works or the works of the law, is summed up in a single verse.

"And by him all that believe are justified from all things, from which ye could
not be justified by the law of Moses" (Acts
13:39).

To think that the believer's good works have any part of
gaining, maintaining, or retaining eternal life is to frustrate
the grace of God. Furthermore, if anyone can add to the
work of Christ in any way, then Christ died for nothing.

"I do not frustrate the grace of God:
for if righteousness come by the law, then
Christ is dead in vain" (Gal. 2:21).

Some seed thoughts.

- Christians aren't sinless, just forgiven.
- Christians aren't sinless, but they should sin less.
- A word about the eleventh hour conversion. I've
  heard professed believers say things such as, "You
  mean to tell me that a person can live a wicked
  life, repent at the last hour and go to heaven?"

Well, yes! That's exactly what the thief on the cross did! It seems unjust to some Christians that God would accept into heaven someone who had little to no good works. Why would God do such a thing? Because salvation is not by man's works and because God is good, that's why! And why shouldn't God be good, the price for salvation has already been fully paid on the cross hasn't it? Those carnal Christians who go to heaven having done little to nothing to serve Christ or have served him for the wrong reasons, as well as those who wait and receive salvation later in life are hurting themselves. These Christians are cheating themselves of eternal rewards. God is good, don't despise him for being more gracious to others than we are ourselves. Finally, those who plan to get right with God at the eleventh hour usually die at ten thirty!

Total Depravity and the Introduction to the TULIP

What is the TULIP? Briefly stated, the TULIP is an acronym for the five major points of the hyper-Calvinism belief system or doctrines. The TULIP stands for:

*T*otal depravity or total inability of man

*U*nconditional election

*L*imited atonement

*I*rresistible grace

*P*erseverance of the saints

What is the difference between Calvinism and hyper-Calvinism? A brief explanation is that Calvin didn't believe in the "L" or limited atonement of Christ, but rather, he believed the plain teaching of the Bible that the blood of Christ is sufficient to save the whole world. Hence the term hyper in hyper-Calvinism designates going beyond what Calvin himself taught. The plain teaching of the Holy Bible is that the Son of God shed his blood for the sins of the world and not just for a certain few. We would need to rewrite or at least reinterpret the Bible with a biased slant in order to make it say otherwise.

> For God so loved *the world*, that he gave his only begotten Son, that whosoever believeth in him should not perish, but have everlasting life. For God sent not his Son into the world to condemn the world; but that *the world through him might be saved.* (John 3:16–17; emphasis mine)

There is a seemingly endless array of variations of Calvinism, but a simplified version of Calvinistic and hyper-Calvinistic logic can be expressed like this:

1. Man is spiritually dead and cannot save himself— *Total depravity*

2. A dead man cannot reason and has no will, therefore, God must choose him for salvation—*U*nconditional election

3. Christ did not waste his blood on nonbelievers and only died for some—*L*imited atonement

4. When God chooses someone for salvation, God calls and man cannot resist—*I*rresistible grace

5. Those whom God chooses for salvation must endure to the end—*P*erseverance of the saints

We will consider each part of the TULIP in a separate chapter, but for now, let's acknowledge one thing. Calvinism, like Christianity itself, is a cognitive belief system and as such, the entire belief system is predicated upon a single belief. What does this mean? For example, Christianity itself being a cognitive belief system is predicated upon a single belief. That single belief is the deity of Christ. If the Lord Jesus was not God in the flesh, then he was an imposter, and God lied when he spoke from heaven and called Jesus Christ "my beloved Son" in Matthew 3:17, Matthew 17:5, Mark 1:11, Mark 9:7, Luke 3:22, Luke 9:35. The point is that Christianity falls apart without

~ 342 ~

the deity of Christ; Christ can save no one, and "we are of all men most miserable" (1 Cor. 15:19). However, since Christ Jesus was God in the flesh, we have hope in him and beyond this life. We will later apply this same reasoning to the teachings of Calvin.

It's noteworthy that divisions among professing Calvinists begin with the very first point—that being man's depravity. Many millions of Bible believers hold that man is totally depraved and totally unable to save himself, yet reject Calvin's total inability doctrine; why is this? The answer is because Calvin's teachings go *beyond* the Bible truth of no salvation by works and adds that man is unable to *repent* and unable to *believe* the Gospel. This is contrary to the Bible and is in fact the reason Bible believers depart from Calvin at this point. Why did Calvin believe that man was so depraved that he couldn't repent of sin or believe the gospel? I submit that Calvinism is predicated upon an incorrect assumption and a misunderstanding of the composition of man. Calvin's human reasoning dictated that a spiritually dead person is "totally depraved" to the point that man cannot repent or believe anything, including the gospel; therefore, man has no free will to choose. This is not what the Bible teaches. The Bible answer to this reasoning is that while man before being regenerated by God is indeed spiritually dead and cut off from God and heaven, the sinner is still a living, thinking, feeling, decision-making being. Even an un-regenerated person with a dead spirit can laugh, cry, reproduce, think, and communicate. The reason a spiritually dead person is able to do these things is because God made man a *living soul*, and it is man's *soul* which encompasses his emotions, appetites, desires, and longings, including his reasoning mind. Un-regenerated persons buy, sell, reason, accept, reject, and function in a busy world in spite of being spiritually dead unto God. The key point to acknowledge is that man repents and believes *not* with his *spirit* which is *dead*, but with his *soul* which is *alive*! After man *believes* the gospel in his *soul* and repents in his heart, Christ, in the person of the Holy Ghost, comes into man's heart. Again, the Holy Ghost comes in only *after* man asks the Lord for salvation as we will see. Below are sixteen questions, which will be answered from the Bible in this chapter.

1. What is meant by the total depravity of man?

2. Can man save himself?

3. Can man call upon God to save him or must he wait for God to save him and then call?

4. What is God's order for salvation? Do we ask and receive or receive, then ask?

5. Does repentance follow eternal life or vice versa?

6. Do we receive eternal life first and afterward believe and have faith in God's word and Son?

7. Does hearing the word of God precede the salvation of the soul?

8. Does receiving God's word precede receiving the Spirit of God?

9. Are we saved before we call upon the Lord or after?

10. Does God believe the gospel for man or does God command man to believe for himself?

11. Did the Lord Jesus teach that some people cannot believe the truth or that they will not believe?

12. Does God repent for man, as Calvin believed, or does God command man to repent for himself?

13. When repentance and belief themes appear in the same verse, is the focus on God repenting for the

would-be believer or on the would-be believer himself?

14. According to scripture, whom does God want to repent?

15. Does God force people to repent; what does the Bible say?

16. What is imputation and how does it relate to salvation?

The total depravity of man

Let's now define the term. Since total depravity is *not a Bible term,* we must allow man to define it. The problem is that there are, in fact, several definitions for this term. To keep it simple, some would define the term as man's inability to repent, believe, or reach out to God in any way. Still, others oversimplify the term and say that total depravity means that man can't save himself. Just allowing these two extremely different definitions causes great confusion among the brethren. This confusion is not of God.

"For *God is not the author of confu-sion*, but of peace, as in all churches of the saints" (1 Cor. 14:33; emphasis mine).

Can man save himself?

The Bible truly teaches that man is totally unable to save himself by his own efforts. If you are unclear on this fact, I encourage you to reread chapters 7 and 8. However, the extreme view that a non-regenerated person is unable to believe, repent, or call out in faith to God is not a Bible doctrine. It's not reasonable to assume that a person who cannot save himself by works must therefore not be able to repent, believe, or call out to someone who can save him. Let's take a look at a simple example. Let's agree that a person chained in a burning building doesn't have the ability to escape. Must we automatically assume that this same person, who can't save himself, must therefore not have the ability to call upon someone else to help him out of his predicament? Of course not. The inability to save one's self, either physically or spiritually, does not mean that the person in jeopardy is excluded from calling upon someone else to save him.

Can man call upon God to save him or must he wait for God to save him and then call?

Example 1:

> "And the publican, standing afar off, would not lift up so much as his eyes unto heaven, but smote upon his breast, saying, *God be merciful to me a sinner*" (Luke 18:13; emphasis mine).

Calvinism teaches that the Holy Spirit comes into a man and then that man repents and believes the gospel. But the Bible teaches that belief and repentance come *before* the Holy Ghost enters; this divine order is clearly taught in scripture. A thorough study of the Bible reveals that God's divine order is that repentance, confessing, calling, trusting, as well as hearing, believing, and having faith in God's word always precedes receiving salvation. Many examples will follow.

What is God's order for salvation? Do we ask and receive or receive then ask?

Example 2: Please notice the order once more, call first, salvation second.

> "For whosoever shall *call* upon the name of the Lord shall be *saved*" (Rom. 10:13; emphasis mine).

Example 3:

> "If ye then, being evil, know how to give good gifts unto your children: how much more shall your heavenly Father *give the Holy Spirit* to *them that ask* him?" (Luke 11:13; emphasis mine)

Does repentance follow eternal life or vice versa?

Example 4:

> "When they heard these things, they held their peace, and glorified God, saying, Then hath God also to the Gentiles granted *repentance unto life*" (Acts 11:18; emphasis mine).

Example 5:

> "For godly sorrow worketh *repentance to salvation* not to be repented of: but the sorrow of the world worketh death" (2 Cor. 7:10; emphasis mine).

Do we receive eternal life first and afterward
believe and have faith in God's word and Son?

Example 6:

"That whosoever *believeth* in him
should not perish, but have *eternal life*"
(John 3:15; emphasis mine).

Example 7:

"For God so loved the world, that
he gave his only begotten Son, that whosoever *believeth* in him should not perish, but have *everlasting life*" (John 3:16;
emphasis mine).

Example 8:

"And this is the will of him that sent
me, that every one which seeth the Son,
and *believeth* on him, may have *everlasting*

life: and I will raise him up at the last day"
(John 6:40; emphasis mine).

Example 9: John wrote his gospel for the purpose of imparting faith resulting in salvation.

> "But these are *written*, that ye might
> *believe* that Jesus is the Christ, the Son of
> God; and that *believing* ye might have *life*
> through his name" (John 20:31; emphasis
> mine).

Example 10:

> "Those by the way side are they that
> hear; then cometh the devil, and *taketh*
> *away the word* out of their hearts, *lest they*
> *should believe* and *be saved*" (Luke 8:12;
> emphasis mine).

Example 11:

"And they said, *Believe* on the Lord Jesus Christ, and thou shalt *be saved*, and thy house" (Acts 16:31; emphasis mine).

Example 12:

"But as many as *received* him, to them gave he power to *become* the *sons of God*, even to them that *believe* on his name" (John 1:12; emphasis mine).

Example 13:

He that *believeth* on me, as the scripture hath said, out of his belly shall flow rivers of living water. (39) (But this spake he of the Spirit, which they that *believe* on him should *receive*: for the *Holy Ghost* was not yet given; because that Jesus was not yet glorified.) (John 7:38–39; emphasis mine)

Does hearing the word of God precede
the salvation of the soul?

Example 14:

> "Wherefore lay apart all filthiness
> and superfluity of naughtiness, and *receive*
> with meekness the engrafted *word,* which
> is able to *save your souls*" (James 1:21;
> emphasis mine).

Does receiving God's word precede receiving the Spirit of God?

Example 15:

> "This only would I learn of you,
> *Received* ye *the Spirit* by the works of the
> law, or *by the hearing* of faith?" (Gal. 3:2;
> emphasis mine).

There are many combinations of these themes in scripture. In every case, salvation, eternal life, receiving the Spirit

of God, etc., are always a result of repentance, faith, hearing, believing, confessing, trusting, and calling on God. These themes always precede the receiving of salvation.

Example 16: Hearing and believing God's word precedes everlasting life.

> "Verily, verily, I say unto you, He that *heareth* my word, and *believeth* on him that sent me, hath *everlasting life*, and shall not come into condemnation; but is passed from death unto life" (John 5:24; emphasis mine).

Example 17:

> "In whom ye also trusted, *after* that ye *heard* the word of truth, the gospel of your salvation: in whom also *after* that ye *believed*, ye were sealed with that holy Spirit of promise" (Eph. 1:13).

Example 18:

> And when there had been much dis-
> puting, Peter rose up, and said unto them,
> Men and brethren, ye know how that a
> good while ago God made choice among
> us, that the Gentiles by my mouth should
> *hear* the word of the gospel, and *believe*.
> (Acts 15:7; emphasis mine)

Are we saved before we, believe, confess, hear,
et. al. and call upon the Lord or after?

Example 19: Believing and confessing or calling upon
the Lord precedes salvation.

> "That *if thou shalt confess* with thy
> mouth the Lord Jesus, and shalt *believe* in
> thine heart that God hath raised him from
> the dead, thou shalt *be saved*" (Rom. 10:9;
> emphasis mine).

Example 20: Calling, believing and hearing all precede salvation.

> "How then shall they *call* on him in whom they have not believed? and how shall they *believe* in him of whom they have not heard? and how shall they *hear* without a preacher?" (Rom. 10:14; emphasis mine).

Example 21: Trusting, hearing, believing, and receiving God's word results in receiving the holy Spirit.

> "In whom *ye* also *trusted, after* that *ye heard* the word of truth, the gospel of your salvation: in whom also *after* that *ye believed, ye were sealed with that holy Spirit* of promise" (Eph. 1:13; emphasis mine).

My old theology teacher used to ask, "How many times does God have to say something for it to be true?" And his answer was always, "One time!"

The proper order of salvation is that salvation, receiving the Spirit of God and forgiveness follow repentance, believing, calling, etc. The proper mechanics of salvation can never be understood until we grasp the true nature of mankind. That is to say, because Calvinism incorrectly teaches that a spiritually dead person can't repent, believe, or hear God's word, it is also assumed that God needs to repent and believe for man, hence the reversed order. If you still have difficulty understanding how a spiritually dead person can reason and repent, please reread chapter 5, "The Three Parts of Man."

Does God believe the gospel for man or does
God command man to believe for himself?

Example 22: Indeed, if mankind were not able to believe God's word, then God, of necessity, must believe the gospel for him. However, do we find clear passages in scripture of God believing the gospel for man or do we find God commanding man to believe for himself?

"And this is his *commandment*, That *we* should *believe* on the name of his Son Jesus Christ, and love one another, as he gave us commandment" (1 John 3:23; emphasis mine).

Example 23: The apostles preached that man must believe in order to be saved.

"And they said, *Believe* on the Lord Jesus Christ, and thou shalt be saved, and thy house" (Acts 16:31; emphasis mine).

Example 24: It was the desire of the Son of God that the world would believe in him.

"That they all may be one; as thou, Father, art in me, and I in thee, that they also may be one in us: that *the world* may *believe* that thou hast sent me" (John 17:21; emphasis mine).

Example 25: Here are more Bible verses that teach that man believes all by himself, as opposed to God believing for him.

"Wherefore, sirs, be of good cheer: for *I believe* God, that it shall be even as it was told me" (Acts 27:25; emphasis mine).

Example 26:

"And he said, Lord, *I believe*. And he worshipped him" (John 9:38; emphasis mine).

Example 27:

"She saith unto him, Yea, Lord: *I believe* that thou art the Christ, the Son of God, which should come into the world" (John 11:27; emphasis mine).

Example 28:

> "And Philip said, If thou believest with all thine heart, thou mayest. And he answered and said, *I believe* that Jesus Christ is the Son of God" (Acts 8:37; emphasis mine).

Man can believe or reject the Gospel because he possesses his own will. Below is a brief outline of the free will of man from chapter 6.

A. God has a will.

> "And the LORD God said, It is not good that the man should be alone; *I will* make him an help meet for him" (Gen. 2:18; emphasis mine).

B. Mankind in general has a will to make choices.

"While it is said, To day *if ye will* hear his voice, harden not your hearts, as in the provocation" (Heb. 3:5; emphasis mine).

C. God expects man to make choices with his will.

"I call heaven and earth to record this day against you, that I have set before you life and death, blessing and cursing: therefore *choose* life, that both thou and thy seed may live" (Deut. 30:19; emphasis mine).

Some of these people made the right choice and some did not.

D. Unsaved man in particular has a will and can make choices.

"O Jerusalem, Jerusalem, thou that killest the prophets, and stonest them which

are sent unto thee, how often would I have
gathered thy children together, even as a hen
gathereth her chickens under her wings, and
ye would not!" (Matt. 23:37; emphasis mine).

E. What is God's will for man pertaining to salvation?

"For this is good and acceptable in the
sight of *God* our Saviour; Who *will* have
all men to be *saved*, and to *come* unto the
knowledge of the truth" (1 Tim. 2:3–4;
emphasis mine).

F. God's will is sometimes contingent upon man's will.

"*Draw nigh* to God, and *he will* draw
nigh to you. Cleanse your hands, ye sinners; and purify your hearts, ye double
minded" (James 4:8; emphasis mine).

Please notice that God places the burden on man to
make the next move. Significant time and space has been

given to the subject of whether or not the Bible teaches the free will of man. If you are unclear about God's will or man's will, I invite you to reread chapter 6.

Does the Bible teach that some people cannot believe or that they will not believe?

Example 29: Nobody appreciates it when another person puts words in his mouth, so let's not be guilty of putting words in God's mouth.

"Art thou the Christ? tell us. And he said unto them, If I tell you, *ye will not* believe" (Luke 22:67; emphasis mine).

Example 30: Here is a second witness from scripture, again from the mouth of the Lord himself.

"Then said Jesus unto him, Except ye see signs and wonders, *ye will not* believe" (John 4:48; emphasis mine).

The Lord did not say in either instance to the people that ye *can not* believe, but that ye *will not* believe.

Example 31: Christ's teachings assert that believing or not believing is a personal choice.

> "If I do not the works of my Father, *believe me not*. But if I do, though ye believe not me, *believe* the works: that ye may know, and believe, that the Father is in me, and I in him" (John 10:37–38; emphasis mine).

Example 32: Another example of the individual choosing to believe.

> "Jesus saith unto her, Said I not unto thee, that, *if thou wouldest believe*, thou shouldest see the glory of God?" (John 11:40; emphasis mine)

Does God repent for man as Calvinism teaches or does God command man to repent for himself?

Example 33:

> "And the times of this ignorance *God* winked at; but now *commandeth* all *men* every where *to repent*" (Acts 17:30; emphasis mine)

Example 34:

> "And saying, The time is fulfilled, and the kingdom of God is at hand: *repent ye*, and *believe* the gospel" (Mark 1:15; emphasis mine).

Example 35:

> "I tell you, Nay: but, except *ye repent*, ye shall all likewise perish" (Luke 13:3; emphasis mine).

Example 36:

> "I tell you, Nay: but, except *ye repent,*
> ye shall all likewise perish" (Luke 13:5;
> emphasis mine).

Example 37: Did God repent for Job or did Job repent for himself?

> "Wherefore *I* abhor myself, and *repent*
> in dust and ashes" (Job 42:6; emphasis
> mine).

When repentance and belief, i.e., faith themes appear in the same verse, is the focus on God repenting for the would-be believer or on the would-be believer himself?

Example 38:

> "And saying, The time is fulfilled,
> and the kingdom of God is at hand: *repent*

ye, and *believe* the gospel" (Mark 1:15; emphasis mine).

Example 39: Paul preached:

"Testifying both to the Jews, and also to the Greeks, *repentance* toward God, and *faith* toward our Lord Jesus Christ" (Acts 20:21; emphasis mine).

Example 40:

"Therefore leaving the principles of the doctrine of Christ, let us go on unto perfection; not laying again the foundation of *repentance* from dead works, and of *faith* toward God" (Heb. 6:1; emphasis mine).

Example 41:

"*Repent ye* therefore, and *be converted,* that your sins may be blotted out, when

the times of refreshing shall come from
the presence of the Lord" (Acts 3:19;
emphasis mine).

According to the Bible, God always places the burden
on man to repent and believe.

Whom does God want to repent?

Example 42:

"The Lord is not slack concerning
his promise, as some men count slackness; but is longsuffering to us-ward, not
willing that any should perish, but that
all should come *to repentance*" (2 Pet. 3:9;
emphasis mine).

Example 43:

"And the times of this ignorance
God winked at; but now commandeth *all*

men every where to *repent*" (Acts 17:30; emphasis mine).

Does this verse exclude any person?

Example 44: The next three verses are in the context of salvation.

> "For *all have sinned,* and come short of the glory of God" (Rom. 3:23; emphasis mine).

Example 45: Since all are sinners, then repentance is for all.

> "But go ye and learn what that meaneth, I will have mercy, and not sacrifice: for I am not come to call the righteous, but *sinners to repentance*" (Matt. 9:13; emphasis mine).

Example 46:

> "When Jesus heard it, he saith unto them, They that are whole have no need of the physician, but they that are sick: I came not to call the righteous, but *sinners to repentance*" (Mark 2:17; emphasis mine).

Example 47:

> "I came not to call the righteous, but *sinners to repentance*" (Luke 5:32; emphasis mine).

Any reasonable person not trained in the teachings of Calvin would conclude that the Lord wants all persons to repent. The plain common-sense interpretation of scriptures here commands more authority than does any private interpretation of scripture.

Does God force people to repent or does God call,
plead, invite, etc.; what does the Bible say?

Example 48:

> "I call heaven and earth to record this
> day against you, that I have set before you
> life and death, blessing and cursing: there-
> fore *choose life,* that both thou and thy seed
> may live" (Deut. 30:1; emphasis mine 9).

Example 49:

> Say unto them, As I live, saith the
> Lord GOD, I have no pleasure in the death
> of the wicked; but that the *wicked turn*
> from his way and live: *turn ye, turn ye*
> from your evil ways; for *why will ye die,*
> O house of Israel? (Ezek. 33:11; emphasis
> mine)

Example 50:

"But go ye and learn what that meaneth, I will have mercy, and not sacrifice: for I am not come to *call* the righteous, but *sinners to repentance*" (Matt. 9:13; emphasis mine).

Example 51:

"When Jesus heard it, he saith unto them, They that are whole have no need of the physician, but they that are sick: I came not to *call* the righteous, but *sinners to repentance*" (Mark 2:17; emphasis mine).

Example 52:

"I came not to *call* the righteous, but *sinners to repentance*" (Luke 5:32; emphasis mine).

What is imputation and how does it relate to salvation?

Imputation, briefly stated, is the act of God whereby God places the righteousness of Christ on the believer. Those who have God's imputation have salvation and vice versa. The important element of imputation in salvation is that imputation is contingent upon the individual's choice to believe, not on God to believe.

Example 53:

"Now it was not written for his sake alone, that it was *imputed* to him; But for us also, to whom it shall be imputed, *if we believe* on him that raised up Jesus our Lord from the dead" (Rom. 4:23–24; emphasis mine).

Example 54: Here is a second witness from scripture.

"And the scripture was fulfilled which saith, *Abraham believed* God, and it was *imputed* unto him for righteousness: and he was called the Friend of God" (James 2:23; emphasis mine).

Example 55: This verse doses not say that if God shalt…but if *thou* shalt…

"That *if thou* shalt confess with thy mouth the Lord Jesus, and shalt *believe* in thine heart that God hath raised him from the dead, thou shalt be saved" (Rom. 10:9; emphasis mine).

Example 56: Do you remember what God said to Cain after his offering was rejected?

"*If thou* doest well, shalt thou not be accepted? and *if thou* doest not well, sin lieth at the door. And unto thee shall be his desire, and thou shalt rule over him" (Gen. 4:7; emphasis mine).

God clearly places the responsibility on the sinner to believe in order that he may receive imputation; this is where the onus belongs. The obvious conclusion from this section is that while it is a Bible fact that man cannot save himself, he can repent, believe the gospel and call upon the Saviour. To suggest that God must repent or believe for man is to take the onus from man, where it belongs, and to place it on God, where it doesn't!

Another important question: Does a person will himself to be saved?

Answer: No, of course not.

Example 57:

> He came unto his own, and his own received him not. But as many as received him, to them gave the power to become the sons of God, even to them that believe on his name: Which were *born*, not of blood, nor of the will of the flesh, *nor of the will of man*, but of God. (John 1:11–13; emphasis mine)

A person is not saved by force of will, but when man's heart is willing to call upon God, then God is willing to save.

Example 58: The teaching of man's willingness to seek God's presence is consistent in scripture, Old Testament and New.

Example 59:

> "And ye shall *seek me*, and *find me*, when ye shall search for me with all your heart" (Jer. 29:13; emphasis mine).

Example 60:

> "For *every one* that asketh receiveth; and he *that seeketh findeth*; and to him that knocketh it shall be opened" (Luke 11:10; emphasis mine).

Example 61:

> "Behold, I stand at the door, and knock: *if any man* hear my voice, and *open the door, I will* come in to him, and will sup with him, and he with me" (Rev. 3:20; emphasis mine).

Let's consider a real-life experience.

While on vacation one year, my wife and I visited what appeared to be a good Bible-teaching church. During the sermon, the preacher preached that it was impossible for anyone to seek after God, quoting Romans 3:11.

> "There is none that understandeth, there is none that seeketh after God" (Rom. 3:11).

The preacher assured the congregation that no man ever sought after God, period. His reasoning flowed from Calvinist doctrine, i.e., because man is spiritually dead, he can't possibly seek God. After the sermon, we shook hands and I asked him to read Jeremiah 29:13.

"And *ye shall seek me, and find me,* when ye shall search for me with all your heart" (Jer. 29:13; emphasis mine).

The man was perplexed and didn't have an answer. Do you have an answer? Which is true, Romans 3:11 or Jeremiah 29:13? The answer is both are true. If you believe that there are contradictions in God's holy word, then the Bible is meaningless and man becomes the final authority and not God. How do we reconcile these two scriptures? All scriptures harmonize perfectly when they are rightly divided. The answer is in the tense of the verbs. By the way, verb tenses are very important and help to define the context of scripture. Romans 3:11 does not say that none ever sought God, but that none seeketh after God. The verb "seeketh" is present tense continual, i.e., none (no person) seeks after God totally and continually without fail; the spirit is willing, but the flesh is weak. Romans 3:11 is not saying that no one ever seeks God at all. On the contrary, the Bible abounds with examples of individuals seeking God. Please do your own study. I'll rest with Jeremiah 29:13 and Psalms 34:4.

> "*I sought* the LORD, and he heard me,
> and delivered me from all my fears" (Ps.
> 34:4; emphasis mine).

Let's alter our beliefs to align with the Bible as opposed to dismissing, changing or reinterpreting the Bible where it doesn't align with our preconceived notions. It's ludicrous to believe that the Bible must line up with what we were taught by Mom, Dad, church or Bible college. Everyone has different life experiences and preconceived ideas. If we don't want to beat our heads against the wall, we must surrender our faith to the Bible itself and believe only the Bible. When the Bible seems to contradict itself or make no sense, then let's admit to ourselves that we don't understand, but the answer is never that the Bible is wrong. Our convictions and doctrines never trump the truth of the Bible.

Here are some end of chapter conclusions for your consideration.

1. The terms total depravity and total inability are not Bible terms.

2. There are multiple meanings to these terms, which causes confusion.

3. Even if we give the term total depravity a more biblically accurate definition such as "man's inability to save himself by his own works," we are still using a misleading term. Those who have been schooled in Calvinism would assume that we believe that man has no ability to repent and call upon God. To avoid confusion, it's therefore wiser not to promote this term at all. When others use these terms, we must always seek clarification of the term.

4. While it is a Bible fact that man cannot save himself, he can call on God to save him. Man can, however, repent and believe the gospel.

5. As was previously mentioned, Calvinism, like Christianity itself, is a cognitive belief system and as such the entire belief system is predicated upon a

single belief. Calvinism teaches that man is totally depraved with a total inability to repent, believe and call upon the Saviour for salvation. Again, this belief sprang from the false assumption that a spiritually dead person can do nothing. We have seen from scripture that man repents and believes not with his *spirit* which is *dead*, but with his *soul* which is *alive*! God has every right to place the burden of repenting, believing and coming to God upon man.

6. If we believe Calvinism to be correct, that man can neither repent or believe the gospel, ask yourself the question, "Why would God command us to do something which he knew we can't do?" God, in fact, in scripture, always puts the onus on man to repent and believe. The simple truth is that God doesn't repent for man, but rather commands man to repent himself.

7. The divine order is that hearing, trusting, and believing the gospel, precede salvation.

"In whom ye also *trusted, after* that ye *heard* the word of truth, the gospel of your salvation: in whom also *after* that ye *believed*, ye were sealed with that holy Spirit of promise" (Eph. 1:13; emphasis mine)

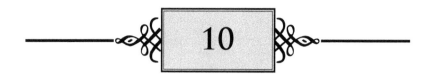

10

Unconditional Election:
The "U" of the TULIP

What is the TULIP? Briefly stated, the TULIP is an acronym for the five major points of the hyper-Calvinism belief system or doctrines. The TULIP stands for...

*T*otal depravity or total inability of man

*U*nconditional election

*L*imited atonement (not believed by John Calvin)

*I*rresistible grace

*P*erseverance of the saints

The "U" of the TULIP stands for unconditional election and is the belief that God chooses individuals for heaven and hell. As with all of terms constituting the TULIP, unconditional election is not a Bible term. Even as the "T" of the TULIP innately caries multiple meanings, so too does the term unconditional election. The way Calvinists understand this term is that God chose some individuals for hell and some for heaven, and no person has any choice or input in the matter. You can be the judge as to whether this is what the Bible teaches or not. A biblical definition for election would be: the act of God whereby God chooses things, places and people, for his glory and service. This simple definition brings us to a fundamental Bible truth, i.e., God's choosing in the Holy Scriptures is always for service and never for salvation. We will consider many scriptures in support of this fact. First, let's consider why Calvinism feels the need for God to choose individuals for salvation. Because Calvinism assumes that a person with a dead spirit couldn't believe, repent or call out to God, it also assumes that God must choose or reject the gospel for man. We have seen in chapter five, that there is no need for this line of reasoning, since the Bible teaches that a lost man can make decisions in his *soul* which is *alive* even though he possesses a *spirit* which is *dead*.

Election is a truly great Bible doctrine! What is Bible based election? Before we come to a definitive conclusion, we must do an exhaustive study of election and choosing, including their derivations throughout scripture. Below are the resulting words with the number of times that each occurs.

- elect = 17x
- elect's = 3x
- election = 6x
- elected = 1x
- total = 27x
- choose = 59x (1 double references)
- chose = 29x (2 double references)
- chosen = 123x (4 double references)
- chooseth = 3x
- choosing = 1x
- total = 215x
- grand total = 242x

I invite you to duplicate the study, which was done in preparation for writing this book, i.e., read all of these verses and their respective contexts. We sincerely want to know what the Bible says for itself and not what others tell us the Bible says, don't we? We would all do well not to believe authors of books or orators simply because they're famous. It's always better to let the scriptures interpret the scriptures. I have a sign in my study that says, "The word of God sheds a great deal of light on Bible commentaries!" Let's now explore God's great doctrine of election in scripture!

We will examine these questions in this chapter.

1. Does God only choose people for service or does he choose things too?
2. Do you remember the important teaching tool of Hebrew poetry?
3. What does Old Testament Hebrew poetry teach that election and choosing are for?
4. What does the New Testament teach that election and choosing are for?
5. Does God force individuals to serve him or does God allow man a free will/choice to serve?
6. Is it possible that election and salvation are the same thing?

7. Are there special choosings that help us to understand that election is for service?

8. According to the Bible, does God place the onus of salvation on himself or on the individual?

Some of God's chosen things.

Example 1: Jerusalem, God's chosen city

"But I have *chosen Jerusalem*, that my name might be there" (2 Chron. 6:6a; emphasis mine).

Example 2: God shall yet choose Jerusalem.

"Cry yet, saying, Thus saith the LORD of hosts; My cities through prosperity shall yet be spread abroad; and the LORD shall yet comfort Zion, *and shall yet choose Jerusalem*" (Zech. 1:17; emphasis mine).

Example 3: God has chosen foolish and weak things.

"But God hath *chosen* the *foolish things* of the world to confound the wise; and God hath *chosen* the *weak things* of the world to confound the things which are mighty" (1 Cor. 1:27; emphasis mine).

Within this same context of foolish and weak things which God has chosen to confound the wise, we also find the "foolish" delivery method of salvation which God has chosen, that being the preaching of his word.

"For after that in the wisdom of God the world by wisdom knew not God, it pleased God by the *foolishness* of *preaching* to save them that believe" (1 Cor. 1:21; emphasis mine).

God chose the method of salvation.

Example 4:

> "But we are bound to give thanks always to God for you, brethren beloved of the Lord, because God hath from the beginning chosen you to salvation through sanctification of the Spirit and belief of the truth" (2 Thess. 2:13).

I appreciate the fact that we can be easily confused if we don't read the Bible as it's written. This verse does not say that God has chosen anyone "for salvation," but "to salvation." Simply put, God is choosing the method of salvation or the method for individuals to be saved and not persons themselves for salvation. In other words, God has chosen the method that you, I or anyone who becomes saved will do so through God's appointed method of sanctification of the Spirit and belief of the truth. It is the method that is being chosen here and not individuals for salvation. There is much more Bible information associated with God's choosing the method of salvation. God also chose that the method of salvation would be a free gift given through faith and not by our works.

Example 5:

> "For by grace are ye saved through faith; and that not of yourselves: it is the *gift* of God: Not of works, lest any man should boast" (Eph. 2:8–9; emphasis mine).

Example 6:

> "*Not by works* of righteousness which we have done, but according to his mercy he saved us, by the washing of regeneration, and renewing of the Holy Ghost" (Titus 3:5; emphasis mine).

Example 7:

> Even so then at this present time also there is a remnant according to the *elec-*

tion of grace. And if by grace, then is it no more of works: otherwise grace is no more grace. But if it be of works, then is it no more grace: otherwise work is no more work. (Rom. 11:5–6; emphasis mine)

In this scripture, God is not choosing people to be recipients of his grace, but rather God is choosing grace itself and not works as the method of salvation. Notice that the scriptures do not say that there is a remnant chosen by grace, but that grace itself is being elected or chosen. A paraphrase could read, "There is a group that is saved according to God's chosen method of grace." In other words, God chose the method of salvation to be by grace through faith, to save a remnant. So once again, God is choosing the *method of* salvation and not individuals *for salvation.* This fact maintains once more that salvation is given as a gift and not a payment for performing works.

Much time and space could be spent to give us a complete picture of God's chosen method of salvation. However, our main focus is not on soteriology, but rather, how election relates to the method of salvation and not to the individual for salvation. Those who choose to come to God through his chosen method of salvation by grace through faith in the blood of God's chosen servant Christ are God's chosen for service. God, therefore, has chosen and ordained that all recipients of eternal life should serve him. These blessed truths are in sharp contrast to Calvinism, which teaches that God loves only his elect and all others he does not.

Example 8:

> "For this is good and acceptable in the sight of *God* our Saviour; *Who will have all men to be saved, and to come unto the knowledge of the truth*" (1 Tim. 2:3–4; emphasis mine).

A refresher in Hebrew poetry.

I trust you recall, how that in chapter 2, we observed the Hebrew poetic style often used in the Bible. The Bible uses rhyming themes or thought patterns, which affords us a tool to help interpret, i.e., rightly divide scripture. Let's refresh our memories with some great examples of Hebrew poetry!

Example 9: Lamp and light

"Thy word is a *lamp* unto my feet, and a *light* unto my path" (Ps. 119:105; emphasis mine).

Note the matching or rhyming thymes of God's word being both a "lamp" and a "light" unto the psalmist's path. A lamp, of course, is a type of light, thus the matching theme.

Example 10: Zion and Jerusalem

"Rejoice greatly, O daughter of *Zion*; shout, O daughter of *Jerusalem*: behold, thy King cometh unto thee: he is just, and having salvation; lowly, and riding upon an ass, and upon a colt the foal of an ass" (Zech. 9:9; emphasis mine).

We see several rhyming thought patterns; one being that Zion is another name for Jerusalem.

Example 11: Seed and children

"O ye *seed* of Israel his servant, ye *children* of Jacob, his chosen ones" (1 Cor. 16:13; emphasis mine).

The Old Testament Hebrew poetry teaches that election and choosing are for service.

Example 12: Israel and Jacob

"O ye seed of *Israel* his servant, ye children of *Jacob*, his chosen ones" (1 Cor. 16:13; emphasis mine).

Here, Israel is matched with Jacob; Israel and Jacob being the same person, with Israel being the name given by his heavenly Father and Jacob given by his earthly. Now, let's go a little deeper for there is another rhyming theme here. Yes, you probably guessed it! Israel is the Lord's "servant" and Jacob is his "chosen." This is a clear, decisive and fundamental doctrine of scripture, i.e., Jacob, as well as the nation of Israel, is chosen for service. But do we have another witness in scripture expressing this truth?

Example 13:

"For Jacob my *servant's* sake, and Israel mine *elect*, I have even called thee by thy name: I have surnamed thee, though thou hast not known me" (Isa. 45:4; emphasis mine).

Example 14:

"And I will bring forth a seed out of Jacob, and out of Judah an inheritor of my mountains: and *mine elect* shall inherit it, and *my servants* shall dwell there" (Isa. 65:9; emphasis mine).

Example 15: An Old Testament account with King Hezekiah addressing the Levites.

> "My sons, be not now negligent: for the LORD hath *chosen* you to stand before him, *to serve* him, and that ye should *minister* unto him, and burn incense" (2 Chron. 29:11; emphasis mine).

Bible election is for service and never for salvation!

Example 16: The Bible teaches that the Lord Jesus is God's elect.

> "Behold my *servant*, whom I uphold; mine *elect*, in whom my soul delighteth; I have put my spirit upon him: he shall bring forth judgment to the Gentiles" (Isa. 42:1; emphasis mine).

Question: Was the Lord Jesus chosen to be saved? No. He was never lost, but the Father chose his Son to serve himself by bringing judgment and eternal life to the Gentiles.

The New Testament teaches that election and choosing are for service, not salvation.

A New Testament example of election for service.

Example 17: "Paul, a *servant* of God, and an apostle of Jesus Christ, according to the faith of God's *elect*, and the acknowledging of the truth which is after godliness" (Titus 1:1; emphasis mine).

Another New Testament example of election for service.

Example 18:

> (For the children being not yet born, neither having done any good or evil, that the purpose of God according to *election* might stand, not of works, but of him that calleth;) It was said unto her, The elder

shall *serve* the younger. (Rom. 9:11–12; emphasis mine)

Not only is the election or choosing for service clearly seen here, but also God's chosen method of grace. You may say that you didn't see the word grace anywhere; no, but the idea is openly expressed in that election stands, "not of works," therefore it must by necessity be by grace!

The choosing of the apostle to replace Judas Iscariot and minister or serve.

Example 19:

And they prayed, and said, Thou, Lord, which knowest the hearts of all men, shew whether of these two thou hast *chosen*, That he may take part of this *ministry* and apostleship, from which Judas by transgression fell, that he might go to his own place. (Acts 1:24–25; emphasis mine)

Did the Father save the Son? No, Christ needed no saving. The Son was chosen to serve.

Example 20:

> "Behold my *servant*, whom I have *chosen*; my beloved, in whom my soul is well pleased: I will put my spirit upon him, and he shall shew judgment to the Gentiles" (Matt. 12:18; emphasis mine).

Let's consider some verses, well-worn and misapplied by students of Calvin.

Example 21:

> "So the last shall be first, and the first last: for many be called, but few chosen" (Matt. 20:16).

Ask yourself, what is the context of this verse? Do you know from memory? Is the word chosen in the text referring to salvation or service? I ask you to take some time to be a student of the Bible and not a student of me, Calvin or your pastor. What is the biblical context? Here is the full text.

For the kingdom of heaven is like unto a man that is an householder, which went out early in the morning to hire *labourers* into his vineyard. And when he had agreed with the labourers for a penny a day, he sent them into his vineyard. And he went out about the third hour, and saw others standing idle in the marketplace, And said unto them; Go ye also into the vineyard, and whatsoever is right I will give you. And they went their way. Again he went out about the sixth and ninth hour, and did likewise. And about the eleventh hour he went out, and found others standing idle, and saith unto them, Why stand ye here all the day idle? They say unto him, Because no man hath hired us. He saith unto them, Go ye also into the vineyard; and whatsoever is right, that shall ye receive. So when even was come, the lord of the vineyard saith unto his steward, Call the labourers, and give them their hire, beginning from the last unto the first. And when they came that were hired about the eleventh hour, they received every man a penny. But when the first came, they supposed that they should have received more; and they likewise received every man a penny. And when they had received it, they murmured against the goodman of the house, Saying, These last have wrought but one hour, and thou hast made them equal unto us, which have borne the burden and heat of the day. But he answered one of them, and said, Friend, I do thee no wrong: didst not thou agree with me for a penny? Take that thine is, and go thy way: I will give unto this last, even as unto thee. Is it not lawful for me to do what I will with mine own? Is thine eye evil, because I am good? So the last shall be first, and the first last: for many be called, but few *chosen*. (Matt. 20:1–16; emphasis mine)

Answer: The context of the choosing in verse sixteen is for servants or labourers in verse 1. The main takeaway here is that this passage has nothing to do with salvation but with service.

Let's consider another verse that some treat as though the interpretation by Calvinists is the only possible interpretation. Let's begin with only half of a verse, for this is how it is most often quoted, which makes it much easier to take out of context.

Example 22:

"Ye have not chosen me, but I have *chosen* you(.)" (John 15:16a)

I placed a period here to express the finality of those who mistakenly quote this verse, believing that it is the final proof that God chooses individuals for salvation. I ask you again, dear reader, do you truly know the context of this verse? Can you quote the entire verse? Have you studied it for yourself or have you been taught what it's supposed to mean? Let's read the entire verse together.

> Ye have not chosen me, but I have chosen you, and ordained you, that ye should go and bring forth fruit, and that your fruit should remain: that whatsoever ye shall ask of the Father in my name, he may give it you. (John 15:16)

Did you learn something new? According to the text, for what purpose was the individual chosen? Were they chosen to be saved? Were they chosen to go to heaven or to be redeemed? No, they were chosen for service, in this case, specifically to bring forth fruit.

> Ye have not chosen me, but I have *chosen* you, and ordained you, that ye should go and bring forth *fruit*, and that your fruit should remain: that whatsoever ye shall ask of the Father in my name, he may give it you. (John 15:16; emphasis mine)

Let's go a little deeper.

Example 23:

> "But ye are a *chosen* generation, a royal priesthood, an holy nation, a peculiar people; that ye should *shew forth the praises* of him who hath called you out of darkness into his marvellous light" (1 Pet. 2:9; emphasis mine).

1. In its context, this verse is referring to the generation to which Paul was speaking—"*ye* are a chosen generation."
2. The text doesn't mention salvation at all, but rather service to God in the form of showing praise.

Paul writing to Timothy, we see again that choosing is for service.

Example 24:

> "No man that warreth entangleth himself with the affairs of this life; that he

may please him who hath *chosen* him to be a *soldier*" (2 Tim. 2:4; emphasis mine).

Once again, the choosing is for service; in this case to serve as a soldier.

Example 25:

"Therefore I endure all things for the *elect's* sakes, *that they may also obtain the salvation* which is in Christ Jesus with eternal glory" (2 Tim. 2:10; emphasis mine).

If election or choosing were for salvation, then we should be able to substitute elect and chosen for saved or redeemed. This method, we find, doesn't work, but let's try. If elect means saved, then this verse would read: Therefore I endure all things for the *saved* sakes, *that they may also obtain the salvation* which is in Christ Jesus with eternal glory.

What? This makes no sense at all. However, if we read election as service it makes perfect sense. Therefore, I endure all things for the *servant's* sakes *that they may also obtain the salvation*, which is in Christ Jesus with eternal glory. Again, Israel is God's elect or chosen nation for service and Paul endured many things that some Jews would obey the gospel and be saved. To be clear, all the Jews were chosen by God for service, i.e., to bear his name, etc., but no Jew or Gentile was ever chosen for salvation. God offers salvation to all that they might choose Christ.

Example 26:

"Wherefore also it is contained in the scripture, Behold, I lay in Sion a chief corner stone, *elect*, precious: and he that believeth on him shall not be confounded" (1 Pet. 2:6; emphasis mine).

The context of the elect or the chosen stone is the Lord Jesus Christ who was chosen to serve the Father and mankind. If we try to substitute saved for elect, the verse is violated.

"Wherefore also it is contained in the scripture, Behold, I lay in Sion a chief corner stone, *saved*, precious: and he that believeth on him shall not be confounded."

This would make no sense. The Lord Jesus was never lost and never needed saving. It makes perfect sense, however, that the Son of God was chosen by the Father to bring salvation to a lost and dying world.

Example 27:

> "Jesus answered them, Have not I *cho-sen* you twelve, and one of you is a devil?"
> (John 6:70; emphasis mine).

If choosing is for salvation, then we must believe that Jesus saved all twelve disciples including Judas Iscariot! No, Judas was chosen, not for salvation, but for service.

We have seen how the Bible teaches, in both the New and Old Testaments, that election is for service, not for salvation, but what about God's call for service?

God doesn't force individuals to serve him, but rather,
God allows man a free will choice to serve.

The Bible teaches that the call for service is a free will choice. Consider the Old Testament willing slave and his free will choice to go or stay.

Example 28:

> And if the servant shall plainly say, I love my master, my wife, and my children; *I will not go out free*: Then his master shall bring him unto the judges; he shall also bring him to the door, or unto the door post; and his master shall bore his ear through with an aul; and he shall *serve* him for ever. (Exod. 21:5–6; emphasis mine)

This very same teaching is outlined in the book of Deuteronomy.

Example 29:

> And it shall be, if he say unto thee, *I will not go* away from thee; because he loveth thee and thine house, because he is well with thee; Then thou shalt take an aul, and thrust it through his ear unto the door, and he shall be thy *servant* for ever. And also unto thy maidservant thou shalt do likewise. (Deut. 15:16–17; emphasis mine)

The great apostle Paul, being a Jew, knowing the Jewish Law, said this.

Example 30:

> "For though I be free from all men, yet have *I made myself servant* unto all, that I might gain the more" (1 Cor. 9:19; emphasis mine).

Was Paul stupid? Do you understand the Bible and the mind of God better than Paul? For Paul said that he made himself a servant, i.e., a willing bond slave. That is, Paul made a conscious choice to serve God as we all do today. God has not created automatons, zombies or mindless robots, but rather creatures in his own image with a free will. Whether Old Testament or New, God encourages people to choose life and service.

Example 31: Angels, which generally means messengers, were created as servants.

> "But to which of the *angels* said he at any time, Sit on my right hand, until I make thine enemies thy footstool? Are they not *all ministering spirits*, sent forth to *minister* for them who shall be heirs of salvation?" (Heb. 1:13–14; emphasis mine)

1. All of the angels were created for service, to be ministering spirits.
2. Some angels left their appointed position; some were judged sooner and some later. "And the *angels*

which *kept not* their first estate, but *left* their own habitation, he hath reserved in everlasting chains under darkness unto the judgment of the great day" (Jude 1:6).

3. Some angels chose to serve God and some not.

Example 32:

"I call heaven and earth to record this day against you, that I have set before you life and death, blessing and cursing: therefore *choose life*, that both thou and thy seed may live" (Deut. 30:19).

Again, the Bible declares that Israel is God's chosen for service.

Example 33:

"Yet now hear, O *Jacob* my *servant*; and *Israel*, whom I have *chosen*" (Isa. 44:1; emphasis mine).

Now let's go down a little deeper and ask ourselves the question, "Does Israel serve God today? Do they promote the Gospel of Jesus Christ nationally? No, of course not. So, what's the point? This is a simple illustration showing that Israel has a *choice* in the matter. In the Old Testament, Israel served God like a yo-yo, serving then not serving. Today, Israel doesn't serve God nationally because they have rejected their Messiah. However, when Israel receives their Messiah, during the tribulation, they will return to God's service nationally. Once again, if a chosen person or nation had no choice, but to do the will of God, then Israel would never have stopped serving God. Therefore, since God's chosen nation Israel does not serve him nationally, it proves the point that service, like salvation, is a free will choice.

Example 34: Jacob was chosen for God's service before he was born, but Jacob, of his own free will, chose to obey God's call to service *after* he tested God and found him faithful.

And Jacob vowed a vow, saying, *If God will be with me, and will keep me in* this way that I go, and will give me bread to eat, and raiment to put on, So that I come again to my father's house in peace; *then* shall the LORD be my God: And this stone, which I have set for a pillar, shall be God's house: and of all that thou shalt give me I will surely give the tenth unto thee. (Gen. 28:20–22; emphasis mine)

Let's recall the wonderful context of this passage. Jacob was fleeing for his very life from his brother Esau. Jacob was not yet fully convinced of God's divine protection, power and provision, so he makes a deal with God. *If* you will do a miracle and keep me, i.e., keep my brother from killing me, and provide me the necessities of life so that I return to Esau in peace, (giving Esau enough time to calm down) *then* you will be my God. Of course, God, knowing the future, answered Jacob's prayer and gained a servant.

How could God choose Jacob for service before he was even born? Simple, God, because of his foreknowledge, knew the future. God knew that Jacob would eventually accept God's will. God did not force Jacob to do anything.

Jacob, like me and you, came to God because he had a need. God didn't need to force anything because he knew the future and made his choice accordingly. A good thing to remember is that knowing the future is very different from controlling the future. We will cover the topic of fore-knowledge in more depth in a later chapter.

Example 35: The principle of volunteer service was taught to Martha by Christ.

> But Martha was cumbered about much serving, and came to him, and said, Lord, dost thou not care that *my sister hath left me to serve alone? bid her therefore that she help me.* And Jesus answered and said unto her, Martha, Martha, thou art careful and troubled about many things: But one thing is needful: and Mary hath chosen that good part, which shall not be taken away from her. (Luke 10:40–42; emphasis mine)

Martha was asking the Lord to *make* Mary serve tables, to which the Lord said, Mary hath chosen that good part. Two large truths are seen here: one, the Lord allowed Mary a choice and two, the Lord didn't force Mary to serve with Martha.

God's election for service and being saved are very different things and when we try to force them together, we violate scripture.

Example 36: Israel's choosing

"For thou art an holy people unto the LORD thy God: the LORD thy God hath *chosen* thee to be a special people unto himself, above all people that are upon the face of the earth" (Deut. 7:6; emphasis mine).

Israel was chosen to serve God as a special people, not that they would have some automatic salvation.

Example 37:

> "For thou art an holy people unto the
> LORD thy God, and the LORD hath *chosen*
> thee to be a peculiar people unto himself,
> above all the nations that are upon the
> earth" (Deut. 14:2; emphasis mine).

In neither one of the previous two verses does God promise eternal life to any person of Israel. Also, it was *after* this *choosing* that Korah, his friends, and all of their families dropped straight down into the earth.

Example 38: We know that Israel is God's elect.

> "For Jacob my servant's sake, and *Israel*
> *mine elect*, I have even called thee by thy name:
> I have surnamed thee, though thou hast not
> known me" (Isa. 45:4; emphasis mine).

If God chose Israel for salvation, then Paul is speaking nonsense when he says in 2 Timothy 2:10:

Example 39:

> "Therefore I endure all things for the
> elect's sakes, that they may also *obtain the
> salvation* which is in Christ Jesus with eter-
> nal glory" (2 Tim. 2:10; emphasis mine).

If the elect are already saved or will be saved regardless of Paul's actions, then why should Paul endure anything that saved persons might obtain salvation? No, Paul
endured many hardships in the hope that some of the people of Israel would obey the gospel and return to the true
service of God. All the Jews are elected for service, no Jew
is chosen for salvation.

If God chose Israel nationally for salvation, then why
would Paul write the following?

Example 40:

> "That I have great heaviness and con-
> tinual sorrow in my heart. For I could wish
> that myself were accursed from Christ for

my brethren, my kinsmen according to the flesh" (Rom. 9:2–3).

Why was Paul so grieved over his kinsmen Israel? This context bears out here, as well as other places, that Paul was grieved because very few individuals from this chosen nation of servants were saved.

Paul also wrote:

Example 41:

> "For I would not, brethren, that ye should be ignorant of this mystery, lest ye should be wise in your own conceits; that *blindness in part* is happened to Israel, until the fulness of the Gentiles be come in" (Rom. 11:25; emphasis mine).

This verse, referring to spiritual *blindness in part*, proves that the nation of Israel is neither totally saved nor totally lost, even though the entire nation is elected for service. As a side note, there will be a time when the entire nation of Israel will be saved to enter the kingdom age after the tribulation.

> "And so *all Israel shall be saved*: as it
> is written, There shall come out of Sion
> the Deliverer, and shall turn away ungod-
> liness from Jacob" (Rom. 11:26; emphasis
> mine).

This makes sense, for why would the Lord start his earthly reign with any unbelieving Jews? This verse does not teach, however, that all Jews throughout all time will somehow miraculously be saved, but that the Jews entering the kingdom age at that time will all be redeemed.

Example 42:

> "As concerning the *gospel*, they are
> *enemies* for your sakes: but as touching the
> *election*, they are *beloved* for the fathers'
> sakes" (Rom. 11:28; emphasis mine).

What? How can a group of people, "they," be "enemies" of the gospel and "beloved" of the Father for "election?" First, it should be as obvious as an elephant in your refrigerator that election cannot mean salvation. For then the Bible would read: "As concerning the *gospel*, they are *enemies* for your sakes: but as touching the *salvation*, they are *beloved* for the fathers' sakes." This would be total nonsense. Okay, let's examine the context very carefully and rightly divide it and it will make sense.

1. The "they" refers to unsaved Jews who are enemies of the cross, not born-again persons.
2. Yet the unsaved Jew is beloved concerning election because God the Father chose them for service and "will yet choose Israel," (Isa. 14:1) for service. Even though Israel as a nation is on the proverbial spiritual shelf, she, as a chosen nation, is precious to God because God *knows* that she will repent and return to proper *service* for the kingdom age. When we reread this verse with this understanding, it makes complete sense.

Let us never forget to whom the original autographs were given.

Example 43:

> "What advantage then hath the Jew? or what profit is there of circumcision? Much every way: chiefly, because that unto them were committed the oracles of God" (Rom. 3:1–2).

The oracles of God are his utterances or the words of God, the Bible. Here's a question for your consideration. If choosing were for salvation and God only chose to save some, would that demonstrate the Almighty's grace, or his partiality? A Calvinist shared an illustration like this with me: There was a moving conveyor belt and people were dropping into hell, so God saved some, proving his compassion and grace. My similar illustration is, if I run into a burning building and I'm only able to save three out of twenty persons, I indeed am being gracious, but if I have the power to save all twenty and I only choose to save three, I become an inhuman monster. Isn't God all powerful? Is not God Almighty powerful enough to save *all* who come unto him by faith? Did he not say that he is able to save to the *uttermost*? Yes, God is able and eager to save every trembling soul who comes to him in faith. A more proper analogy would be that of all humanity being on thin ice. Consider all humanity as being on the shore of a vast frozen lake. On the near side, the ice is very thick; on the far side, it's too thin to support anyone and all who attempt it will certainly drown in the cold water shortly after they break through. Today, as individuals walk toward the thin ice on eternity's shore and certain death, God calls out to each one and warns all of their impending doom. Those who heed God's warning and turn back will be saved, while those who heed not, will be lost. God warns all, yet some chose to obey the warning and others do not. With this illustration in mind, ask yourself the question, what is the Holy Spirit's job in relation to salvation?

Example 44:

> Nevertheless I tell you the truth; It is
> expedient for you that I go away: for if I go
> not away, the Comforter will not come unto

you; but if I depart, I will send him unto you. And when he is come, *he will reprove the world of sin*, and of righteousness, and of judgment: Of sin, because they believe not on me. (John 16:7–9; emphasis mine)

The answer is that the Comforter (which is the holy Ghost, John 14:26) has the job of reproving (convicting) the world (everyone in the world) of their sin of unbelief. Now, we have two choices: either the Holy Ghost does his job or he doesn't. Since we all agree that the Holy Ghost does his job, then we must also agree that everyone either has been or will be convicted by God's Spirit at some point. So, if God chooses people to be saved and if election were for salvation, why would God waste his time convicting those persons in the world who can't be saved?

Special choosings

Example 45: The next verse is referring to the original Old Testament context of Isaiah 42, where God the Father chose or elected his Son.

"Behold my *servant,* whom I have
chosen; my beloved, in whom my soul is
well pleased: I will put my spirit upon
him, and he shall shew judgment to the
Gentiles" (Matt. 12:18; emphasis mine).

Once more, it should be obvious that God didn't
choose his Son to be saved, for the Son of God was never
lost. The Father chose the Son to complete the service or
job, of salvation.

Example 46: Let's look at this verse again. The Son of
God chose all of the apostles, including Judas Iscariot.

"Jesus answered them, Have not I *chosen* you twelve, and one of you is a *devil*?"
(John 6:70; emphasis mine).

If Christ chose his servants for salvation, then Judas
Iscariot would have been saved. No, the Lord Jesus didn't
choose the apostles for salvation, but for service. All of the

apostles were chosen to preach, including Judas Iscariot, which they did.

> "And as ye go, *preach*, saying, The kingdom of heaven is at hand" (Matt. 10:7; emphasis mine).

Example 47: Persons who want to serve God should be merciful, kind etc. in order to draw others to Christ.

> "Put on therefore, as the *elect* of God, holy and beloved, bowels of mercies, kindness, humbleness of mind, meekness, longsuffering" (Col. 3:12; emphasis mine).

According to the Bible, God places the burden of coming to God for salvation on individuals and not on himself.

The teaching that man has no free will to come to God for salvation creates an insurmountable problem, that being, it reverses the onus. If we release man from his God-given obligation, the burden then falls upon God! Indeed, if man cannot repent, believe or seek God for salvation, then the Bible should say, "If God," but instead we find God saying to man, "If thou." God, in a definitive way, places the onus on man. Let's not be guilty of reversing it! Let's recall an example from the previous chapter dealing with the order of salvation.

Example 48:

> "In whom ye also trusted, *after* that ye *heard* the word of truth, the gospel of your salvation: in whom also *after* that ye *believed*, ye were sealed with that holy Spirit of promise" (Eph. 1:13; emphasis mine).

Within this divine order, God also places the obligation to trust, hear and believe upon the individual.

> "In whom *ye* also *trusted*, after that *ye heard* the word of truth, the gospel of

your salvation: in whom also after that
ye believed, ye were sealed with that holy
Spirit of promise" (Eph. 1:13; emphasis
mine).

Other examples expressing this same truth.
Example 49:

"And *ye* shall *seek* me, and find me,
when *ye* shall *search* for me with all your
heart" (Jer. 29:13; emphasis mine).

Example 50: One of my personal favorites.

"*I sought* the LORD, and he heard me,
and delivered me from all my fears" (Ps.
34:4; emphasis mine).

God hasn't changed his MO; he puts the onus on man
to obey. The little word "if" appears in 1,420 verses and is
found more than once in several of these verses. Here are

some excerpts from an old message of mine entitled "The Onus Is on Us!"

I. The onus was on us (mankind) from the beginning in the garden.

"But of the tree of the knowledge of good and evil, *thou shalt not eat of it*: for in the day that thou eatest thereof thou shalt surely die. God puts the onus on-us, i.e., the burden on mankind!" (Gen. 2:17; emphasis mine)

II. Post-Eden the onus is on us to bring a blood sacrifice.

"*If thou* doest well, shalt thou not be accepted? and *if thou* doest not well, sin lieth at the door. And unto thee shall be his desire, and thou shalt rule over him" (Gen. 4:7; emphasis mine).

The burden "if thou" was placed on man. This was not a works salvation, but an offering of faith in God's blood sacrifice. This offering entailed repentance toward sin and faith toward God's chosen method, i.e., the blood. We understand that the Old Testament blood sacrifice only covered sin until the Lord Jesus completely took away the sin of the world by the offering of his blood. Four points are in order:

A. Sin cannot be taken away without blood.

   "And almost all things are by the law purged with blood; and without shedding of blood is no remission" (Heb. 9:22).

B. Sin cannot be taken away by animal blood.

   "For it is not possible that the blood of bulls and of goats should take away sins" (Heb. 10:4.)

C. Sin cannot be taken away unless the blood sacrifice is sinless.

"For we have not an high priest which cannot be touched with the feeling of our infirmities; but was in all points tempted like as we are, yet without sin" (Heb. 4:15).

D. Sin cannot be taken away eternally without eternal blood.

But *Christ* being come an high priest of good things to come, by a greater and more perfect tabernacle, not made with hands, that is to say, not of this building; Neither by the blood of goats and calves, but by his own *blood* he entered in once into the holy place, having obtained *eternal* redemption for us. (Heb. 9:11–12; emphasis mine)

Only the sinless, eternal blood of the Son of God, Jesus Christ, can take away human sin.

Here's an interesting point. The devil loves to shift the blame or the burden away from where it belongs. Case in point: The phrase "if thou" in the Bible appears for the first time in Genesis 4:7 where God clearly places the onus on man. The first New Testament appearance of "if thou," appears in Matthew 4 where the devil is addressing the Lord Jesus.

> "And when the tempter came to him, he said, *If thou* be the Son of God, command that these stones be made bread" (Matt. 4:3; emphasis mine).

Do you see what Satan did? He tried to redirect the onus and place it on Christ! This is the same thing the Calvinistic doctrine does. Sadly, I know a man who is a dyed-in-the-wool Calvinist, and he will tell you that he doesn't know if he's saved. His reason is that he doesn't know if he's chosen for salvation or not, so he's waiting on God to choose him and bring assurance. Honestly, if we had to wait on God to choose us for salvation, how could we know if we've ever been chosen or not? The answer is we couldn't. Assurance comes from believing God's word. The Bible says in Romans 10:

> That if thou shalt confess with thy mouth the Lord Jesus, and shalt believe in thine heart that God hath raised him from the dead, thou shalt be saved. For with the heart man believeth unto righteousness; and with the mouth confession is made unto salvation." When we believe what God says and act upon it, then we can have confidence that God did his part. God says our confession is made unto salvation. (Rom. 10:9–10)

God said so and that makes it true. In other words, if we do our part, we can trust the Almighty to do his part, Amen.

III. Today the onus is still on us for salvation.

"Behold, I stand at the door, and knock: *if any man hear* my voice, *and open* the door, I will come in to him, and will sup with him, and he with me" (Rev. 3:20; emphasis mine).

"That *if thou* shalt confess with thy mouth the Lord Jesus, and shalt believe in thine heart that God hath raised him from the dead, thou shalt be saved" (Rom. 10:9; emphasis mine).

"*If we confess* our sins, he is faithful and just to forgive us our sins, and to cleanse us from all unrighteousness" (1 John 1:9; emphasis mine).

"I am the door: by me *if any man* enter in, he shall be saved, and shall go in and out, and find pasture" (John 10:9; emphasis mine).

IV. The burden of evangelism and church growth is on us to lift up Christ.

> "And I, *if I be lifted up* from the earth, will draw all men unto me" (John 12:32; emphasis mine).

V. The onus is on us for service that we may rule and reign with Christ.

> "*If we* suffer, we shall also reign with him: *if we* deny him, he also will deny us" (2 Tim. 2:12; emphasis mine).

VI. The privilege of being close to God is also an onus that's on us.

> "*Draw nigh to God,* and *he will draw nigh to you.* Cleanse your hands, ye sinners; and purify your hearts, ye double minded" (James 4:8; emphasis mine).

The context is not one of salvation, but fellowship. In other words, if we want to have fellowship with God, we must take the first step. This principle of fellowship is made clearer in 1 John 1.

"But *if we* walk in the light, as he is in the light, we have fellowship one with another, and the blood of Jesus Christ his Son cleanseth us from all sin" (1 John 1:7; emphasis mine).

VII.   Having a prosperous and blessed country is an onus that's on us.

"*If my people*, which are called by my name, shall humble themselves, and pray, and seek my face, and turn from their wicked ways; then will I hear from heaven, and will forgive their sin, and will heal their land" (Chron. 7:14; emphasis mine).

Notice the Bible does not say if the heathen... The onus is on us as believers to fear the Lord and to depart from evil.

"Be not wise in thine own eyes:
fear the LORD, and depart from evil"
(Prov. 3:7).

End of chapter ponder points.

1. If you were God and election were for salvation, then wouldn't you choose everyone or at least, most everyone and not just a few? Wouldn't you show your abundant mercy by saving all?

2. Every time a Bible doctrine is compromised, it leaves the door open for another false teaching to come in. When the Bible doctrine of the free will of man is removed, it opens the door for the necessity of unconditional election.

3. The God of the Bible doesn't choose some for heaven. In fact, it's God's will and desire that all people be saved.

"The Lord is not slack concerning his promise, as some men count slackness; but is longsuffering to us-ward, not willing that any should perish but that all should come to repentance" (2 Pet. 3:9).

4. Would a holy and righteous God punish people for not responding to the gospel if they were not able to respond? This would be the same as punishing a paraplegic person in a wheelchair for not walking. Everyone is able to respond to the gospel, but not all are willing.

"For God so loved the world, that he gave his only begotten Son, that *whosoever* believeth in him should not perish, but have everlasting life" (John 3:16; emphasis mine).

5. Do you believe the Bible the way it's written or do you need to rewrite or reinterpret hundreds of Bible passages in order to make it fit your beliefs? Doesn't whosoever mean whosoever?

"To him give all the prophets witness, that through his name *whosoever* believeth in him shall receive remission of sins" (Acts 10:43; emphasis mine).

6. And the Spirit and the bride say, Come. And let him that heareth say, Come. And let him that is athirst come. And *whosoever* will, let him take the water of life freely" (Rev. 22:17; emphasis mine).

"For the wages of sin is death; but the *gift* of God is *eternal life* through Jesus Christ our Lord" (Rom. 6:23; emphasis mine).

"And they of the circumcision which believed were astonished, as many as came with Peter, because that on the Gentiles also was poured out the *gift* of the *Holy Ghost*" (Acts 10:45; emphasis mine).

A gift, by its nature, cannot be forced; that nullifies it as a gift. A gift must be willingly received.

"But *as many as received* him, to them gave he power to become the sons of God, even to them that believe on his name" (John 1:12; emphasis mine).

Please notice that this verse doesn't say, 'But as many as God has chosen," but "...*as many as received* him..." Receiving and believing are action verbs for man to obey; not words that God must obey.

7. When the idea of election and choosing is substituted for the idea of service, it always fits. When the principle of election and choosing is substituted for the principle of salvation, it doesn't fit.

8. Wouldn't choosing individuals for heaven and hell make God a respecter of persons?

"Then Peter opened his mouth, and said, Of a truth I perceive that God is no respecter of persons" (Acts 10:34).

11

Limited Atonement: The "L" of the TULIP

No term of the TULIP is a Bible term, including the term "limited atonement." The doctrine of the limited atonement of the blood of Christ was not believed by John Calvin, most probably because of the overwhelming scriptures against it. A simple definition of the word atonement is: the means by which sin is forgiven. In the Old Testament, sin was temporarily covered by the blood of animals until Christ's blood sacrifice. In the New Testament, sin was atoned for, i.e., completely taken away by the blood of Christ.

Example 1:

> "The next day John seeth Jesus coming unto him, and saith, Behold *the Lamb of God*, which *taketh away* the sin of the world" (John 1:29; emphasis mine).

Example 2:

> "And ye know that *he* was manifested
> to *take away our sins*; and in him is no sin"
> (1 John 3:5; emphasis mine).

Example 3:

> "Blotting out the handwriting of
> ordinances that was against us, which was
> contrary to us, and *took it out of the way*,
> nailing it to his cross" (Col. 2:14; emphasis mine).

The reasoning behind the idea of limited atonement is that if God only chooses some people for salvation, then Christ's blood and saving power must be limited only to them. For if Christ died for the whole world and only some partake, then our Lord's blood would be wasted somehow. This line of reasoning is purely humanistic and has no root in the reality of scripture. In simple terms, we must never reason that for each person, one literal drop of blood must be shed and if there were some blood left over, it's somehow wasted. The teaching of scripture is that if you or I were the only person in the world needing redemption, it still would have required *all* of Christ's blood to redeem one individual. To make a modern example, we could think of redemption as a heart defibrillation machine. If we want to shock someone back to life, we must have the entire working machine and not one part for each person on which we intend to use it. Once we have the entire machine, we can "save" one or one million with the same machine. We don't use a part of the machine for each patient, but the whole machine for each one or as many as need it. Again, we need the whole machine or life is not restored, and without Christ's death on the cross, i.e., all of his life's blood, his sacrifice would have meant nothing. To make it more plain, if our Lord could have been crucified, shedding some of his blood, but taken down and revived without dying, his shed blood would have had no saving value. By the same token, if our Lord had died a sacrificial death by strangulation without shedding any of his blood, his death would equally have been without value. Both Jesus' death and the shedding of his blood were absolutely necessary to provide redemption for humanity! Concerning Christ's death by crucifixion on the cross, the Bible teaches that there was no other alternative possible, for the Lord Jesus said:

Example 4:

> "And he went a little further, and fell on his face, and prayed, saying, O my Father, *if it be possible*, let this cup pass from me: nevertheless not as I will, but as thou wilt" (Matt. 26:39; emphasis mine).

Example 5:

> "And he went forward a little, and fell on the ground, and prayed that, *if it were possible*, the hour might pass from him" (Mark 14:35; emphasis mine).

The Father's answer, of course, was silence because there was no other way possible to redeem anyone.

Example 6: Believers are reconciled to God by the death of the Lord Jesus.

> "For if, when we were enemies, we were *reconciled* to God *by the death* of his Son, much more, being reconciled, we shall be saved by his life" (Rom. 5:10; emphasis mine).

Example 7:

> And you, that were sometime alienated and enemies in your mind by wicked works, yet now hath he *reconciled*. In the body of his flesh through *death*, to present you holy and unblameable and unreproveable in his sight. (Col. 1:21–22; emphasis mine)

Example 8: We are also reconciled to God and redeemed by the blood of the Lord Jesus.

> "And, having made peace through the *blood* of his cross, by him to *reconcile* all things unto himself; by him, I say, whether they be things in earth, or things in heaven" (Col. 1:20; emphasis mine).

Example 9:

> "In whom we have *redemption* through his *blood*, even the forgiveness of sins" (Col. 1:14; emphasis mine).

The Calvinist view is that individuals are chosen by God for salvation and only a selected few can possibly be saved. The theory is that God only loves some and not all. In our quest for truth, we need to answer some very pertinent questions with scripture.

1. According to the Bible, whom did God love so much that he gave his Son?

2. According to the Bible, whom did the Lord Jesus seek for salvation?

3. According to the Bible, whom does the Holy Ghost reprove (convict) of sin?

4. According to the Bible, Jesus shed his blood and died to satisfy the payment for whose sins?

5. According to the Bible, for whom did the Lord Jesus taste death?

6. According to the Bible, to whom did God send his Son and for what purpose?

7. According to the Bible, God is the Saviour of whom?

8. According to the Bible, God sent his Son to be the Saviour of whom?

9. According to the Bible, whom does God want to come to repentance and whom does God want to perish?

10. According to the Bible, whose sin does Jesus take away?

11. According to the Bible, whom will Christ come in to and sup with?

12. According to the Bible, whom does God want to be saved and to come unto the knowledge of the truth?

13. According to the Bible, whom does God command to repent?

14. According to the Bible, whom did the Lord Jesus call to repentance?

15. According to the Bible, to who were the good tidings of great joy given at the birth of baby Jesus?

16. According to the Bible, why did John the Baptist bear witness that Christ was the Light of the world?

17. According to the Bible, to whom does the grace of God that brings salvation appear?

18. According to the Bible, are there any other scriptures that express the non-limited power of the redeeming blood of Christ?

According to the Bible, whom did God
love so much that he gave his Son?

Example 10:

"For *God so loved the world, that he*
gave his only begotten *Son,* that whosoever
believeth in him should not perish, but have
everlasting life" (John 3:16; emphasis mine).

Not some of the world, but all of it.

According to the Bible whom did The Lord Jesus seek for salvation?

Example 11:

"For *the Son of man* is come *to seek*
and to save that which was lost" (Luke
19:10; emphasis mine).

The question is, were only the elect lost? It's quite the
dilemma, isn't it? If we say, only the elect were lost, then

we're saying that the non-elect were not lost and didn't need salvation. If we say the elect were not lost, then the Lord didn't come to save them. No, the whole world was lost in the darkness of sin, everyone in the whole world. Election is always for service and this is why the Lord Jesus *died* and shed his *blood* for the whole world.

Example 12:

"For the Son of man is come to save that which was lost" (Matt. 18:11).

That is to say, the whole world was lost.

According to the Bible, whom does the Holy Ghost reprove (convict) of sin?

Example 13:

Nevertheless I tell you the truth; It is expedient for you that I go away: for if I go not away, *the Comforter* will not come unto you; but if I depart, I will send him unto you. (8) And when he is come, he *will reprove the world* of sin, and of righteousness, and of judgment. (John 16:7–8; emphasis mine)

Why would God have the Holy Ghost convict the whole world if only a certain few could possibly be saved?

According to the Bible, Jesus shed his blood and died to satisfy the payment for whose sins?

Example 14:

My little children, these things write I unto you, that ye sin not. And if any man sin, we have an advocate with the Father, Jesus Christ the righteous: And he is *the propitiation for* our sins: and not for ours only, but also for the sins of *the whole world*. (1 John 2:1–2; emphasis mine)

Do you believe that the Father is satisfied with the sacrifice of Jesus Christ for the *whole* world like the Bible says or only a part of the world? The Father was satisfied with the sacrifice of his Son on behalf of *the whole world*. This action was foretold in the Old Testament.

Example 15:

"He shall see of the travail of his soul, and shall be satisfied: by his knowledge shall my righteous servant justify many; for he shall bear their iniquities" (Isa. 53:11).

The Father was satisfied with the atonement of his Son. Some individuals rejected the atonement and were not justified, but many were justified.

According to the Bible, for whom did the
Lord Jesus die or taste death?

Example 16:

> "But we see *Jesus*, who was made a lit-
> tle lower than the angels for the suffering of
> death, crowned with glory and honour; that
> he by the grace of God should *taste death*
> for *every man*" (Heb. 2:9; emphasis mine).

The Bible clearly states that the Lord Jesus tasted death
for every man, not every elect man only. If you're trying to
add or subtract words in order to make these verses fit your
paradigm, then please reread chapter seven "the name game."

Example 17:

> For the love of Christ constraineth
> us; because we thus judge, that if one
> *died for all*, then were all dead: (15) And
> that *he died for all*, that they which live
> should not henceforth live unto them-

selves, but unto him which died for them, and rose again. (2 Cor. 5:14–15; emphasis mine)

According to the Bible, to whom did God send his Son and for what purpose?

Example 18:

"For God sent not *his Son* into the world to condemn the world; but that *the world* through him *might be saved*" (John 3:17; emphasis mine).

According to the Bible, God is the Saviour of whom?

Example 19:

"For therefore we both labour and suffer reproach, because we trust in the living *God*, who *is the Saviour of all men,* specially of those that believe" (2 Tim. 4:10; emphasis mine).

The Bible truth is that God is the Saviour of all men and Christ died for the whole world. This does not mean, however, that every person in the world will enter heaven, but rather that every person in the world is offered salvation. The Saviour can offer eternal life to all because his blood is sufficient to save one and all.

According to the Bible, God sent his Son to be the Saviour of whom?

Example 20:

"And we have seen and do testify that the Father sent the *Son* to be *the Saviour of the world*" (1 John 4:14; emphasis mine).

According to the Bible, whom does God want to come to repentance and whom does God want to perish?

Example 21:

> "*The Lord is* not slack concerning his promise, as some men count slackness; but is longsuffering to us-ward, *not willing that any should perish*, but that *all* should come to repentance" (2 Pet. 3:9; emphasis mine).

According to the Bible, whose sin does Jesus take away? I'm going to put a mistake in the next example to prove a point. Are you ready to pick out the mistake?

Example 22:

> "The next day John seeth Jesus coming unto him, and saith, Behold the Lamb

of God, which taketh away the sin of the elect" (John 1:29).

I'm sure you caught it. The Bible actually reads:

> "The next day John seeth Jesus coming unto him, and saith, Behold *the Lamb* of God, which *taketh away the sin of the world*" (John 1:29; emphasis mine).

There is no reason not to believe the Bible as it's written. Yes, individuals still need to come to Christ to be forgiven, but the way to life is open to all.

According to the Bible, whom will Christ come in and sup with?

Example 23:

> "Behold, I stand at the door, and knock: if *any man* hear my voice, and open the door, *I will come in* to him, and

will *sup* with him, and he with me" (Rev. 3:20; emphasis mine).

The Bible answer is "any man." This would be a false invitation if Calvinism were true!

According to the Bible, whom does God want to be saved and to come unto the knowledge of the truth?

Example 24:

> "For this is good and acceptable in the sight of God our Saviour; Who will have *all men* to be *saved*, and to *come unto the knowledge of the truth*" (1 Tim. 2:3–4; emphasis mine).

God's will is for all men to be saved, but man most often rejects and neglects God's offer.

According to the Bible, who does God command to repent?

Example 25:

> "And the times of this ignorance *God* winked at; but now *commandeth all men* every where *to repent*" (Acts 17:30; emphasis mine).

This verse includes everyone in the world and excludes no one.

According to the Bible, whom did the Lord Jesus call to repentance?

Example 26:

> "And Jesus answering said unto them, They that are whole need not a physician; but they that are sick. *I came not to call the righteous, but sinners to repentance*" (Luke 5:31–32; emphasis mine).

Example 27: Ask yourself, who has sinned?

> "For *all* have sinned, and come short of the glory of God" (Rom. 3:23; emphasis mine).

Not some, but all.

> "As it is written, There is *none* righteous, no, not one" (Rom. 3:10; emphasis mine).

According to the Bible, to whom were the good tidings of great joy given at the birth of baby Jesus?

Example 28: I'm sure you remember the announcement to the angel at the birth of Christ which said:

> "And the angel said unto them, Fear not: for, behold, I bring you good tidings of great joy, which shall be *to the elect only.*" (Luke 2:10).

Sorry, that sounded ridiculous didn't it? The verse actually reads:

> "And the angel said unto them, Fear not: for, behold, I bring you *good tidings of great joy*, which shall be to *all people*" (Luke 2:10; emphasis mine).

Not to a certain few.

According to the Bible, why did John the Baptist bear witness that Christ was the Light of the world?

Example 29:

> "The same came for a witness, to bear witness of the Light, that *all men* through him might believe" (John 1:7; emphasis mine).

Do you believe the Bible the way it's written or must you change the clear meaning of hundreds of verses to fit a belief system?

According to the Bible, to whom does the grace of God that brings salvation appear?

Example 30:

"For *the grace of God* that bringeth salvation hath appeared to *all men*" (Titus 2:11; emphasis mine).

Everyone agrees that no man can be saved without God's grace, so the grace that brings salvation is offered to *all men*.

According to the Bible, are there any other scriptures that express the non-limited power of the redeeming blood of Christ?

Example 31:

"And the *Spirit* and the bride *say*, Come. And let him that heareth say, Come. And let him that is athirst come. And *whosoever will*, let him take the water of life freely" (Rev. 22:17; emphasis mine).

Could God invite "whosoever will" to "come," unless Christ's blood were sufficient for all? The answer is no.

Example 32:

> "Wherefore come out from among them, and be ye separate, saith the Lord, and touch not the unclean thing; and *I will receive you*" (2 Cor. 6:17; emphasis mine).

Again, God couldn't give this blanket invitation for any Bible reader to come unless Christ's blood were sufficient for all. Next is a real-world application of the limited atonement doctrine. C. H. Spurgeon was a popular hyper-Calvinist preacher. He was hyper-Calvinist because he went beyond Calvin's beliefs and accepted the doctrine of limited atonement. In Spurgeon's sermon #52, printed in tract form, he says,

> "May I go out and tell them—Jesus Christ died for every one of you? May I

say—there is righteousness for every one
of you, there is life for every one of you?
No; you may not."

End of excerpt. You must decide if what Spurgeon said
lines up with the clear teaching of Bible truth.

Q & A: Clear questions with direct answers in summary.

1. According to the Bible, whom did God love so
   much that he gave his Son?

   A: the world

2. According to the Bible, whom did The Lord Jesus
   seek for salvation?

   A: that which was lost

3. According to the Bible, whom does the Holy
   Ghost reprove (convict) of sin?

   A: the world

4. According to the Bible, Jesus shed his blood and
   died to satisfy the payment for whose sins?

   A: the whole world

5. According to the Bible, for whom did the Lord Jesus taste death?

A: every man

6. According to the Bible, to whom did God send his Son and for what purpose?

A: the world, that through him all might be saved.

7. According to the Bible, God is the Saviour of whom?

A: all men

8. According to the Bible, God sent his Son to be the Saviour of whom?

A: the world

9. According to the Bible, whom does God want to come to repentance and whom does God want to perish?

A: God wants all to repent and God is not willing that any should perish

10. According to the Bible, whose sin does Jesus take away?

A: the sin of the world

11. According to the Bible, whom will Christ come in to and sup with?

A: any man

12. According to the Bible, who does God want to be saved and to come unto the knowledge of the truth?

    A: all men

13. According to the Bible, who does God command to repent?

    A: all men everywhere

14. According to the Bible, whom did the Lord Jesus call to repentance?

    A: sinners

15. According to the Bible, to whom were the good tidings of great joy given at the birth of baby Jesus?

    A: all people

16. According to the Bible, why did John the Baptist bear witness that Christ was the Light of the world?

    A: that all men through him might believe

17. According to the Bible, to whom does the grace of God that brings salvation appear?

    A: all men

18. According to the Bible, are there any other scriptures that express the non-limited power of the redeeming blood of Christ?

    A: yes, several

Q & A: In summary.

According to the Bible, God loved the world and gave his Son to the world, who shed his blood to be the Saviour of the world. God is satisfied that the sin payment for the whole world is paid in full. Consequently, the blood of the Saviour of the world has taken away the sin of the world. The Lord Jesus himself said that he came to seek and to save that which was lost and to call sinners to repentance. This encompasses every person on earth for the Bible teaches that all were lost and that all are sinners. God is the Saviour of all men and will have all men to be saved. God is not willing that any should perish but desired all to come to repentance. However, those who reject God's payment for sin and offer of eternal life must pay for their own sins with eternal torment. God commands all men everywhere to repent and wants all men (not just some) to come unto the knowledge of the truth. The Lord Jesus promises to come in and sup with any man because he personally tasted death for every man (you), because he loves every man (you).

The angel announced good tidings of great joy to all people at the birth of baby Jesus and later, John Baptist bears witness that Christ was the Light of the world so that all men might believe. Please believe the Bible when it teaches that God gave his Son for everyone and that Christ Jesus wants everyone to be saved, and to prove it, he sends his Spirit to reprove the world and to bring saving grace to all men.

Some closing thoughts.

1. Once more, Calvin didn't believe in the limited atonement doctrine.

    "He that loveth not knoweth not God; for God is love" (1 John 4:8).

2. The Bible declares that God *is* love, which means He is *all* love or as we would say "God is all loving." Since God is *all* loving and love demonstrated is giving, we should see this giving love expressed to *all*. "For God so loved the world, that he gave his only begotten Son, that whosoever believeth in him should not perish, but have everlasting life" (John 3:16). The point being that if God only gave

his Son for a select few, he would not be an all loving God.

3. The Bible declares the blood of Christ is able to reconcile all things, which would include all men.

"And, having made peace through the blood of his cross, by him to reconcile *all things* unto himself; by him, I say, whether they be things in earth, or things in heaven" (Col. 1:20; emphasis mine).

To believe that only some people can be saved is to deny the sufficiency of the blood of Christ.

4. The only limiting power of the blood of Christ is mankind's willingness to repent and believe.

O Jerusalem, Jerusalem, thou that killest the prophets, and stonest them which are sent unto thee, how often would I have gathered thy children together, even as a hen gathereth her chickens under her wings, and *ye would not!* (Matt. 23:37; emphasis mine)

O Jerusalem, Jerusalem, which killest the prophets, and stonest them that are sent unto thee; how often would I have gathered thy children together, as a hen doth gather her brood under her wings, and *ye would not!* (Luke 13:34; emphasis mine)

5. The collective will and intentions of the Father, Son and Holy Ghost are in perfect harmony.

    The Father gave his Son because he loved the world, the Son willingly died for the world, and the holy Ghost reproves the world.

6. Some deeper truth; God told Abraham in Genesis 12:3:

    "And I will bless them that bless thee, and curse him that curseth thee: and in thee shall *all families of the earth* be blessed" (Gen. 12:3; emphasis mine).

How is it that all families of the earth are blessed through Abraham? The answer is that through Abraham's line the Lord Jesus was born of Mary, and through Christ, the world, or all families of the earth, are offered salvation, not just some. If only some families (the elect families) would be blessed, then the Bible would be incorrect the way God wrote it.

7. Our job as ambassadors is to tell the world of God's offer of salvation through Christ and the Bible. "To wit, that *God* was in Christ, *reconciling the world* unto himself, not imputing their trespasses unto them; and *hath committed unto us the word of reconciliation*" (2 Cor. 5:19; emphasis mine).

8. The resurrection of the Lord Jesus was, by God's testimony, for assurance to all men.

"Because he (God) hath appointed a day, in the which he will judge the world in righteousness by that man (Jesus) whom he hath ordained; whereof *he hath given assurance unto all men*, in that he hath raised him from the dead" (Acts 17:31; emphasis mine).

9. The only limiting factor on the blood of Christ is man's willingness to repent and believe the gospel, for the Lord will force his salvation on no one.

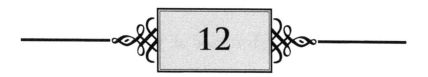

Irresistible Grace: The "I" of the TULIP

Irresistible grace is that doctrine which teaches that God only calls some for salvation and those whom he calls are unable to resist his call. Irresistible grace is not a Bible term, but a synthetic term to help explain Calvin's belief system. Does this doctrine jive with the Bible? You can decide for yourself. Before we delve deeper into this subject, let's consider a fundamental question. If God only chooses to save some and not others, would that demonstrate God's grace or his partiality? Let's reconsider a portion from the unconditional election chapter. A Calvinist once shared an illustration with me, like this. There was a moving conveyor belt and people were dropping into hell, so God saved some, proving his compassion and grace. My similar illustration is, if we run into a burning building and are only able to save three out of twenty, we indeed are being compassionate and gracious, but if we have the ability to save all twenty and we only choose to save three, then we're an inhuman monster. Isn't God all powerful? Is not God Almighty able to save *all* who come unto him by faith? Did the Bible not say that Christ is able to save to the *uttermost*? A more proper analogy would be that of all humanity being on thin ice. Consider all humanity as being on the shore of a vast frozen lake. On the near side the ice is very thick; on the far side it's too thin to support anyone and all who attempt it will certainly drown in the cold water shortly after they break through. Today, as individuals walk toward the thin ice on eternity's shore and certain death, God calls out to each one and warns all of their impending doom. Those who heed God's warning and turn back will be saved, while those who heed not, will be lost. God warns all, yet some chose to obey the warning and others do not. With this illustration in mind, ask yourself the question, what is the Holy Spirit's job in relation to salvation?

Below is a short list of reasonable questions.

1. If God can save some through irresistible grace, why not save all?
2. Is the doctrine of irresistible grace needed?
3. Is it possible to resist the grace of God?

4. Is irresistible grace an oxymoron?

5. If man has no free will like Calvinists believe, then why would God need to use irresistible grace?

6. When you say irresistible grace, do you apply it to salvation or service?

7. Is irresistible grace the same as sovereignty?

If God can save some through irresistible grace, why not save all?

I ask in all humility and humanity, if you were an all-powerful, all-loving God and you chose individual souls for heaven and hell, would you only save some of your creation or would you at least offer to save all? The only way in which God can be righteous is if he offers salvation to all. If God offers salvation to all mankind and some reject it, then God is still righteous. However, if God only offers salvation to a select few and then proceeds to punish those who had no opportunity to respond, God would be unjust. Some may use the doublespeak argument that this is a contradiction in the mind of man, but not in the mind of God. No, this line of reasoning makes no sense to man or God. What is the answer to why God doesn't save all via irresistible grace? The answer is because God saves no one through irresistible grace because it doesn't exist; there is no such thing in the Bible. How can we be sure that there is no such thing? Please consider the next point.

Is the doctrine of irresistible grace needed?

No, Calvinists teach it's needed because they believe that a spiritually dead person can't respond to the gospel. We have seen from the Bible that man believes with his soul, which is alive and not with his spirit, which is dead. The simple truth is, once we have a proper understanding of the composition of man, the need for the irresistible grace evaporates. If you are still unsure, you may want to reread chapter 5.

Is it possible to resist the grace of God?

If we can produce a single Bible example of one or more persons resisting the grace of God, then we must conclude that there is no such thing as irresistible grace.

Consider Stephen's speech to his executioners while he was being stoned to death.

> "Ye stiffnecked and uncircumcised in heart and ears, *ye do always resist the Holy Ghost*: as your fathers did, so do ye" (Acts 7:51; emphasis mine).

Note that these people didn't only resist the Holy Ghost once in a while, but always. It's very possible that at least some of these Jews resisted the calling of the Holy Ghost for salvation on the day of Pentecost in chapter 2. Regardless, the Lord wants us to know that Stephen was "full of the Holy Ghost" when he shared the information about individuals resisting the Holy Ghost.

> "But he, being *full of the Holy Ghost*, looked up stedfastly into heaven, and saw the glory of God, and Jesus standing on the right hand of God" (Acts 7:55; emphasis mine).

Another example of people resisting, in this case, it's called rebelling, against the holy Spirit.

> "But *they rebelled,* and *vexed his holy Spirit*: therefore he was turned to be their enemy, and he fought against them" (Isa. 63:10; emphasis mine).

These people rebelled against the holy Spirit, plain and simple. Now, we have seen two very clear Bible passages that show people resisting the Holy Ghost; if these won't convince the reader that the Holy Ghost can be resisted, then I dare say more passages will not help. If no one can resist or rebel against the Holy Spirit, why are we commanded not to quench him?

> "Quench not the Spirit" (1 Thess. 5:19).

If no one can resist or rebel against the Holy Spirit, why are we commanded not to grieve him?

"And grieve not the holy Spirit of God, whereby ye are sealed unto the day of redemption" (Eph. 4:30).

In my dealings with my Calvinist friends, I find that they often like to jump ship and dive to another topic when they're faced with hard truth. For example, some may say the resisting and rebelling against the holy Ghost is only in reference to persons before salvation. First, unless you believe that the individuals in Acts 7:51 were Stephen's *born-again brothers* stoning him to death, their rebellion was before salvation. Second, this resisting was against the call of salvation as well. If you carefully consider this passage, Stephen told them, in his salvation message, that they were guilty of killing their Messiah, the Just One. Third, if we say that individuals can only resist the Holy Ghost after they're saved, then please tell me, from where did this special, mysterious, and resistive power appear? No, people are by their first nature rebellious and resist God's grace before and after salvation. Was it God's will for Lucifer to rebel and become Satan? That would be absurd, of course not. Lucifer chose to rebel against God's will; the same held true for the angels that sinned, Adam and Eve, and also holds true for all of us today, both before and after salvation. The following verse teaches that some accept the will of God and some reject it.

"For therefore we both labour and suffer reproach, because we trust in the living God, who is the Saviour of all men, specially of those that believe" (1 Tim. 4:10).

Some will believe and some will not, yet God is still the Saviour of all men because he paid the sin debt for one and all and offers eternal life to one and all. Some answer the calling of the Holy Spirit and some resist.

If there were such a thing as irresistible grace, then all men would be saved, because God's saving grace has appeared to all men!

"For the *grace of God* that *bringeth salvation hath appeared to all men*" (Titus 2:11; emphasis mine).

Make no mistake, saving grace has appeared to all men, but all are not saved because some resist and reject it.

We have seen in chapter ten that the choosing of God is always for service and never for salvation. However, if we return to the Calvinist way of thinking for a moment and suppose that choosing is for salvation, then how would we explain Matthew 22:14?

"For many are called, but few are chosen" (Matt. 22:14).

Do you see the problem? If persons are chosen for salvation and no one called can resist the Lord's call, then everyone called should also be chosen, for every elect person must answer the call. In other words, if irresistible grace were true, then the verse should read, "For many are called and many are chosen." How could many be called, but only a few chosen if God's call cannot be resisted? The Bible answer is simple, God calls many, i.e., the whole world (as we have seen previously) for salvation, but God only chooses for service, those who answer salvation's call, i.e., the few. This understanding of scripture is both simple and non-contradictory. Let's reconsider again what is the Holy Spirit's job in relation to salvation.

> Nevertheless I tell you the truth; It is expedient for you that I go away: for if I go not away, the Comforter will not come unto you; but if I depart, I will send him unto you. And when he is come, *he will reprove the world of sin*, and of righteousness, and of judgment: Of sin, because they believe not on me. (John 16:7–9; emphasis mine)

The Comforter (which is the Holy Ghost, John 14:26) has the job of reproving or convicting the world, everyone in the world, of their sin of unbelief. As we have already considered, we have two choices, either the Holy Ghost does his job or he doesn't. Since we all agree that he does his job, then we must also conclude that everyone either has been or will be convicted by God's Spirit at some point in time. Hence, if no one can resist the calling of the Holy Spirit and he calls all, sooner or later, then every person would be saved. Since we know that every person is not saved, then we must conclude that there is no such thing as irresistible grace. I had a Calvinist friend who believed that no person could resist the Holy Spirit. His reasoning was that the grace of God cannot be frustrated. Let's consider this Bible text:

> "I do not frustrate the grace of God:
> for if righteousness come by the law, then
> Christ is dead in vain" (Gal. 2:21).

This text dealing with God's grace being frustrated has nothing to do with the *calling* of the Holy Spirit. It has everything to do with the *method* of salvation, which is by grace, not works. In fact, God's grace can be frustrated and is frustrated every time someone believes that he or she can be made righteous by their own good works or by keeping the law. Paul was meaning that he didn't frustrate the grace of God by trusting in his good works for salvation, but there were those in the church at Galatia who did. Therefore, God's grace can be frustrated by the stubbornness of man.

One last example in this section: can people resist or do despite to God's Spirit of grace?

> Of how much sorer punishment, suppose ye, shall he be thought worthy, who hath trodden under foot the Son of God, and hath counted the blood of the covenant, wherewith he was sanctified, an unholy thing, and *hath done despite* unto the Spirit of grace? (Heb. 10:29; emphasis mine)

People can and do frustrate the grace of God, and can and do despise God's Spirit of grace, at their own peril.

Is irresistible grace an oxymoron?

What is grace? A simple working Bible definition is undeserved or unmerited favor. God's grace is never earned but is always offered and never forced. If "it" can't be resisted, then "it" isn't grace, it's force! God doesn't *force* us to *love* him, *serve* him or *receive* him, and if he did, wouldn't he force *everyone* to love, serve, and receive him? If God forced salvation on anyone, even for their own good, then salvation would be by God's force and not by God's offered grace. Irresistible grace is an oxymoron, it's like being given a mandatory option or a compulsory choice.

If man has no free will like Calvinists believe, then why would God need to use irresistible grace?

This question should be self-evident. Along the same line of reasoning, was Paul given irresistible grace to obey the gospel like Calvinists believe or did Paul receive grace because he obeyed the gospel?

> "By whom we have *received grace* and apostleship, *for obedience* to the faith among all nations, for his name" (Rom. 1:5; emphasis mine).

The Bible order is clear; grace follows obedience.

*When you say irresistible grace, do you
apply it to salvation or service?*

We have answered both sides of this question under number four, but let's look at a clear account of service.

But Martha was cumbered about much serving, and came to him, and said, Lord, dost thou not care that *my sister hath left me to serve alone? bid her therefore that she help me.* And Jesus answered and said unto her, Martha, Martha, thou art careful and troubled about many things: But one thing is needful: and Mary hath chosen that good part, which shall not be taken away from her. (Luke 10:40–42; emphasis mine)

This is the same point made under unconditional election. Martha was asking the Lord to *make* Mary serve tables to which there are three points.

A. The Lord wouldn't make her serve.

B. Mary was serving already, i.e., sitting and learning at the feet of the Lord Jesus is service.

C. Mary had a choice in the matter, for the Lord said, "Mary hath chosen that good part."

Yes, we make a conscious choice to serve or not to serve. Some may believe that people are forced to serve and quote the Psalms:

> "The steps of a good man are ordered
> by the LORD: and he delighteth in his way"
> (Ps. 37:23).

Please think clearly, does this verse really teach that God forces a good man to serve? No, it says that the steps of a good man are ordered by the LORD. When I was in the Air Force, we all were given orders to obey, however, not everyone obeyed those orders, and when they didn't penalties were paid. When I follow the LORD's orders, I'm a "good man;" when I don't obey the LORD's orders, I'm not a "good man." Regardless, I'm the LORD's either way, as a good servant or a bad one.

> "For whether we live, we live unto the
> Lord; and whether we die, we die unto the
> Lord: whether we live therefore, or die, we
> are the Lord's" (Rom. 14:8).

Is irresistible grace the same as sovereignty?

When asked the question, "Is God sovereign?" most Christians will probably answer yes. What is the correct answer; is God indeed sovereign? I have tried to establish a logical and biblical precedent to all such questions by requiring that terms be defined before any conclusions can be reached. It is absolutely necessary to define the terms first; otherwise, the discussion is confused and the loudest voice usually wins. When a Calvinist says God is sovereign, he may mean one thing while another person using the same term, may mean something very different. Please note that I'm painfully aware that not all Calvinists believe the same thing, even as all Arminians don't believe the same thing. Few persons want to be shoved into an unbending mold! My goal is to consider what the Bible teaches without preconceived ideas, man-made terms and explanations. Let's go back and consider the idea of God's sovereignty from a traditional Calvinistic view. If we agree that God is sovereign, then the Calvinist will probably *assume* that we believe that God chooses individuals for salvation and others for hell. As we have seen, the supposed necessity for God to choose persons for salvation is born out of the misunderstanding of the three parts of man, also referred to as man's tripartite composition, threefold nature, or the trichotomy of man. If you have jumped to this chapter without reading the previous chapters in their entirety, you will likely misunderstand the points presented. Briefly put, a Calvinistic idea of God's sovereignty is that God must choose individuals for heaven and believe the gospel for them because unsaved man has a dead spirit and no will or ability to choose. The misunderstanding, again, is in thinking that unsaved man is incapable of making decisions because he possesses a dead spirit, when in fact a natural man is capable of making rational decisions, including the decision to receive Christ, because he possesses a living soul. Please reread chapter 5 if you are unsure what the Bible teaches regarding the composition of man.

If the word sovereignty doesn't mean that God chooses individuals for heaven and hell, what then does it mean? Let me remind the reader that neither sovereign or sovereignty is a Bible word. Please go to your computer or haul out your concordance to verify my statement. Incidentally, just because the word sovereignty isn't in the Bible doesn't mean that the term itself is bad. We can use non-Bible terms to describe or label events, doctrines, processes and so on. The word rapture isn't found in the Bible, but it's a term which describes a biblical event. The word Bible isn't in the Bible, but is a descriptive term meaning "*the* book" or "*the* ultimate book of authority." There is no problem using the word sovereignty, but the fault is in the false assumptions people make surrounding its meaning.

Before we define the word "sovereignty," let's establish a few Bible facts regarding God's attributes and character. Let's remind ourselves that we are not seeking to establish or promote a denomination, paradigm, or system of belief, but to acknowledge the Bible itself as the final authority for all faith and practice. Our goal is to understand the

Bible as it is written and not through a man-made filter of reinterpretation.

Some Bible facts:

Fact 1. God is omnipotent.

> "And I heard as it were the voice of a great multitude, and as the voice of many waters, and as the voice of mighty thunderings, saying, Alleluia: for the Lord *God omnipotent* reigneth" (Rev. 19:6; emphasis mine).

Nine other times the Greek word, here translated omnipotent, is translated Almighty. If we profess to believe the Bible, we must also agree that the Bible clearly stated that God is all powerful.

> "Saying, We give thee thanks, O Lord God *Almighty*, which art, and wast, and art to come; because thou hast taken to

PASTOR KEVIN KLINE

thee thy great power, and hast reigned"
(Rev. 11:17; emphasis mine).

The fact that God is all powerful in no way mandates that he forces people to become saved or forces saved people to do his perfect will. More about this later.

Fact 2. There are a few things God cannot do. Even though God is all powerful, there are things God can't do because of his holy nature and character. Let's consider a few specific things which God cannot do.

Fact 3. God cannot deny himself.

"If we believe not, yet he abideth faithful: *he cannot* deny himself" (2 Tim. 2:13; emphasis mine).

The word "he" in its context is God. This is to say, that once God gives his word, he can't go back on it.

~ 492 ~

Fact 4. God cannot be tempted with evil.

"Let no man say when he is tempted, I am tempted of God: for *God cannot* be tempted with evil, neither tempteth he any man" (James 1:13; emphasis mine).

Fact 5. God cannot lie.

"In hope of eternal life, which *God*, that *cannot* lie, promised before the world began" (Titus 1:2; emphasis mine).

Fact 6. God cannot look on iniquity.

Art thou not from everlasting, O LORD my God, mine Holy One? we shall not die. O LORD, thou hast ordained them for judgment; and, O mighty *God*, thou hast established them for correction. Thou art of purer eyes than to behold evil, and *canst not* look on iniquity: wherefore lookest thou upon them that deal treacherously, and holdest thy tongue when the wicked devoureth the man that is more righteous than he? (Hab. 1:12–13; emphasis mine)

In summary, God can do anything he chooses to do, however, God's holy nature limits what he chooses to do.

Defining the word sovereignty: The dictionary definition of sovereignty is…

1. Supremacy of authority or rule as exercised by a sovereign or sovereign state.
2. Royal rank, authority, or power.
3. Complete independence and self-government.
4. A territory existing as an independent state.

Let's agree to eliminate definition four since God isn't a territory. Is God a completely independent and self-governing being as in number three? Yes, God doesn't need to ask anyone for advice! Is God of royal rank, authority, or power? Yes, all three and King of the universe too! Additionally, the first definition applies to God and his governorship of the universe. Yes, God is the Supreme authority in the universe. To summarize, we agree that God is a Supreme, self-governing, King. To all of this, we may add the well-established Bible fact that God is omnipotent, meaning all powerful. So then, if our definition of sovereignty is that God is all powerful as the Bible declares, then I agree that God is sovereign. If the definition of sovereignty is that since God is all powerful, he must therefore overpower man's will at all times, then I disagree. A problem was created when we made the wrong assumption that since God is all powerful, he must therefore always overpower man. We have seen numerous examples in chapter 6, where man's will was not overpowered by God. Indeed, if God's will always trumps man's will, then all men would be saved since the Holy Spirit convicts all! (John 16:7–8).

Furthermore, the clear teaching of the Bible is that God's will is for all men to be saved.

"For this is good and acceptable in the sight of *God* our Saviour; Who *will* have all men to be saved, and to come unto the knowledge of the truth" (1 Tim. 2:3–4; emphasis mine).

The Bible answer is that God *will* have all men to be saved, but some men refuse and *will not* be saved. Some folks may have the notion that if God wants all men, i.e., all the people of the world to be saved and some individuals refuse to be saved, that somehow God's sovereignty is threatened. Nothing could be further from the truth. *The fact that people refuse God's gift of eternal life in no way challenges God's authority!* God is still on the throne and his character is not impugned in the slightest simply because some have rejected his offer. The character of the person who rejects God is impugned and not God's character. When the Bible declares that a relative few will enter heaven, it in no way suggests that God failed. Indeed, God succeeded in paying for and offering eternal life to every single person in the world!

"For therefore we both labour and suffer reproach, because we trust in the living God, who is the Saviour of all men, specially of those that believe" (1 Tim. 4:10).

Those who rejected eternal life failed God; God did not fail them. God's authority and power are not diminished one bit by those who reject his offer. God is still able to save to the uttermost those who are willing to come to him by faith in Christ. Let's consider a fun illustration. Let's make you a magnanimous, philanthropic multimillionaire! You enter a room filled with financially needy people, and you offer each and every one a very large stack of new $100 bills. Most think it's too good to be true and walk out; others believe the offer, but think that there's a catch and leave; still, others are afraid that it's stolen and won't take the offer. Soon, for one reason or another, everyone is gone except for one person who receives the legitimate gift with joy. Are you, the generous millionaire, lessened in power, character or honor because most refused your offer? No, in no way. By the same token, if God offers eternal life to all and most reject it, God is no less sovereign because of detractors, but it is the detractors themselves who are lessened.

God is always sovereign regardless of man's actions. Remember, God made the rules and not man. God's sovereignty is seen in that he alone chose the plan of salvation, the method of salvation, as well as the means and conditions of salvation and not man. Those who violate God's command for "all men every where" to repent and believe the gospel (Acts 17:30), will ultimately be judged and punished by the same all-powerful God whose law they have broken. God gives man choices, but God made the rules and he has *the last say* because he is the only "Sovereign," Almighty, Potentate.

Please consider the simplicity of accepting God's word at face value.

> O Jerusalem, Jerusalem, thou that killest the prophets, and stonest them which are sent unto thee, how often *would* *I* have gathered thy children together, even as a hen gathereth her chickens under her wings, and *ye would not*! (Matt. 23:37; emphasis mine)

God's will was to gather the people of Jerusalem, but the people refused. I see this as a microcosm of the world in relation to the gospel.

Let's now reconsider the definition of the word sovereignty. Which definition would you choose?

A. God is all powerful.

B. God is all powerful, therefore he must control everything, including man's will.

Again, what does sovereignty mean and how do we define it? Since sovereignty isn't a Bible word, the Bible offers no definition; the closest Bible words are Almighty and omnipotent. Almighty and omnipotent mean all powerful. Scholars may assume or may have been taught that God's omnipotence, somehow, means he must totally overpower or control man's will, but this is not the case. Man often goes against God's will, both saved and unsaved alike.

God's will for the unsaved.

"The *Lord is* not slack concerning his promise, as some men count slackness;

but is longsuffering to us-ward, *not willing that any should perish*, but that *all* should come to repentance" (2 Pet. 3:9; emphasis mine).

God doesn't desire anyone to perish, not even the scoffers who walk after their own lusts (2 Pet. 3:3), but God wants all of them to repent. We all agree that God is sovereign, at least in some form, but does God exercise his total power at all times?

"Will a man rob God? Yet ye have robbed me. But ye say, Wherein have we robbed thee? In tithes and offerings" (2. Malachi 3:8).

God asks a sharp question, "Will a man rob God?" The answer is certainly yes, because of the next sentence, "Yet *ye have* robbed me." Yes, men have robbed God, men will rob God, and men will continue to do so. It would be silly to argue that God *wants* anyone to rob him, therefore the Bible presents us with a case where man is willfully going against God's will. This is not to say that man's will is stronger than God's will, for that would be equally silly. The answer is that God gives man a choice to obey his will or not, while God remains a sovereign Lord over all men. God's sovereignty is manifest in God's ultimate judgment of man, where God meets out the consequences of man's choices. Let's look at some other Bible examples:

God's will for the saved:

"For this is the will of God, even your sanctification, that ye should abstain from fornication" (1 Thess. 4:3).

God's sovereign will for every believer is to abstain from fornication, but do some Christians ever choose fornication regardless? Yes, they do, but they do so against God's will and will suffer the negative consequences of their chosen actions.

"In every thing give thanks: for this is the will of God in Christ Jesus concerning you" (1 Thess. 5:18).

I trust we can all identify with this one. Our Holy God wants us to be thankful in everything, as the scripture says, "this is the will of God," yet we often fall short of God's will and suffer the consequences.

The fact that God is the only supreme all-powerful king of the universe in no way suggests that God forces people to be saved, to serve him or that man can never go against God's will. God's sovereignty does dictate, however, that mankind will ultimately answer to him and God himself will levy judgment based on the choices each has made. Speaking to Christians, 2 Corinthians 5:10 says:

"For we must all appear before the judgment seat of Christ; that every one may receive the things done in his body, according to that he hath done, whether it be good or bad" (2 Cor. 5:10).

Let's go a little deeper. I made a huge statement earlier when I wrote; the fact that God is the only supreme all-powerful king of the universe in no way suggests that God forces people to be *saved*, to *serve* him, or that man can never go against God's will. Let's examine that statement in reverse order. First, can people go against God's will? The full Bible answer is both yes and no. What do I mean; how can it be yes and no? First, the yes side. Once more, according to Malachi, is it God's will for man to rob God? No. But does man rob God? Yes.

> "Will a man rob God? Yet ye have
> robbed me. But ye say, wherein have
> we robbed thee? In tithes and offerings"
> (Mal. 3:8).

Even though God's will is for man not to rob him, man will and does rob God. God allows man to do some horrific sins against his will to prove the sinfulness of man as well as God's longsuffering and great forgiveness. Is it God's will for people to murder people? No. Do people murder people? Yes, every day! People can and do go against God's will every single day and a long list could be made. However, there are God-placed boundaries against man's will infringing upon God's will. If some people had their way they would murder every Christian and stamp out every vestige of Christianity. This is a good example of where God draws the line.

> "And I say also unto thee, That thou art Peter, and upon this rock I will build my church; and the gates of hell shall not prevail against it" (Matt. 16:18).

This verse can be parsed in several ways, but one thing is clear, God will not allow evil men, devils, or Satan himself to prevail against the born-again body of Christ, the church. In other words, man's will and desire may be to prevail against God's church, but God says in essence, "No, you will not!" Does this mean that God will not allow any believer to be persecuted? No, quite the contrary, for the Bible teaches in 2 Timothy:

> "Yea, and all that will live godly in Christ Jesus shall suffer persecution" (2 Tim. 3:12).

THE DOCTRINE OF ETERNAL LIFE

God will never allow anyone or anything to eradicate all of the born-again believers on earth, neither will God allow any single born-again person to be lost though all the devils of hell unite. In this, God is both almighty and sovereign!

Let's consider God's sovereignty in relation to service.

Was Moses, for example, in God's perfect will? The correct answer would be sometimes. The Lord wanted Moses to be the spokesperson for Israel, but Moses refused because he was "slow of speech, and of a slow tongue." God was angry with Moses and told him to take his brother Aaron with him to do the speaking. This account is recorded in Exodus 4. So, originally it was God's will to have Moses do the speaking, but when Moses refused, God allowed Aaron to become the main speaker. This simple account proves that God has more than one will. God has his perfect will and his permissive or allowable will. Believers live mostly in God's permissive will. We may do God's perfect will often, but not in a continual, unbroken fashion. I believe that the Lord Jesus was the only person who continually did the Father's will.

"And he that sent me is with me: the Father hath not left me alone; for *I do always* those things that please him" (John 8:29; emphasis mine).

We mere mortals spend most of our lives in God's permissive will, i.e., we fall short of God's perfect will every day, yet God still delights in using us. If, however, we stray too close to the edge of God's permissive will, God is sovereign and we are in danger of angering our creator, as Moses did. This is the situation of first Corinthians:

"For this cause many are *weak* and *sickly* among you, and *many sleep*" (1 Cor. 11:30; emphasis mine).

When people get too close to the edge of God's permissible or allowable will, the Lord may warn them with infirmities and even death eventually. Another way to say it is that because God is sovereign, he puts limits on man, because of the choices of man.

Some closing thoughts on the concept of irresistible grace. When I was in the military, we used a special device called an aerospace darkness penetrator, otherwise known as a flashlight! The point is that giving something a fancy name does not increase its legitimacy. If such a thing as irresistible grace existed, it would be indistinguishable from pure raw force. Biblical grace is always offered and never forced. God offering salvation to all is grace, while God selecting persons for salvation or only offering the grace that brings salvation to some, would be unjust partiality. It is a clear teaching of scripture that God's eternal life is a free gift.

> "For the wages of sin is death; but *the gift of God is eternal life* through Jesus Christ our Lord" (Rom. 6:23; emphasis mine).

God's grace that brings salvation is a gift as well.

> "For by *grace* are ye *saved* through faith; and that not of yourselves: *it is the*

> *gift of God*: Not of works, lest any man should boast" (Eph. 2:8–9; emphasis mine).

If eternal life were a payment for doing good works, then salvation would not be by grace, nor would it be a gift, but a payment. On the other hand, if eternal life were forced upon any individual without choice, neither would salvation be by grace, nor would it any longer be a gift, for a gift must be willingly received.

Consider a common-sense approach to biblical sovereignty versus unbiblical Calvinistic sovereignty. Yes, God is the Almighty, but no, he doesn't force some to be saved and others into hell with no offer of salvation.

Why would God Almighty plead and invite persons to come to him for salvation or service if the individuals have no choice in the matter? This point bears consideration. If God overpowers individuals to be saved, why would God waste his time pleading with them? If you like to do original research, look up all occurrences of the word "come" in the Bible. There are over 1,800 references of the word and some of the general categories are: God's invitation to come to him for rest, refreshment, learning, consideration of God's ways, repentance, restoration, worship, fellowship, salvation, and service. Let's confine ourselves to a short study of God's invitation to man to come for salvation and service, both directly and through his prophets.

God's pleading invitation to man to come for salvation

> "*Come now*, and let us reason together, saith the LORD: though your sins be as scarlet, they shall be as white as snow; though they be red like crimson, they shall be as wool" (Isa. 1:18; emphasis mine).

> "But to Israel he saith, *All day long I have stretched forth my hands* unto a disobedient and gainsaying people" (Rom. 10:21).

> "The Lord is not slack concerning his promise, as some men count slackness; but is longsuffering to us-ward, not willing that any should perish, but that *all* should *come* to repentance" (2 Pet. 3:9; emphasis mine).

"And the Spirit and the bride say, *Come*. And let him that heareth say, *Come*. And let him that is athirst *come*. And whosoever will, let him take the water of life freely" (Rev. 22:17; emphasis mine).

Again, why would God plead with man to come to him if man has no choice?

God's pleading invitation to come to him and follow him for service.

"Jesus said unto him, If thou wilt be perfect, go and sell that thou hast, and give to the poor, and thou shalt have treasure in heaven: and *come and follow me*" (Matt. 19:21; emphasis mine).

"Then said Jesus unto his disciples, If any man *will come* after me, let him deny himself, and *take up* his cross, and *follow me*" (Matt. 16:24; emphasis mine).

"And Jesus said unto them, *Come* ye after me, and I will make you to become *fishers of men*" (Mark 1:17; emphasis mine).

Lastly, should we serve God through irresistible grace or in sincerity?

"Now therefore fear the LORD, and *serve* him in *sincerity* and in truth: and put away the gods which your fathers served on the other side of the flood, and in Egypt; and serve ye the LORD" (Josh. 24:14; emphasis mine).

"For we are not as many, which corrupt the word of God: but as of *sincerity*, but as of God, in the sight of God speak we in Christ" (2 Cor. 2:17; emphasis mine).

Irresistible grace is not a Bible term, but a confusing man-made term.

13

Perseverance of the Saints: The "P" of the TULIP

The term, "perseverance of the saints" is not a Bible term; neither are the words persist, persistent, or persevere, found in the Bible. The word perseverance is found in only one verse, which has nothing to with eternal life or the security of the believer's soul, but with being faithful in prayer.

> "Praying always with all prayer and supplication in the Spirit, and watching thereunto with all *perseverance* and supplication for all saints" (Eph. 6:18; emphasis mine).

The scripture most often used to promote the concept of the perseverance of the eternal souls of the saints stems from a well-known verse, taken out of context, that being Matthew 24:13.

"But he that shall endure unto the end,
the same shall be saved" (Matt. 24:13).

First, let's be mindful that the salvation spoken of here is a physical salvation and not a spiritual salvation. We must not lump the two together if we hope to rightly divide the word of truth. Other examples of physical salvation in the Bible follow.

"And Adam was not deceived, but the woman being deceived was in the transgression. Notwithstanding she shall be *saved* in childbearing, if they continue in faith and charity and holiness with sobriety" (1 Tim. 2:14–15; emphasis mine).

Obviously, a woman isn't granted eternal life for surviving childbirth. Another example of physical salvation is seen in 1 Samuel 11:13.

"And Saul said, There shall not a man be put to death this day: for today the

LORD hath wrought salvation in Israel" (1 Sam. 11:13).

The physical salvation expressed in Matthew 24:13 is repeated in Matthew 24:22.

"And except those days should be shortened, there should no *flesh* be *saved*: but for the elect's sake those days shall be shortened" (Matt. 24:22; emphasis mine).

Second, let's refresh our memories concerning the context of Matthew 24. Matthew was written before Acts 2 and the day of Pentecost, sometimes referred to as the birthday of the church of Christ. The theme of Matthew is Christ the king of the Jews, understanding that Christ is never referred to as the King of the church. You may recall that in chapter three of this book, we observed from Matthew's gospel, chapters 23–25, the following:

Matthew 23 records the rejection of the Lord Jesus as king by the leaders of the Jewish nation. Matthew 24 records the return of the Lord Jesus as king to the Jewish nation. Matthew 25 records the subsequent restoration of the Jewish nation or "kingdom of heaven."

The context of Matthew 24 is not that of Christ coming for his *bride* before the tribulation, but Christ the Jewish Messiah coming to the nation of *Israel* after the tribulation!

> Immediately *after the tribulation* of those days shall the sun be darkened, and the moon shall not give her light, and the stars shall fall from heaven, and the powers of the heavens shall be shaken: And then shall appear the sign of the Son of man in heaven: and then shall all the tribes of the earth mourn, and they shall see the *Son of man coming* in the clouds of heaven with power and great glory. (Matt. 24:29–30; emphasis mine)

The term "Son of man" is also a decidedly Jewish term. Therefore, Matthew 24:13 is not referring to any born-again person striving to gain or keep eternal life. The context bears out that the salvation referred to is that of a physical nature and not a spiritual nature as in the case of eternal life. In other words, those believing Jews in Matthew 24, who physically endure to the end and survive the tribulation period (Jacob's trouble), will be saved physically to enter the millennial reign.

Please allow me to inject a personal opinion here, using the word perseverance in relation to eternal life is misleading. Perseverance means persistence, which genders thoughts of human effort. God Almighty never uses the words perseverance or persistence in relation to eternal life; he uses a far better term which we will consider momentarily. You, the reader, may think that only Arminians don't believe in the perseverance of the saints. I'm not an Arminian, i.e., I believe in eternal life—life which cannot be undone, taken away, or end. However, I don't believe in the perseverance of the saints, but rather in the *preservation* of the saints. We have seen that the Holy Bible in no way teaches the perseverance of the saints in regards to eternal life, but does it clearly teach the preservation of the saints?

God's preservation, example 1:

> "And the Lord shall deliver me from every evil work, and will *preserve me* unto his heavenly kingdom: to whom be glory *for ever and ever.* Amen" (2 Tim. 4:18; emphasis mine).

Please notice that the preservation context is unto his heavenly kingdom and not unto some earthly kingdom. Secondly, the Lord's preservation is eternal. Also, notice that the great Apostle Paul isn't making any effort here to do anything, but he rests in the promise of the Lord to preserve him. The eternal preservation of the soul of the believer is also taught in the Old Testament.

God's preservation, example 2:

> "The LORD shall *preserve* thee from all evil: he *shall preserve thy soul.* The LORD shall *preserve* thy going out and thy com-

ing in from this time forth, and even *for evermore*" (Ps. 121:7–8; emphasis mine).

God's preservation, example 3:

"For *the* LORD loveth judgment, and forsaketh not *his saints*; *they are preserved for ever*: but the seed of the wicked shall be cut off" (Ps. 37:28; emphasis mine).

The eternal preservation of the soul goes beyond the earthly existence, not because people persevere, but because they are preserved, i.e., kept by the power of God. A good Bible definition of preservation is to be kept by the power of God.

God's preservation, example 4:

Blessed be the God and Father of our Lord Jesus Christ, which according to his abundant mercy hath *begotten us again* unto a lively hope by the resurrection of

Jesus Christ from the dead, To an inheritance incorruptible, and undefiled, and that fadeth not away, reserved in heaven for you, *Who are kept by the power of God* through faith unto salvation ready to be revealed in the last time. (1 Pet. 1:3–5; emphasis mine)

All begotten or born-again believers are kept by the power of God unto salvation. The faith mentioned here in verse 5 is not some fickle or changeable future faith, but the saving faith that was exhibited at the moment of salvation. We will see this more clearly when we later examine the promises of God in scripture. There is also a wonderful parallel between the preservation of God's word and the preservation of the soul of God's child.

God's words are preserved by God's power.

God's preservation, example 5:

"The words of the LORD are *pure words*: as silver tried in a furnace of earth, purified seven times. Thou shalt keep

them, O LORD, thou *shalt preserve* them
from this generation *for ever*" (Ps. 12:6–7;
emphasis mine).

God's child is likewise preserved by God's power.

God's preservation, example 6:

"And the *Lord shall* deliver me from
every evil work, and will *preserve me* unto
his heavenly kingdom: to whom be glory
for ever and ever. Amen" (2 Tim. 4:18;
emphasis mine).

We, as human beings, like to lump doctrines into easy
piles, however, life is never that easy. Bible doctrines, criss-
cross denominational, ethnic and geographical boundaries. The trinity, or triune Godhead, is neither Calvinist or
Arminian, but is a Bible doctrine. The deity of Christ isn't
Jewish, Arab or American, but a Bible doctrine. The sealing of the Holy Spirit at the moment of salvation is neither a Pentecostal nor a Baptist doctrine, but a great Bible

doctrine. Likewise, the preservation of the soul, or if you'd rather, the eternal security of the believer is not a doctrine of Calvin, but a Bible doctrine.

In clear speech, the term "perseverance of the saints" belongs to John Calvin, while the concept of the believer's soul being preserved by the power of God is a Bible doctrine and belongs to God.

God's preservation, example 7:

"Jude, the servant of Jesus Christ, and brother of James, to them that are sanctified by *God the Father*, and *preserved in Jesus Christ*, and called" (Jude 1:1; emphasis mine).

Once again, the Bible uses the word preserved in direct relationship to man's soul.

God's preservation, example 8:

"And the very God of peace sanctify you wholly; and I pray God your whole

spirit and *soul* and body be *preserved* blameless unto the coming of our Lord Jesus
Christ" (2 Thess. 5:23; emphasis mine).

In this next section, we will review some of the scripture we considered in chapter 7. The preservation of the
believer's soul by God was clearly understood by the New
Testament Bible writers. If the writers of scripture believed
that salvation could be lost, or if believers themselves had
to somehow endure to the end to receive eternal life, then
how could God make these following Bible promises?

God's promise, example 1:

"That if thou shalt confess with thy
mouth the Lord Jesus, and shalt believe in
thine heart that God hath raised him from
the dead, *thou shalt be saved*" (Rom. 10:9;
emphasis mine).

If it were possible for the soul to be lost, or eternal
life to be somehow undone, the statement "thou shalt be

saved" would not be true. Rather, the scriptures would of necessity require a qualifier such as "unless," "as long as" or other conditions stated. Praise God that once the conditions of repentance and faith are combined with the heart calling out (in this case the heart calling out via the mouth) to God, spiritual salvation is given, promised and guaranteed! You may have been taught that individuals can somehow fall away from eternal life. The doctrine of eternal life, however, mandates that if the spiritual life one has been given can be taken away, then it's not eternal life, but rather conditional life, temporary life, or some other kind of life foreign to God. We will examine the concepts of falling away and backsliding later in this chapter, but for now let's bask in the promises of God to preserve our eternal souls.

God's promise, example 2:

> "Beloved, now are we the sons of God, and it doth not yet appear what we shall be: but we know that, when he shall appear, *we shall be like him*; for we shall see him as he is" (1 John 3:2; emphasis mine).

The single point here is simple; how could the prophet who penned down this scripture possibly declare to *all* the children of God that *we shall* (not just I shall, but we shall) be like him? If there were the slightest possibility of any child of God losing eternal life, this statement would be false. If any child of God could possibly lose their eternal life, then the apostle would have to have written something like, "Beloved, now are we the sons of God, and it doth not yet appear what we shall be: but we know that, when he shall appear, *some of us might be like him if we have maintained sufficient good works and have not done too many bad works*; for *then maybe* we shall see him as he is." No, the apostle writes to all the children of God and boldly declares that we (all of us, each one of us) shall be like him, which means we will see and be glorified like him. The only way this verse makes sense is when we know the proper understanding of the doctrine of eternal life, which is God's gift of everlasting, spiritual life that God gives to every believer at the moment of salvation, promising his child that he will never perish.

God's promise, example 3:

> "Verily, verily, I say unto you, *He that* heareth my word, and *believeth* on him that sent me, *hath everlasting life*, and *shall not come into condemnation*; but is passed from death unto life" (John 5:24; emphasis mine).

The Lord himself declared that he that believeth (believes) hath (has) eternal life and *shall not* come into condemnation. This verse does not say anything such as, "he that continues to believe and do good works…" There are no exceptions or qualifiers given. Once we believe, we do have eternal life and we shall not come into condemnation. Others may say, "and *might* not come into condemnation," but the Lord said *shall* not. Whom will you believe; the interpretation of man or the promise of God? Also, the final promise of God at the end of the verse is no less spectacular, "but is passed from death unto life." This couldn't be made any clearer. Each and every believer at the moment of salvation "is passed from death unto life," i.e., taken from the punishment of hell and the lake of fire and is guaranteed a place in heaven.

God's promise, example 4:

> "And to wait for his Son from heaven, whom he raised from the dead, even Jesus, which *delivered* us from the wrath to come" (1 Thess. 1:10; emphasis mine).

Please notice that the tense of the verb is past tense, declaring a finalized transaction which is nothing less than the promise of God. This epistle, written to born-again believers, declares that we all have been delivered, again, past tense and a completed action, from the wrath to come without exception.

God's promise, example 5:

> "For whosoever shall call upon the name of the Lord *shall* be saved" (Rom. 10:13; emphasis mine).

The proper context of this verse is someone with repentance and saving faith. Does this verse then teach that whosoever shall call upon the name of the Lord *might* be saved as long as they do many good works and few bad works or does it teach that they *shall* be saved?

God's promise, example 6:

> "And this is the will of him that sent me, that every one which seeth the Son, and believeth on him, may have everlasting life: and *I will raise him up at the last day*" (John 6:40; emphasis mine).

The word "may" here doesn't mean maybe, but is a word of permission, i.e., yes, he may (can) have everlasting life. This is followed by the best part which is the promise of Christ himself, "I will raise him up at the last day." This promise is extended to "every one" that "believeth," because our eternal life is founded upon the finished work of Christ Jesus and our faith at the moment of salvation and not on our future works or future faith. Our future works after our salvation determine our rewards in heaven, while our eternal life is secured by the finished work of Christ.

God's promise, example 7:

> "And though after my skin worms destroy this body, yet in my flesh *shall I see God*" (Job 19:26; emphasis mine).

Even Old Testament saints carried the assurance of God's promise of eternal life. Job could not make this statement honestly if he were depending on his good works to solidify his salvation or if he believed that he had to endure faithfully to the end. Job was trusting in God's power and not his own when he declared, "...shall I see God."

God's promise, example 8:

> "And this is the record, that God *hath given* to us *eternal life*, and this life is in his Son" (1 John 5:11; emphasis mine).

Please notice the tense of the verb; God hath (has) given. This is a past perfect tense which indicates a condition that has happened in the past and continues into the future, in this case, into eternity. Another way to express this is to say that God has already, in the past, given us eternal life the moment we believed, and this life can never end.

God's promise, example 9:

> "He that hath the Son *hath life*; and
> he that hath not the Son of God hath not
> life" (1 John 5:12; emphasis mine).

Clearly, a person is either saved or lost with no in-between or limbo! Even as a lost person without eternal life should have absolutely no hope of heaven, a saved person possesses eternal life and should have absolutely no fear or doubt of losing it. We should, however, be on guard at all times not to lose our rewards.

"Look to yourselves, that we lose not
those things which we have wrought, but
that we receive a full reward" (2 John 1:8).

But our eternal life, which is the salvation of our soul, needs to rest in Christ. Paul wrote "For the which cause I also suffer these things: nevertheless I am not ashamed: for I know whom I have believed, and am persuaded that *he is able to keep* that which I have committed unto him against that day" (2 Tim. 1:12).

Paul committed his very soul unto the Lord for safe keeping! This is God's intention for every child of his. To illustrate: a believer may erroneously think of eternal life as a gold coin or a diamond ring, which although very precious, may be possessed today and lost tomorrow. This is not what the Bible teaches. Our eternal life, biblically speaking, is like a gold coin or diamond ring too precious to be entrusted to a child until they are fully grown. Although the possession belongs to the child, the thing of value is locked in a safe by the parent until the child is grown. Once the child reaches maturation, he receives his inheritance from the safe. In like manner, the Bible teaches that the Lord keeps our souls and not we ourselves; for who but God could be trusted with something so precious as an eternal soul? Please remember, dear believer, how precious you are to God. God in Christ left heaven and became a man. God, in the flesh, suffered, bled and died as a man, was buried, and rose again after three days and three nights in the grave. He did this because he loves *you* and wants *you* to have eternal life and the assurance and knowledge of eternal life. The only possible way to have assurance of eternal life is to receive it as a gift (Rom. 6:23) and trust by faith in the finished work of the Lord Jesus and not in our own works. Consequently, our individual souls are more safe, being kept by the power of God (1 Pet. 1:5), than any coin in any earthly safe!

God's promise, example 10:

> "For *we know* that if our earthly house of this tabernacle were dissolved, we have a building of God, an house not made with hands, *eternal* in the heavens" (2 Cor. 5:1; emphasis mine).

Here, Paul is referring to our *eternal* heavenly bodies (see verse 6), but please notice his confidence. Paul says we know, not just I know, but *we know*. Did Paul know any carnal Christians? Yes, of course, the Corinthian church was loaded with carnal Christians! The only way Paul could have made this bold statement is if *all* born-again children of God had eternal life based upon the finished work of Christ and not based upon their own future works.

If I ask an honest Arminian friend, "When you die will you go to heaven?" he will likely answer, "I hope so." Not yes and not no; why is this? Because he has been taught that his eternal life depends on his performance, persistence, or perseverance of good works, either to get eternal life, to keep eternal life, or both. Indeed, if we had to keep eternal life by our good works we would lose it every day. Conversely, every believer can have Paul's very same confidence if he simply believes the Bible promise of God that he has already given us eternal life at the moment of conversion.

> "And this is the promise that he hath *promised* us, even *eternal life*" (1 John 2:25; emphasis mine).

Not conditional or temporary life.

> "For *all the promises* of God in him
> are yea, and in him Amen, unto the glory
> of God by us" (2 Cor. 1:20).

So, when a born-again child of God is asked, "When you die, will you go to heaven?" if they're trusting in their works, they should answer no. If they're trusting in the finished work of Christ, they should answer yes, like Paul and James.

> "let your yea be yea" (James 5:12).

It is not arrogant or proud for a born-again believer in Christ to have full assurance of eternal life. Having confidence in the promise of eternal life is no different than believing the promise of Christ's return or the promise of the New Jerusalem. It's very wrong to glory in self and the works of man, but perfectly holy to glory in the finished work of Christ on the cross.

"But God forbid that I should glory,
save in the cross of our Lord Jesus Christ,
by whom the world is crucified unto me,
and I unto the world" (Gal. 6:14).

There is no difference in boasting in the finished work of Christ on the cross and the promise of eternal life to us as believers, for they are one in the same to the born-again believer.

God's promise, example 11:

"These things have I written unto you that believe on the name of the Son of God; that ye may *know* that *ye have eternal life*, and that ye may believe on the name of the Son of God" (1 John 5:13; emphasis mine).

Can a person know he's saved? Job and Paul did in chapter 7, and there are many more examples in scripture. Perhaps the more pertinent question is, does God want us to guess, hope, feel, or know that we have eternal life? What saith the scriptures? God Almighty gave the scriptures to us that we would not doubt his unspeakable gift of eternal life. Some believers could possibly stumble at the word "may." The word "may," in this context, does not mean maybe, but can. If someone asks you if they may go to the store and you reply yes, you may; you don't mean maybe; you mean, yes, you can, you have permission. God tells us that we are permitted to know and can know that we have eternal life. My personal experience of nearly forty years of leading persons to Christ has shown that the majority of individuals who lack the assurance of their salvation have never been born again. Others lacking assurance often are trusting in their own fickle works and feelings from day to day, rather than the finished and unchanging work of Christ. Those trusting in their own works to obtain, maintain or retain eternal life have every reason to doubt their final end, while those who trust in the finished work of Christ alone have no room for doubt.

God's promise, example 12:

> "He that hath an ear, let him hear what the Spirit saith unto the churches; He that overcometh *shall not* be hurt of the second death" (Rev. 2:11; emphasis mine).

Remember, according to 1 John 5:5, an overcomer is a believer in Jesus, the Son of God.

> "Who is he that overcometh the world, but he that believeth that Jesus is the Son of God?" (1 John 5:5).

If it were possible for a believer to lose eternal life, God could not promise in Revelation 2:11 that he "*shall not* be hurt of the second death." This is indeed God's promise of eternal life.

God's promise, example 13:

> "For whatsoever is born of God over-
> cometh the world: and this is the victory
> that overcometh the world, even our *faith*.
> Who is he that overcometh the world, but
> he that *believeth* that Jesus is the Son of
> God?" (1 John 5:4–5; emphasis mine).

In verse 4, the apostle tells us that the overcomer overcame the world by faith and faith alone, not by faith plus
works. This principle is repeated in verse five; the overcomer overcomes by his belief only, not by his belief plus
sufficient good works and minimal bad works.

God's promise, example 14:

> "He that overcometh, the same *shall
> be* clothed in white raiment; and *I will
> not* blot out his name out of the book of
> life, but *I will* confess his name before my

Father, and before his angels" (Rev. 3:5; emphasis mine).

The Lord Jesus Christ our Saviour promises (see Rev. 1:1) that every believer will be clothed in white, his name will not be blotted out, and his name will be confessed before the Father. Would you rather believe your human Sunday School teacher and doubt, or trust Christ and have peace?

God's promise, example 15:

> "Let your conversation be without covetousness; and be content with such things as ye have: for he hath said, *I will never leave thee*, nor forsake thee" (Heb. 13:5; emphasis mine).

This is God's direct promise to every born-again believer without qualification. That is to say, God doesn't say "unless…" Dear reader, if the Holy Bible needs to be altered in any way to make any doctrine understandable, then that doctrine is not biblical. In chapter 7 entitled "The Name Game," we examined the proper application of James 2. Perhaps James will be clearer to us now that we have a deeper understanding of God's promise of eternal life.

Understanding James 2.

> Even so faith, if it hath not works, is dead, being alone. Yea, a man may say, Thou hast faith, and I have works: shew me thy faith without thy works, and I will shew thee my faith by my works. Thou believest that there is one God; thou doest well: the devils also believe, and tremble. But wilt thou know, O vain man, that faith without works is dead? Was not Abraham our father justified by works, when he had offered Isaac his son upon the altar? Seest thou how faith wrought with his works, and by works was faith made perfect? And the scripture was fulfilled which saith, Abraham believed God, and it was

imputed unto him for righteousness: and he was called the Friend of God. Ye see then how that by works a man is justified, and not by faith only. (James 2:17–24)

Let me assure you that I believe every word of this text just as it is written. However, what those of Arminian faith are taught James says and what James is actually saying are two very different things. The typical Arminian believes in a formula of "faith plus his good works equals salvation" based heavily on his misunderstanding of this portion of scripture. Let's examine each verse.

Verse 17. "Even so faith, if it hath not works, is dead, being alone."

We all agree that a person who exhibits no good works has no genuine faith.

Verse 18. "Yea, a man may say, Thou hast faith, and I have works: shew me thy faith without thy works, and I will shew thee my faith by my works."

Here, here! Genuine saving faith will always produce good works.

Verse 19. "Thou believest that there is one God; thou doest well: the devils also believe, and tremble."

Monotheistic faith is not sufficient for salvation. The Jews and Muslims have faith in a single Creator God but reject the deity of his Son. The devils believe and have even seen the one true God but believing in the existence of God is not repentance and faith, neither is it the same as calling out for salvation.

Verse 20. "But wilt thou know, O vain man, that faith without works is dead?"

A person without saving faith can only produce dead works.

Verse 21. "Was not Abraham our father justified by works, when he had offered Isaac his son upon the altar?"

Abraham certainly was completely and totally justified by works!

Verse 22. "Seest thou how faith wrought with his works, and by works was faith made perfect?"

Yes, yes. Abraham's works made his faith perfect i.e. complete.

Verse 23. "And the scripture was fulfilled which saith, Abraham believed God, and it was imputed unto him for righteousness: and he was called the Friend of God."

Please notice that Abraham's faith or belief was imputed unto him for righteousness with God.

Verse 24. "Ye see then how that by works a man is justified, and not by faith only."

Yes, Abraham was justified by his works and by his faith; with this I wholeheartedly agree!

By now, my Arminian friends may be totally confused. Let me assure you that I completely agree with the Holy Bible, but not in the Arminian interpretation of the Bible. What do I mean? As with Calvinism, Bible words are retranslated or at best misunderstood skewing their meanings and changing Bible doctrines.

Here's what traditional Arminians think verse 24 says:

"Ye see then how that by works a man
is *saved*, and not by faith only."

What the Bible actually says:

> Verse 24. "Ye see then how that by works a man is *justified*, and not by faith only."

You may say that saved and justified mean exactly the same thing and that false assumption is the root cause of the problem. Justification has more than one application; therefore, justification is not always synonymous with salvation. There are two kinds of justification in the Bible— justification before God and justification before man. To see this more clearly, let's use what I call the Newton's law principle of scripture. Newton's law in the natural world states that, "for every action, there is an equal and opposite reaction." This, of course, is a law of physics, which is the study of God's physical universe. In God's word, there is a congruent, unstated law which dictates that for every scripture there is an equal and opposite scripture. In other words, if we have trouble understanding one scripture, God has given us another scripture to help balance out our understanding. Such is the case of James 2:24, when God states that Abraham was justified by works. God was not meaning that Abraham was saved by works. How do we know? First, being justified by works in the sight of God violates many scriptures, including the clear teaching of Galatians 2:16.

> Knowing that a man is not justified by the works of the law, but by the faith of Jesus Christ, even we have believed in Jesus Christ, that we might be justified by the faith of Christ, and not by the works of the law: for *by the works* of the law *shall no flesh be justified.* (Gal. 2:16; emphasis mine)

Second, the balancing scriptures on this very same topic as James 2 are found in Romans 4.

> What shall we say then that Abraham our father, as pertaining to the flesh, hath found? For if Abraham were justified by works, he hath whereof to glory; but not

before God. For what saith the scripture? Abraham believed God, and it was counted unto him for righteousness. Now to him that worketh is the reward not reckoned of grace, but of debt. But to him that worketh not, but believeth on him that justifieth the ungodly, his faith is counted for righteousness. Even as David also describeth the blessedness of the man, unto whom God imputeth righteousness without works, Saying, Blessed are they whose iniquities are forgiven, and whose sins are covered. Blessed is the man to whom the Lord will not impute sin. (Rom. 4:1–8)

Here, God wonderfully balances out the eight verses of James 2 with these eight verses from Romans 4.

Verse 1. "What shall we say then that Abraham our father, as pertaining to the flesh, hath found?"

Notice that our attention is focused on that which pertains to the flesh or human good works.

Verse 2. "For if Abraham were justified by works, he hath whereof to glory; but not before God."

Paul writes in the hypothetical when he says, "For if Abraham were justified by works," and we do agree that Abraham was indeed justified by his works according to James 2:24. However, God, through Paul, goes on to say in Romans 4:2 that Abraham was *not justified* before God by works. Ask yourself this question, did Abraham's works justify him before God? The answer must be no. What did justify Abraham before God? Let's continue.

Verse 3. "For what saith the scripture? Abraham *believed* God, and *it* was counted unto him for righteousness."

Abraham's belief or faith, justified him before God. What happens to any person who tries to use his works to be justified before God? The Bible has the answer.

Verse 5. "Now to him that worketh is the reward not reckoned of grace, but of debt."

Our works will not buy us God's grace nor cancel our sin, but will reckon unto us debt. Let's be perfectly clear, all of our good works combined could never cancel out one lie, or prideful thought! That's why our Saviour came and shed his blood! What can wash away my sin? Nothing, but the blood of Jesus.

Verse 6. "Even as David also describeth the blessedness of the man, unto whom God imputeth righteousness without works."

God always imputes, i.e., places on the account of the believer in Christ, righteousness without works.

Verse 7. "Saying, Blessed are they whose iniquities are forgiven, and whose sins are covered."

The blessed or happy man is one who accepts God's forgiveness as a gift, without trying to, as it were, pay God back for salvation by doing good works.

Verse 8. "Blessed is the man to whom the Lord will not impute sin."

We can be truly blessed when we take God at his word and receive the blood of Christ as the complete payment for our sin and not try to offer our pitiful works as partial payment. Please remember, Isaiah 64:6.

> "But we are all as an unclean thing,
> and *all our righteousnesses are as filthy rags*;
> and we all do fade as a leaf; and our iniq-

uities, like the wind, have taken us away"
(Isa. 64:6; emphasis mine).

So then, faith and faith alone without works justified
Abraham before God, while works and works alone outwardly justified Abraham before man. This is the proper
context of James 2:24.

"Ye see then how that by *works* a man
is justified, and not by *faith* only" (James
2:24; emphasis mine).

Works are seen outwardly because men cannot see
our faith, but they can see our actions. God however, can
see our hearts and does not require works for justification
before him, but faith only. This is the doctrine of twofold
justification. Justified before God by our faith alone and
justified before man by our works alone. The Greek word
for justification means to be innocent or righteous. At the
moment of salvation, God declares the believer in Christ
to be innocent and righteous by faith without the believer's
works. Why? Because at the moment of salvation, all of our

sins are forgiven, and the Father sees the finished work of Christ as the final and complete payment for our sin. So then, Abraham was made perfect or complete because he had faith before God and works before man. Is it possible for a person to be justified in one way and not the other? Of course! These two types of justification are not the same and are not mutually exclusive. In other words, a man may have one and not the other, both, or neither. Is there further scriptural evidence demonstrating that a person may be justified by works before men, but not before God? Yes.

> "And he said unto them, *Ye are they which justify yourselves before men*; but God knoweth your hearts: for that which is highly esteemed among men is abomination in the sight of God" (Luke 16:15; emphasis mine).

A person may be kind and do many good works outwardly being justified before men while never being born-again. Have you ever heard someone say something like, "If anyone makes it to heaven, it'll be Mrs. Smith. She's not a Christian, but she's the kindest soul…?" Bible-believers know that persons are not justified before God by their works, including works of kindness.

> "For if Abraham were justified by works, he hath whereof to glory; but not before God" (Rom. 4:2).
>
> "Not by works of righteousness which we have done, but according to his mercy he saved us, by the washing of regeneration, and renewing of the Holy Ghost" (Titus 3:5).

Mrs. Smith would be an example of a person with dead works, having never called upon the Lord, lacking saving faith. The opposite can also be true. That is, a person may be truly born-again, but because of his life's circumstances, he may not appear to be a mature, saved Christian because he lacks basic and proper Christian works. An example would be a child of seven years old from a heathen household who was allowed to attend a gospel-preaching church one time. The child receives the Lord and with joy goes home and shares their faith with their parents. The parents sharply rebuke that child and never allow the child to ever attend church again. This child stays in a wicked household of cursing, lying, drunkenness, drug abuse and so on, until young adulthood. No one can expect this child to act like a decent, knowledgeable or moderately obedient Christian. They may not be justified by their works before men, but God knew their heart and sincere prayer of faith the moment they called on Christ for salvation. Death bed conversions and conversions that were followed soon after by death are other examples of believers who may not appear to men as having saving faith.

Are there any Bible examples explaining the teaching of Romans 4; that a person is not justified by good works before God? Yes, of course. Let's consider a man who thought he was justified by good works before God.

Two men went up into the temple to
pray; the one a Pharisee, and the other a
publican. The Pharisee stood and prayed
thus with himself, God, I thank thee, that
I am not as other men are, extortioners,

unjust, adulterers, or even as this publican. I fast twice in the week, I give tithes of all that I possess. And the publican, standing afar off, would not lift up so much as his eyes unto heaven, but smote upon his breast, saying, God be merciful to me a sinner. I tell you, this man went down to his house justified rather than the other: for every one that exalteth himself shall be abased; and he that humbleth himself shall be exalted. (Luke 18:10–14)

Please ask yourself, how is it that the person with many good works went away unjustified while the person without any apparent good works went away justified? The answer is manifold. First, the Romans 4 principle is in play here. A man may be justified before other men by his works as seen in James 2, but never before God as seen in Romans 4. Second, the Bible teaches us that a man is not justified before God by works, but by faith. The Pharisee was trusting in his works to be justified in the sight of God and went away unjustified while the publican knew his works were worthless and put his faith in God's mercy. Probably every reader would agree that repentance and faith are the two necessary ingredients for salvation. If not, I invite you to do your own study now of all the verses on this subject. Look up all forms of the words "faith" and "believe" in close proximity to all forms of the word "repent."

For individuals who do have repentance toward God and faith toward Christ, the only thing lacking is to call out to God. This is another reason why the publican went away justified without any works and the Pharisee went away unjustified with many good works. Moreover, the Pharisee never asked God for salvation or mercy, but the publican did.

> "And the publican, standing afar off, would not lift up so much as his eyes unto heaven, but smote upon his breast, saying, God be merciful to me a sinner" (Luke 18:13).
>
> "yet ye have not, because ye ask not" (James 4:2b).
>
> "That *if thou shalt confess* with thy mouth the Lord Jesus, and shalt believe in

thine heart that God hath raised him from the dead, *thou shalt be saved*" (Rom. 10:9; emphasis mine).

Before we move on, we should be clear on these points.

1. Eternal life is not temporary life, which has an end.
2. Eternal life is not conditional life; that which can be lost is not eternal.
3. Eternal life is by definition everlasting life; life which can never end or perish.
4. Eternal life is everlasting life, which is given to sinners as a gift and not earned by his feeble works.
5. Eternal life is everlasting life, which the believer does not maintain by his feeble works.
6. Eternal life is never ending life, which God himself keeps for all of his children.
7. Eternal life is God keeping his children by God's own power.

Once we understand the importance of not elevating good works to the level of a savior, to obtain, maintain or retain salvation, we appreciate the proper balance and importance of good works as seen in chapter 8 of this book. Always remember that the believer's good works do yield eternal rewards, but they do not get us saved, make us saved or keep us saved. The believer's good works are not influential for his salvation, but for the salvation of others. You may appreciate rereading chapter eight. I would like to ask you the question again, "Can you prove your doctrine without adding to, taking away or replacing any Bible words, or must you play the name game?"

A few words on backsliding:

You may have been taught that the term *backsliding* means "losing eternal life," but we have demonstrated that eternal life by its very definition is never-ending life. Backsliding is an Old Testament term that generally means to turn back, to draw back, or go away from. A nation can go away from God or return to God; an individual may be close to God at times and further away at other times. If a person is a child of God, he may be a good child at times and a disobedient child at other times, but alas, he's still God's child. The Bible term backsliding applies to service, not salvation. If we must make an application to salvation, it would apply to someone who rejected the truth of the gospel, but never received it.

"But if ye be without chastisement, whereof all are partakers, then are ye bastards, and not sons" (Heb. 12:8).

A person who is not a child of God may seek to understand spiritual things and then backslide or turn away from revealed truth. The person who rejects an offer of salvation, for instance, didn't lose eternal life for he never had it, while a saved person who turns away from truth forfeits peace, joy, and rewards, but never eternal life.

"But we are not of them who draw back unto perdition; but of them that believe to the saving of the soul" (Heb. 10:39).

One last scripture.

"Now the just shall live by faith: but
if any man draw back, my soul shall have
no pleasure in him" (Heb. 10:38).

This context is a believer drawing back and refusing to
serve God any more. Please notice that the Lord doesn't say
that they will perish in the flames of hell or lose eternal life.
The scriptures simply tell us that God will have no pleasure
in us if we choose to draw back. Even as a child who refuses
to pitch in and do his part is a disappointment to his father,
so too is a child of God who draws back and refuses to live
by faith. Nevertheless, he remains forever a child of God.

For more information on the security of the believer's
soul, reread chapter 7 entitled "The Name Game." Finally,
the Bible never teaches the perseverance of the saints, but
it does clearly teach the preservation of the believer. If you
the reader, have even the slightest doubt concerning your
eternal soul, please read chapter 19 on God's salvation plan.

Foreknowledge, Foreordained, and Predestination

We will now consider these Bible doctrines in order: foreknowledge, foreordained, and predestination. A word to the wise; when we don't understand a complicated doctrine or scripture, we must put more weight on the easy to understand scripture and less weight on the difficult. For the difficult must always fit within the simple, rather than reinterpreting the simple to make it fit into the complex doctrine. Also, put more emphasis on the many scriptures that agree and less emphasis on the few isolated scriptures that don't seem to agree.

By this time, I trust that you appreciate the value of not lumping terms together. Even when these terms appear in close proximity to each other within a verse, terms must remain separate and distinct in meaning if we are to clearly understand the Holy Scriptures. Foreknowledge is a great Bible doctrine that teaches that God knows what will happen before it does. Since God is all knowing, his foreknowledge is total. The word foreknowledge is used in two Bible verses, Acts 2:23 and 1 Peter 1:2, with one occurrence of the word "foreknow" in Romans 8:29 and one use of the word "foreknew," in Romans 11:2. It should be noted that this doctrine is also taught using other words and terms as well. For example, our Lord said:

> "Now *I tell you before it come*, that, when it is come to pass, ye may believe that I am he" (John 13:19; emphasis mine).
> "And now *I have told you before it come to pass*, that, when it is come to pass, ye might believe" (John 14:29; emphasis mine).

Here, the Lord demonstrated his foreknowledge in order to gender faith, "That, when it is come to pass, ye may believe that I am he" and "*when it is come to pass, ye might believe.*" God the Father uses this same technique in the Old Testament. The doctrine of the foreknowledge of God should be understood as part of God's omniscience, which is his all-knowing-ness. God not only sees tomorrow more clearly than we see today, but he also remembers yesterday as clearly as he sees tomorrow. Remembering the past, as well as knowing the future, is all part of God's omniscience. We will consider three major points related to God's foreknowledge.

I.   Knowing the future doesn't mean that God is causing or forcing the future.
II. God uses his foreknowledge to make choices, including selecting servants.
III. Foreknowledge is not foreordination, neither is foreordination, predestination.

*Knowing the future is not causality, making
or forcing the future to happen.*

Some folks may have been taught that since God is all knowing and all powerful that he must somehow totally control the future. Have they considered that position in the light of scripture? Knowing the future and causing the future are two entirely different things. Having the power to control everybody and everything does not mean that God chooses to do so. For now, let's consider the idea that knowing the future does not equate to causing the future to happen.

For example, let's say you're sitting at an outdoor coffee shop and someone pulls up in a car and parks very close to you. You hear the sound of air hissing, and looking over, you see a nail sticking out of the car's tire. Based on your foreknowledge of tires, when the person gets out, you inform him that there's a nail in his tire and that the tire will soon go flat. The driver tells you that he'll get it fixed tomorrow, but you insist that you know it won't last that long and that it will go flat soon. The man promptly ignores your advice and sits down and drinks a cup of coffee. Minutes later, the driver of the car returns to find the tire flat and proceeds to blame you for causing his tire to go flat, because you "knew" it would happen. You indeed had foreknowledge. You foreknew that his tire would go flat, but you certainly did not cause it to go flat. I trust that this simple illustration demonstrates that foreknowledge is not causality. Let's consider a few Bible examples showing that knowing the future is not forcing the future.

Bible example 1: The Lord Jesus said in John's gospel:

> "I am come in my Father's name, and
> ye receive me not: if another shall come in
> his own name, *him ye will receive*" (John
> 5:43; emphasis mine).

I'm sure we would all agree that the Lord Jesus fore-knew all things. With that in mind, this scripture demands a choice; either the Lord, by his declaration, is *forcing* people to receive a false messiah by saying "him ye will receive," or the Lord is simply *telling* people what is going to happen in the future. Let's consider the fuller context of John 5.

> And ye have not his word abiding
> in you: for whom he hath sent, him ye
> believe not. Search the scriptures; for in
> them ye think ye have eternal life: and they
> are they which testify of me. And ye will
> not come to me, that ye might have life. I
> receive not honour from men. But I know
> you, that ye have not the love of God in

you. I am come in my Father's name, and
ye receive me not: if another shall come in
his own name, him ye will receive. (John
5:38–43)

In verse 38, we learn that this group of people had no
faith in Christ, "*ye believe not.*"

In verse 39, the Lord encourages them to "Search the
scriptures," in order to gain saving faith, because "faith cometh
by hearing, and hearing by the word of God" (Rom. 10:17).

In verse 40, the Lord does not say, "ye cannot come to
me," but "ye *will not* come to me that ye might have life,"
indicating that they had a choice and that the Lord *knew*
what choice they would make! This is extremely important
to remember.

In verse 41, the Lord was interested in truth and not
being honored of men.

In verse 42, our Lord said, "I know you," which is
comparable to John 2:25. "And needed not that any should
testify of man: for *he knew what was in man.*"

And finally, in verse 43, the Lord is simply telling this
group that they will not come to him and that they will

receive another who comes in his own name. This declaration is based on the foreknowledge of the Son of God and not on the Lord forcing anyone to react in a certain way.

Bible example 2: Recorded in the synoptic gospels is the account of Peter denying the Lord.

Did the Lord predestine or force Peter to deny him, or did our Lord simply know the future?

> "Jesus said unto him, Verily I say unto thee, That this night, before the cock crow, *thou shalt deny me* thrice" (Matt. 26:34; emphasis mine).
>
> "And Jesus saith unto him, Verily I say unto thee, That this day, even in this night, before the cock crow twice, *thou shalt deny me* thrice" (Mark 14:30; emphasis mine).
>
> "And he said, I tell thee, Peter, the cock shall not crow this day, before that *thou shalt* thrice *deny* that thou knowest *me*" (Luke 22:34; emphasis mine).

We are confronted with two options; either the Lord *forced* Peter to deny him or the Lord simply *knew* that Peter would deny him and *foretold* the event. It's absurd to think that the Lord wanted Peter to deny him and forced him to do so. The only other option is that the Lord was merely foretelling the future. Foretelling the future is not forcing the future even as forecasting the weather is not forcing the weather. Let's appreciate the fact that the Lord foretelling us what Peter would do brings glory to himself, even though Peter never thought he would deny his Saviour.

> "The heart is deceitful above all things, and desperately wicked: who can know it?" (Jer. 17:9).

Bible example 3: Concerning the betrayal of Christ by Judas Iscariot

> "And he answered and said, He that dippeth his hand with me in the dish, *the same shall betray me*" (Matt. 26:23; emphasis mine).

Obviously, the Lord didn't *force* Judas to betray him, but was simply manifesting his omniscience. However, we may make a strong argument that someone may have forced Judas to betray the Lord. Yes, the other guy!

> "And after the sop *Satan entered into him.*
> Then said Jesus unto him, That thou doest,
> do quickly" (John 13:27; emphasis mine).

Hopefully, the point clearly emerges that, knowing the future and forcing the future are two very different things. The Lord can "know" the future without "forcing" the future. Believing that God totally forces the future leads to fatalism, which is a self-defeating doctrine. If the future is written in stone and people are merely puppets with no choice of freewill, then why sacrifice one's self for a greater cause? Why suffer needlessly for that which cannot be altered? If man can affect no change in any area of life, then why would Paul write such beautiful words such as…

> "For I speak to you Gentiles, inas-
> much as I am the apostle of the Gentiles,

I magnify mine office: If by any means I may provoke to emulation them which are my flesh, and *might save some of them*" (Rom. 11:13–14; emphasis mine).

"To the weak became I as weak, that I might gain the weak: I am made all things to all men, *that I might by all means save some*" (1 Cor. 9:22; emphasis mine).

Brother Paul was no fool. He chose to obey his calling for service and suffered greatly for the cause of Christ, for which we are extremely blessed. I'm afraid that this is one of those things that either people "get" or "don't get" and a thousand Bible examples will make no difference. The great Apostle Paul didn't have a fatalist view, i.e., he believed in preaching the gospel to everyone so that each individual might choose, resulting in the salvation of some.

Bible example 4: Concerning the crucifixion of Christ

"Him, being delivered by the *determinate counsel* and *foreknowledge* of God, ye

have taken, and by wicked hands have crucified and slain" (Acts 2:23; emphasis mine).

We would all agree that God had the crucifixion
planned before the creation. God, because of his foreknowledge, determined that the blood of Christ would be
the only remedy for man's sin. However, God didn't predestinate or force anyone to participate in the crucifixion,
but he did know who would. Perhaps the best example of
all—to demonstrate that election, predestination, and foreknowledge have nothing to do with force—is the crucifixion of the Son of God. God's Son was chosen/elected by
the determinate counsel and foreknowledge of God to be
crucified, yet the Lord Jesus said:

Therefore doth my Father love me,
because *I lay down my life*, that I might
take it again. *No man taketh it from me*, but
I lay it down of myself. I have power to lay
it down, and I have power to take it again.
This commandment have I received of my
Father. (John 10:17–18; emphasis mine)

The Lord Jesus was selected, chosen, and *elected* to die for mankind because he was willing. He was not elected and then forced to be made willing. We see this same principle with Mary, the mother of baby Jesus.

Bible example 5: God didn't force Mary; he received her permission.

Mary was foreordained/predestined to bring forth baby Jesus, not simply because God chose her to do so, but God chose Mary because he *foreknew* that she would be willing. Even so, the scriptures record Mary's consent, which was absolutely necessary for the Holy Ghost to proceed.

> And the angel answered and said unto her, The Holy Ghost shall come upon thee, and the power of the Highest shall overshadow thee: therefore also that holy thing which shall be born of thee shall be called the Son of God. And, behold, thy cousin Elisabeth, she hath also conceived a son in her old age: and this is the sixth month with her, who was called barren.

For with God nothing shall be impossible. *And Mary said,* Behold the handmaid of the Lord; *be it unto me according to thy word.* And the angel departed from her. (Luke 1:35–38; emphasis mine)

Bible example 6: Jacob

Jacob was chosen for God's service before he was born, but Jacob, of his own free will, chose to obey God's call to service after he tested God and found him faithful.

And Jacob vowed a vow, saying, *If* God will be with me, and will keep me in this way that I go, and will give me bread to eat, and raiment to put on, So that I come again to my father's house in peace; *then* shall the LORD be my God: And this stone, which I have set for a pillar, shall be God's house: and of all that thou shalt give me I will surely give the tenth unto thee. (Gen. 28:20–22)

Let's recall the wonderful context of this passage. Jacob was fleeing for his very life from his brother Esau. Jacob was not yet fully convinced of God's divine protection and power, so he makes a deal with God. *If* you will do a miracle and keep me (keep my brother from killing me) and give me the necessities of life, so that I return to Esau in peace, (giving Esau enough time to calm down), *then* you will be my God. Of course, God, knowing the future, answered Jacob's prayer and gained a servant. How could God choose Jacob for service before he was even born? Simple, God, because of his foreknowledge, knew the future. God knew that Jacob would eventually accept the Lord's will. God did not force Jacob to do anything; God didn't need to because he knew the future.

Bible example 7: Adam and Eve

Adam and Eve fell by choice, rejecting God's word not to eat, in favor of the devil's promise to be as gods. God knew what man would choose and, because of his foreknowledge, made provision for fallen mankind's redemption. God in no way wanted Adam and Eve to make the wrong decision that led to separation and eventual death, but he did foreknow all.

God uses his foreknowledge to make choices, including selecting servants.

Example 1. The context here in Romans eleven is the Jewish nation.

> "God hath not cast away *his people* which he foreknew. Wot ye not what the scripture saith of Elias? how he maketh intercession to God against *Israel,* saying" (Rom. 11:2; emphasis mine).

In this context, "his people" refers to the nation of Israel. Let's see a fuller context.

> I say then, Hath God cast away his people? God forbid. For I also am an Israelite, of the seed of Abraham, of the tribe of Benjamin. God hath not cast away

his people which he *foreknew.* Wot ye not what the scripture saith of Elias? how he maketh intercession to God against *Israel,* saying, Lord, they have killed thy prophets, and digged down thine altars; and I am left alone, and they seek my life. But what saith the answer of God unto him? I have reserved to myself seven thousand men, who have not bowed the knee to the image of Baal. Even so then at this present time also there is *a remnant according to the election of grace.* And if by grace, then is it no more of works: otherwise grace is no more grace. But if it be of works, then is it no more grace: otherwise work is no more work. (Rom. 11:1–6; emphasis mine)

We may imagine some mysterious force choosing individuals for eternal life and excluding others. However, nothing could be further from the truth. God has chosen Israel for service, i.e., to do certain jobs such as, to bear his name among the Gentiles, to bring forth the scriptures, and to bear the Messiah. The world has the scriptures and a Saviour today because of the Jews.

> "What advantage then hath the Jew? or what profit is there of circumcision? Much every way: chiefly, because that unto them were committed the oracles of God" (Rom. 3:1–2).

The Jewish nation, through Mary, brought forth Christ, the Saviour of the world. The Jewish nation is, at present, not doing a very good job of bearing the name of God to the world, but God will yet choose Israel for service, because he alone knows the future. God knows that during the tribulation, Israel will repent nationally and return to God, but in the meantime, or as Paul states, at this present time also, there is a remnant according to the election of grace. Paul isn't teaching some weird doctrine here, but is merely stating two facts. One: that there are a few Jews (a remnant) believing the gospel of grace and not the false gospel of works. Two: this remnant of Jews who have believed in Christ has been chosen to serve God by

His grace. In other words, every person who receives Christ as Saviour is chosen (elected) by God's grace to serve him. The Gentiles are the majority of the election according to grace and the Jews are the minority or remnant of the election according to God's grace.

Example 2: Peter's service and God's foreknowledge

> Peter, an apostle of Jesus Christ, to the strangers scattered throughout Pontus, Galatia, Cappadocia, Asia, and Bithynia, *Elect* according to the *foreknowledge* of God the Father, through sanctification of the Spirit, unto obedience and sprinkling of the blood of Jesus Christ: Grace unto you, and peace, be multiplied. (1 Pet. 1:1–2; emphasis mine)

Here, the apostle Peter declares himself to be elect according to the foreknowledge of God. Peter is simply saying that God chose him for service; in this case, to be an apostle based upon God's foreknowledge. A problem is created when people are taught that election is for salvation when it's not. Election is never for salvation; it's always for service. If you find a verse that seems to suggest that election is for salvation, it's because you are not rightly dividing it. God choosing individuals for service, based upon his foreknowledge, is the entire Bible pattern of God's election. God chooses all, each and every servant based on his foreknowledge. Let's look at a very simple illustration to see how practical God is.

The Bible teaches that humans are made in the image of God, and we, like God, make choices every day based on our foreknowledge. For example, if you need to move a piano, do you choose people alphabetically, by singing ability, or based on your foreknowledge of who's the strongest? Some individuals are better suited to some jobs based on their abilities, so we tend to choose our helpers based on our foreknowledge of their potential performance. The point is that if we have enough common sense not to pick the smallest and weakest people to move a piano, God can certainly elect and choose individuals for service based on his complete foreknowledge. Just like us, God may not always choose the biggest and strongest to move his piano or provide some other service. Sometimes, our choice must be the willing souls and not the most qualified. Although it may take smaller, weaker people more time and effort to move a piano, those willing to do the work, will get the job. In like manner, the Lord chose all of his servants. Moses said that he was "slow of speech, and of a slow tongue," while Paul declared that "I be rude in speech." We would all like to have the speaking ability of these great men of God, but they didn't see themselves as talented. We know that Aaron could "speak well" and Paul was not counted among James and John, the sons of Zebedee, who were called "the sons of thunder," but that's God's point. The Lord chooses for each believer a task which *he knows* they are able to do. Our chosen tasks may not be easy, but God knows, because of his foreknowledge, which task to assign to whom. This is God's election; choosing believers for service based on his foreknowledge. You may say, "But God elected people before he even made the world!" Yes, of course our omniscient Lord didn't need to force anyone to be saved or to serve him. God, because of his fantastic foreknowledge, simply knew who would repent and receive Christ, and who would have what abilities and willingness for his service. God made his election and selections based on his foreknowledge without any force to anyone. Our Saviour is also our greatest example of service. Looking deeper into our Saviour's election for service based upon the foreknowledge of the Father, we learn several things. Firstly, the Father chose the Son to provide salvation to the world, knowing that only he *could* do the job.

> "And he is the propitiation for our sins: and not for ours only, but also for the sins of the whole world" (1 John 2:2).

Second, the selection and election of the Son by the Father was based upon the Father's foreknowledge.

> Forasmuch as ye know that ye were not redeemed with corruptible things, as silver and gold, from your vain conversation received by tradition from your fathers; But with the precious blood of Christ, as of a lamb without blemish and without spot: Who verily was *foreordained*

before the foundation of the world, but was manifest in these last times for you. (1 Pet. 1:18–20; emphasis mine)

Third, the Father not only knew Christ's ability to do redemption's work, but also his *willingness* to do it, because of his foreknowledge. Thus, Christ Jesus was chosen to bring salvation because the Father knew he *would* do it.

Therefore doth my Father love me, because I lay down my life, that I might take it again. No man taketh it from me, but *I lay it down of myself.* I have power to lay it down, and I have power to take it again. This commandment have I received of my Father. (John 10:17–18; emphasis mine)

My dear friends, God is not the God of force. That's the other guy! God is a God of love and compassion. Following are just a few examples out of many.

"But thou, O Lord, art a God *full* of *compassion*, and gracious, longsuffering, and plenteous in mercy and truth" (Ps. 86:15; emphasis mine).

"But when he saw the multitudes, he was moved with *compassion* on them, because they fainted, and were scattered abroad, as sheep having no shepherd" (Matt. 9:36; emphasis mine).

"And Jesus went forth, and saw a great multitude, and was moved with *compassion* toward them, and he healed their sick" (Matt. 14:14; emphasis mine).

"Then Jesus called his disciples unto him, and said, I have *compassion* on the multitude, because they continue with me now three days, and have nothing to eat: and I will not send them away fasting, lest they faint in the way" (Matt. 15:32; emphasis mine).

I understand that Hollywood made a movie entitled *The Passion of the Christ.* We would do well to forget about that movie and consider and have more appreciation for the *compassion* of the Christ.

Regardless of our belief system, we would all agree that we serve a great God. Let's consider two scenarios in order to see which one speaks to the greater God. In scenario number one, God chooses some people for heaven and some people for hell based on his own will. He proceeds to create mankind and control him by calling some with irresistible grace while withholding this grace from others, so as to arrive at his desired outcome. In scenario number two, God wants all people to be saved and enjoy heaven. However, God knows before he creates man that he will fall, so he provides salvation's plan in advance for all. God also pleads with mankind to receive life and, after salvation, to serve him with the promise of rewards. He gives each person a free will to choose for both salvation and service, but because he is omniscient, he can choose his servants based upon those whom he knows will be willingly saved and want to serve. Which is the greater God, the one who chooses some individuals for salvation and forces his desired outcome, or the God who gives every person a free will and foreknows the choices of every man and fashions his plans accordingly? The latter is the greater God by far.

Example 3: Let's return to the account of Moses to appreciate God's foreknowledge.

> And Moses said unto the LORD, O my Lord, I am not eloquent, neither heretofore, nor since thou hast spoken unto thy servant: but I am slow of speech, and of a slow tongue. And the LORD said unto him, Who hath made man's mouth? or who maketh the dumb, or deaf, or the seeing, or the blind? have not I the LORD? Now therefore go, and I will be with thy mouth, and teach thee what thou shalt say. And he said, O my Lord, send, I pray thee, by the hand of him whom thou wilt send. And the anger of the LORD was kindled against Moses, and he said, Is not Aaron the Levite thy brother? I know that

he can speak well. And also, behold, he cometh forth to meet thee: and when he seeth thee, he will be glad in his heart. (Exod. 4:10–14)

Observe:

1. God wanted Moses to be the chief speaker.
2. Moses refuses to be the chief speaker.
3. God became angry with Moses.
4. God foreknew Moses's stubbornness and was not caught off guard, he simply substituted Aaron.

Foreknowledge is not foreordination, neither is foreordination, predestination.

Here are some simple definitions for your consideration:

- foreknowledge: God knowing what will happen before it does.
- foreordain: God planning what will happen before it does.

- predestination: God bringing to pass what he determined would happen.

Those who repent and believe the gospel are predestined for heaven and those who reject the gospel are predestined for hell. The fact that God knows what decision each person will eventually make has absolutely no bearing on man's freewill to choose. Do you recall the illustration of the car and the flat tire? Did you know the tire would go flat based on your foreknowledge? Yes, but did you cause the tire to go flat? No. Does God know who will reject the gospel? Yes. Does God cause them to reject the gospel? No. Does God know who will accept the gospel? Yes. Does God cause them to accept the gospel? No. Once more, knowing the future is not causing the future to happen. Below are a few more examples.

Example 1: Back to the example of Peter's denial.

If my grandson asks me for a pocketknife and he's allowed to have one, I know, before I give him one, that sooner or later he will cut himself. If I then give him a pocketknife and tell him to be careful, it can't be said that

I forced him to cut himself. If we compare this to Peter's denial of the Lord, we can see that Peter didn't want to deny his Lord, and his Lord certainly didn't want to be denied by Peter, yet because of Peter's human failings, he failed as the Lord knew he would. Simply put, the Lord didn't predestinate or foreordain anyone to betray him, but he did foreknow all the details and wove it into salvation's plan.

Let's look at another example that may be a little more difficult.

Example 2: The church creeps!

> "For there are certain men crept in unawares, who were before of old ordained to this condemnation, ungodly men, turning the grace of our God into lasciviousness, and denying the only Lord God, and our Lord Jesus Christ" (Jude 1:4).

God isn't ordaining certain individuals by name and forcing them to do these evil works, as it may seem, but rather, God is ordaining that those persons who will creep in will be ungodly, lascivious, Christ denying, etc. The point is that the Lord isn't ordaining or condemning any individuals to do a deed, but he is ordaining, based upon his foreknowledge, that the culprits who will do these deeds will be of a certain type. In other words, God has ordained that those who are condemned to do these dastardly deeds are of a certain type. So, God is ordaining or electing/choosing the type of individuals and not the individuals themselves. We are told that certain men crept in and then God proceeds to tell us their certain character or type. This is yet another example of God demonstrating his foreknowledge, ordaining things based upon his foreknowledge. We must always keep in mind that foreknowledge and ordaining are separate actions.

Example 3: The election and foreordaining of our Saviour.

God the Father did love, choose and foreordain his only begotten Son before the creation, to redeem mankind by his blood, based on his foreknowledge.

Father, I will that they also, whom thou hast given me, be with me where I am; that they may behold my glory, which thou hast given me: for thou lovedst me *before the foundation of the world*. (John 17:24; emphasis mine)

Forasmuch as ye know that ye were not redeemed with corruptible things, as silver and gold, from your vain conversation received by tradition from your fathers; But with the precious blood of Christ, as of a lamb without blemish and without spot: Who verily was *foreordained before the foundation of the world*, but was manifest in these last times for you. (1 Pet. 1:18–20; emphasis mine)

God's choosing is never for salvation but is always related to service. The Son of God was both loved by the Father before the foundation of the world and foreordained by him to bring salvation to a lost and dying world. Even as we, as humans, will make preparations before a tragedy (buy supplies etc.), so, too, did the Father make preparation for the fall of mankind before the world was even created; this being done in love based on God's foreknowledge.

Example 4: Another choosing/or foreordaining, based on God's foreknowledge.

> "According as he hath chosen us in
> him before the foundation of the world,
> that we should be holy and without blame
> before him in love" (Eph. 1:4).

This verse does not say that every believer was chosen *for* salvation before the foundation of the world, as some believe. Neither does it say that believers were chosen *to be* in Christ before the foundation of the world. Rather, this verse is teaching that God has chosen, before the foundation of the world, that those who will be in Christ, i.e., born-again, should also be holy and without blame before him in love. The choosing or foreordaining is that every believer in Christ should be of a certain character. Please notice that it doesn't even say that we *must be* holy and without blame…, but that we *should be.* Yes, Christ has chosen before the foundation of the world that every believer "in him," (born-again person) "should be holy and without blame before him in love:" The next verse in Ephesians is much the same.

> "Having predestinated us unto the adoption of children by Jesus Christ to himself, according to the good pleasure of his will" (Eph. 1:5).

All born-again believers are predestined, i.e., slated to be adopted by God. Persons are not predestinated to be born-again believers, but those who become born-again believers, *are* predestinated to also be adopted as God's children, which is also according to the good pleasure of his will. It is God's will and pleasing to him that every born-again believer in Christ also be adopted. Please allow me a short rabbit trail here. I wondered about this next thought for years, that is, if we are born into the family of God, why do we need to be adopted? No one goes to the authorities and asks to adopt a naturally born child into their family, do they? So, are we adopted into the family of God or are we born into it? Well, man is a tripartite being (spirit, soul and body) with two major components; the physical and the spiritual. Spiritually speaking, the human creature is born into the family of God at the moment of conversion. Man's physical component, however, his flesh and the lusts thereof, is foreign and abhorrent to God.

> "For all that is in the world, the lust
> of the flesh, and the lust of the eyes, and
> the pride of life, is not of the Father, but is
> of the world" (1 John 2:16).

For a clearer picture, please read Galatians 5. The spirit of man is born of God. It is the flesh and its nature which must be changed, then adopted by God. The Spirit of adoption is the glorification of man, including the redemption of his body.

> "For ye have not received the spirit of
> bondage again to fear; but ye have received

the Spirit of adoption, whereby we cry, Abba, Father" (Rom. 8:15).

"And not only they, but ourselves also, which have the firstfruits of the Spirit, even we ourselves groan within ourselves, waiting for *the adoption*, to wit, *the redemption of our body*" (Rom. 8:23; emphasis mine).

I appreciate that a person who has been trained to think one way for a long time may have difficulty thinking another way, even if the old way is inferior and the new superior. To use a Bible example; the transition from the Old Testament to the New was such a fantastic, mind-shifting endeavor that God Almighty wrought many miracles, both before, during and after Pentecost, to prove that a change was taking place, away from the Law and Judaism, to a New Covenant. Change can be difficult, but good change is always worth the effort. Aren't you so glad that we don't live under the Old Testament Law? What do you think about those Old Testament believers who were unwilling to change their thinking?

Example 5: More foreknowledge and predestination.

Let's continue in Romans for a bit and examine an often misapplied verse.

> "For whom he did *foreknow*, he also did *predestinate* to be conformed to the image of his Son, that he might be the firstborn among many brethren" (Rom. 8:29; emphasis mine).

First, this verse is not saying, "for whom God did foreknow, he also did predestinate to be saved." Let's separate the individual doctrines here rather than lump them all together, as is often the case. The phrase, "for whom he did foreknow," just means that God knew beforehand those who would receive eternal life. In other words, "For whom he did foreknow," in no way suggests that God chose anyone for salvation. We have seen that foreknowing is not choosing or predestinating; it's only God knowing something in advance. God, here, did not choose in advance individuals to be saved, but rather, he chose in advance that those who would be saved, would also be conformed to the image of his Son. In plain speak, this verse has nothing to do with God choosing anyone for heaven, but rather, deals with God choosing that all believers would be worked on by the Holy Spirit to become more Christlike and conformed to his image. This is the same doctrine taught in Ephesians 1:4 and in the book of Philippians.

> "Being confident of this very thing, that he which hath begun a good work in you will perform it until the day of Jesus Christ" (Phil. 1:6).

The fact that the Holy Ghost will continue to work on each believer *after* salvation is predetermined and written in stone. This fact, however, in no way suggests that believers are chosen to go to heaven *before* salvation. Furthermore, after anyone accepts the Saviour, their conformity is predetermined, i.e., the Holy Spirit will work on him in this life to be conformed to Christ's image. The unsaved either resist or yields to the Holy Ghost for salvation and likewise, believers either yield to or resist the working of the Holy Ghost in their lives after salvation. It's noteworthy that even though every believer in Christ is predestinated to be conformed to the image of Christ, that the Bible still commands the Christian not to quench or grieve the Spirit of God.

> "Quench not the Spirit" (1 Thess. 5:19).
>
> "And grieve not the holy Spirit of God, whereby ye are sealed unto the day of redemption" (Eph. 4:30).

It should be obvious to everyone that the work of the Holy Spirit is never done in man's lifetime. Because man resists the working of the Spirit of God, and other factors as well, the total transformation of man will take place upon death.

Example 6: A quick look at all of the Bible verses using the word predestinate, et. al. together.

1. God predestinated that all believers be conformed to the image of Christ.

"For whom he did foreknow, he also did *predestinate* to be conformed to the image of his Son, that he might be the firstborn among many brethren" (Rom. 8:29; emphasis mine).

2. All believers in Christ were predestinated to be conformed to the image of Christ and were also called.

"Moreover whom he did *predestinate*, them he also called: and whom he called, them he also justified: and whom he justified, them he also glorified" (Rom. 8:30; emphasis mine).

3. God predestinated that all his children, who were born-again, would also be adopted.

"Having *predestinated* us unto the adoption of children by Jesus Christ to himself, according to the good pleasure of his will" (Eph. 1:5; emphasis mine).

4. All the children of God have a predestinated purpose to serve and to obtain an inheritance.

> "In whom also we have obtained an inheritance, being *predestinated* according to the purpose of him who worketh all things after the counsel of his own will" (Eph. 1:11; emphasis mine).

So then, even as election is not God choosing anyone for salvation, neither is predestination God choosing anyone for heaven or hell. God has, however, predestinated that those who accept Christ have a predetermined place, i.e., heaven, and those who reject Christ have a predetermined place, i.e., hell and ultimately, the lake of fire. We may say then with confidence, based upon the clear teachings of the Bible, that *individuals* are not elected to heaven, but are elected to serve God based upon the Lord's foreknowledge; God knowing who will receive Christ. In like manner, *individuals* are not predestined to heaven or hell before they accept or reject Christ, but the *location* of anyone who neglects to accept Christ is predetermined to be hell. Likewise, the *location* of anyone who accepts Christ is predetermined to be heaven. It is therefore the location that God has predetermined based upon the individual's decision and not God predetermining the individual himself to a location before birth, without regard to that person's decision or faith. God's promise once more is…

> "Behold, I stand at the door, and knock: if any man hear my voice, and open the door, I will come in to him, and will sup with him, and he with me" (Rev. 3:20).

Please, appreciate the simplicity of Revelation 3:20 taken at face value and with childlike faith.

1. The Lord is on the outside of man's heart and will not trespass. He must be asked in or let in.

2. The obligation is on man to open the door, for the Lord Jesus will not force it.

3. The Lord promises, "I will come in," not maybe, but "I will," if you will ask me to.

4. To whom is this promise? The Lord said "if any man." Dear reader, please believe God's word with childlike faith and not with some endless complicated system of theology. When the Lord says, "if any man," he means it. Man's way brings frustration and sadness, but God's way brings joy and peace.

5. The simple truth is that if God chose or predestinated individuals to hell, then Revelation 3:20 would be a lie.

Calvinistic thinking is often backwards. One may reason that if God knows that person "X" won't get saved, that this means that person "X" therefore, can't get saved. This is backward thinking. We have seen that, God knowing who will receive or reject salvation, has no bearing on the individual's decision to accept or reject God's salvation. Remember, God wants "all men everywhere" to be saved, the Lord Jesus tasted death for "every man," the Holy

Ghost's job is to reprove "the world" of sin, and the Lord Jesus, in the person of the Holy Spirit, will come in to "any man." If person "X" rejects God's gift of eternal life, then he will appear in the predetermined place called hell. If person "X" receives God's gift of eternal life, then he will appear in the predetermined place called heaven. It's that simple.

Along these same lines, I've heard people defending the belief that God chose some people for heaven and some for hell by stating that, since God did it, it must be right. This, too, is backward thinking. Proper thinking order commands that, if it's not right, then God *didn't* do it! I've also heard the argument that Calvinistic beliefs are a contradiction in the mind of man, but not in the mind of God. This thinking is also backwards, because Calvin's doctrine is assumed to be correct. So, we must accept it, even if it contradicts common sense, rather than putting the doctrine on trial with the Bible as the judge. If we assume that the teachings of any Bible scholar are correct and we must wrest or twist scripture (2 Pet. 3:16) to make it fit what the scholar teaches, then we are flawed in our method of reasoning. Using this method of dishonest scholarship, anyone can make any doctrine "fit."

"That be far from thee to do after this manner, to slay the righteous with the wicked: and that the righteous should be as the wicked, that be far from thee: *Shall not the Judge of all the earth do right?"* (Gen. 18:25; emphasis mine).

Example 7: Let's examine another often misunderstood Bible verse.

"And when the Gentiles heard this, they were glad, and glorified the word of the Lord: and as many as were *ordained* to eternal life believed" (Acts 13:48; emphasis mine).

First, this verse doesn't say ordained *for* eternal life, but ordained *to* eternal life. Second, the Greek word used here for ordained is elsewhere (Acts 15:2) translated determined. This is to say, all of the Gentile individuals of Acts 13:48 who heard the gospel and were determined to receive the gift of eternal life believed. Everyone who has repentance and faith, coupled with a willing heart to call out to Christ, is ordained to eternal life.

Example 8: Foreordination and common sense.

> "And as it is appointed unto men
> once to die, but after this the judgment"
> (Heb. 9:27).

We know, because of this verse and others, that mankind is appointed unto death. We all have an appointment with death, but notice that we are only appointed to die once! Yet, we know that there are two deaths; one physical and one spiritual. The death to which all men are appointed in Hebrews 9:27 is physical. However, all men are *not* appointed to the second "lake of fire" death, which is spiritual.

> "And death and hell were cast into *the*
> *lake of fire.* This is *the second death*" (Rev.
> 20:14; emphasis mine).

The point is that if some people were foreordained to heaven and others to hell, this verse would read something like, "And as it is appointed unto *some* men once to die, and *other men twice* to die, but after this the judgment."

Example 9: Predestination is God's promise to all who receive eternal life.

Once we receive eternal life, all born-again believers are predestined for heaven; otherwise, this next verse could not be true.

> "That *if* thou shalt confess with thy mouth the Lord Jesus, and shalt believe in thine heart that God hath raised him from the dead, *thou shalt be saved*" (Rom. 10:9; emphasis mine).

The Bible does not say, "might be saved, as long as you endure to the end or as long as you keep the faith and do good works to the end." Some born-again believers may very well believe and teach that they can lose their salvation, but what does the Bible say? First, it says, "Thou shalt be saved," not thou might be saved. Second, there is a principle in scripture that God will do what he said he would do, whether or not man believes him.

> "For what if some did not believe?
> shall their unbelief make the faith of God
> without effect?" (Rom. 3:3).

The proper context is about some Jews, who did not believe God's words, but the principle is the same. The principle is that even though some Jews didn't believe the prophecies of God, they still came true regardless of their unbelief. Today, some born-again Christians don't believe God's promise of eternal life. They believe in conditional life or temporary life, which they believe they themselves keep or lose. God, on the other hand, promises to keep the believer by his awesome power (1 Pet. 1:5) apart from man's efforts. In short, once you've been born-again, you're predestined for heaven, whether you believe God's promise or not! If you haven't been born-again, you had better hurry to the cross!

Example 10: God's appointment of those disobedient to the gospel.

> "And a stone of stumbling, and a rock of offence, even to them which stumble at the word, being disobedient: whereunto also they were appointed" (1 Pet. 2:8).

Some may have been taught that this verse means that certain individuals were appointed to disobey the gospel, but this is an incorrect private interpretation. God isn't appointing anyone to be disobedient to the gospel. He is appointing those who choose to be disobedient to the gospel, to stumble or be offended by the rest of the Bible. Again, the appointment here is to those who reject the gospel being disobedient to it. These individuals as disobedient persons to the gospel, are appointed to stumble at the rest of God's word. This is common sense, i.e., if a person rejects the simplest expression of God's love for them as seen in the gospel, how could they possibly understand the deeper Bible truths? They will utterly stumble at the deeper truths of the Bible. So then, the appointment here isn't for anyone to disobey the gospel, but to those who choose to disobey it, they are appointed to stumble. Those who obey the gospel are appointed both Christ as the Rock of their salvation, and further understanding of the word. Conversely, to those who are disobedient to the gospel, Christ is an offence and they are appointed to stumble at the word.

A brief overview of Romans 8:28–39
with a few short comments.

> "And we know that all things work
> together for good to them that love God,
> to them who are the called according to
> his purpose" (Rom. 8:28.)

Everything will eventually work out for good, for those who are saved and are serving God according to his purpose.

> "For whom he did foreknow, he also
> did predestinate to be conformed to the

image of his Son, that he might be the first-
born among many brethren" (Rom. 8:29).

God knew who would be saved and he decided before
anyone was saved, that all those who would be saved, would
begin to be molded to become more Christlike.

"Moreover whom he did predestinate,
them he also called: and whom he called,
them he also justified: and whom he justified, them he also glorified" (Rom. 8:30).

God calls all for salvation, but those whom he knew
would accept Christ, he called and also determined beforehand that they would also be conformed to his likeness.

What shall we then say to these
things? If God be for us, who can be
against us? He that spared not his own
Son, but delivered him up for us all, how
shall he not with him also freely give us
all things? Who shall lay any thing to the

charge of God's elect? It is God that justifieth. (Rom. 8:31–33)

God himself will eventually judge his servants and no
one else.

God himself will judge his servants.

> Who is he that condemneth? It is
> Christ that died, yea rather, that is risen
> again, who is even at the right hand of
> God, who also maketh intercession for
> us. Who shall separate us from the love
> of Christ? shall tribulation, or distress, or
> persecution, or famine, or nakedness, or
> peril, or sword? (Rom. 8:34–35)

What can take away our eternal life? The inference is
that nothing can.

> As it is written, For thy sake we are
> killed all the day long; we are accounted
> as sheep for the slaughter. Nay, in all

these things we are more than conquerors through him that loved us. For I am persuaded, that neither death, nor life, nor angels, nor principalities, nor powers, nor things present, nor things to come. Nor height, nor depth, nor any other creature, shall be able to separate us from the love of God, which is in Christ Jesus our Lord. (Rom. 8:36–39)

Once we receive Christ as our Saviour, nothing can separate us from him.

Is the Future Written in Stone?

What a great question to ponder! Is the future written in stone or can it be altered? The answer must come from examining and comparing the scriptures and not from the mind of man. You may recall my personal testimony, where I stated that I threw away all of my preconceived ideas and let the Bible teach me everything I believe. Have you done this concerning your belief of the future? Have you searched the entire Bible to see what it says itself concerning future events, and the possibility of the timing of future events being changed based upon the believer's prayers? To say the future is written in stone is to suggest that God is forcing the future. To say that the future is random is to suggest that God doesn't know the future. Both of these extreme views gender problems. To make it plain, there are events which God Almighty has ordained to happen that must and will come to pass, but the timing of these events can be changed by prayer.

God sees the future clearly not because he forces his will totally, but because he knows what he himself and every creature will do. People and angels, for example, still make their own decisions; some yielding to God's will and others not. However, the Lord has already made his plans knowing what man will do. The quick answer to this question, "Is the future written in stone?" is yes and no. We will consider several scriptures to back up the yes and no answer, but first the yes.

I. Is The future written in stone? Yes, the future is written in stone!

Example 1: "From that time forth began Jesus to shew unto his disciples, how that he *must* go unto Jerusalem, and suffer many things of the elders and chief priests and scribes, and be killed, and be raised again the third day" (Matt. 16:21).

Example 2: "And ye shall hear of wars and rumours of wars: see that ye be not troubled: for *all these things must come to pass,* but the end is not yet" (Matt. 24:6; emphasis mine).

Example 3: "And they asked him, saying, Why say the scribes that Elias *must* first come? And he answered and told them, Elias *verily cometh first,* and restoreth all things; and how it is written of the Son of man, that he must suffer many things, and be set at nought" (Mark 9:11–12; emphasis mine).

Example 4: "And when ye shall hear of wars and rumours of wars, be ye not troubled: for such things *must* needs be; but the end shall not be yet" (Mark 13:7; emphasis mine).

Example 5: "I was daily with you in the temple teaching, and ye took me not: but the scriptures *must* be fulfilled" (Mark 14:49; emphasis mine).

Example 6: "For as yet they knew not the scripture, that he *must* rise again from the dead" (John 20:9; emphasis mine).

Example 7: "For he *must* reign, till he hath put all enemies under his feet" (1 Cor. 15:25; emphasis mine).

Example 8: "For we *must* all appear before the judgment seat of Christ; that every one may receive the things done in his body, according to that he hath done, whether it be good or bad" (2 Cor. 5:10; emphasis mine).

Example 9: "For the time is come that judgment *must* begin at the house of God: and if it first begin at us, what shall the end be of them that obey not the gospel of God?" (1 Pet. 4:17; emphasis mine)

Example 10: "The Revelation of Jesus Christ, which God gave unto him, to shew unto his servants things which *must* shortly *come to pass*; and he sent and signified it by his angel unto his servant John" (Rev. 1:1; emphasis mine)

These verses are self-evident, proclaiming things which are written in stone and *must*, therefore, come to pass.

II. Is The future written in stone? No, the future isn't written in stone!

Do you believe that prayer changes things? If not, then there is no reason to pray and we become fatalistic. However, if you believe the Bible, then you believe that prayer changes things. In the next section, let's consider *prayers that changed the future*!

Example 1: Before I was born-again, my future was hell, and now that I have received Christ as my Saviour, my future is heaven. Indeed, had I done nothing, and not called upon the name of Jesus, my neglect would have assured me a place in hell. The fact that the Almighty knew that I would believe the gospel, and even when I would believe, had no bearing on my decision to choose Christ. What changed my future? Prayer!

"That *if* thou shalt confess with thy
mouth the Lord Jesus, and shalt believe in
thine heart that God hath raised him from

the dead, *thou shalt be saved*" (Rom. 10:9; emphasis mine).

"For *whosoever shall call* upon the name of the Lord *shall be saved*" (Rom. 10:3; emphasis mine).

Example 2:

In those days was Hezekiah sick unto death. And the prophet Isaiah the son of Amoz came to him, and said unto him, *Thus saith the* LORD, Set thine house in order; *for thou shalt die, and not live.* Then he turned his face to the wall, and prayed unto the LORD, saying, *I beseech thee, O* LORD, remember now how I have walked before thee in truth and with a perfect heart, and have done that which is good in thy sight. And Hezekiah wept sore. And it came to pass, afore Isaiah was gone out into the middle court, that *the word of the* LORD came to him, saying, Turn again, and tell Hezekiah the captain of my people, *Thus saith the LORD*, the God of David thy father, *I have heard thy prayer*, I have seen thy tears: behold, *I will heal thee*: on the third day thou shalt go up unto the house of the LORD. And *I will add unto thy days fifteen years*; and I will deliver thee and this city out of the hand of the king of Assyria; and I will defend this city for mine own sake, and for my servant David's sake. (2 Kings 20:1–8; emphasis mine)

King Hezekiah was told to set his house in order because he was going to die. Hezekiah prayed and fifteen years were added to his life! His prayer certainly changed his future! Later, the king asked the prophet for a sign that he would be healed. Hezekiah was allowed to choose which sign he wanted, but it was the prophet Isaiah's prayer that moved the hand of God!

Example 3:

> And Hezekiah said unto Isaiah, What
> shall be the sign that the LORD will heal
> me, and that I shall go up into the house
> of the LORD the third day? And Isaiah said,
> This sign shalt thou have of the LORD,
> that the LORD will do the thing that he
> hath spoken: shall the shadow go forward
> ten degrees, or go back ten degrees? And
> Hezekiah answered, It is a light thing for
> the shadow to go down ten degrees: nay,
> but let the shadow return backward ten
> degrees. And Isaiah the prophet cried unto
> the LORD: and he brought the shadow
> ten degrees backward, by which it had
> gone down in the dial of Ahaz. (2 Kings
> 20:8–11)

We could consider many other prayers that changed
lives, battles, and the natural course of history. There are
specified events that must happen, because God has said

that they must. There are also specified events that God can change. There are events which man cannot change, such as death, yet there are events which man can change; the greatest of these being his eternal destination through the salvation prayer. We live in a world surrounded by good and evil, and man often chooses the evil, but this is not to say he can't choose the good. I didn't grow up in a Christian home, but one with fighting, yelling and confusion. I decided as an unsaved person that when I grew up, I would have a household free of turmoil. My wife and I had a peaceful household for three years before I was saved, but after my salvation it got even better! My salvation prayer changed my entire life for the better.

What seems to be written in stone often isn't. Events that the Lord said must take place will take place, but it's the timing that is subject to change. In other words, we must all die (save for the rapture), but it's the *timing* that is subject to change. I'm sure you'll agree that the choices we make in life can have a great bearing on our longevity. In a general way, those who are irresponsible with their diets and life habits have a shorter life span on average than do others. Christians are warned that they can be made sick and shorten their lives by partaking of the Lord's table unworthily.

> Example 4: "For he that eateth and drinketh unworthily, eateth and drinketh damnation to himself, not discerning the Lord's body. For this cause many are weak and *sickly* among you, and many *sleep*" (1 Cor. 11:29–30; emphasis mine).

The point here is that the *timing* of our death *is* subject to change based on *our* choices. Remember King Hezekiah? Are there other things which must come to pass, but the timing thereof is subject to change? You decide based on scripture.

> Example 5: The manifestation of the kingdom of heaven

> 1. John the Baptist: "And saying, Repent ye: for the kingdom of heaven *is at hand*" (Matt. 3:2; emphasis mine).

2. The Lord Jesus: "From that time Jesus began to preach, and to say, Repent: for the kingdom of heaven *is at hand*" (Matt. 4:17; emphasis mine).

3. The disciples: "And as ye go, preach, saying, The kingdom of heaven *is at hand*" (Matt. 10:7; emphasis mine).

The kingdom of heaven is the millennial, or the thousand year, reign of Christ on earth. The question is, were all of these preachers pulling peoples' legs by declaring that the kingdom of heaven was at hand? No, of course not, but the kingdom of heaven has still never come. How then could it have been said that it was at hand? Simple, it was! Had the Jewish leadership received Christ as the Messiah, the Lord would have ushered in the kingdom age. I believe that the present church age would have followed the kingdom age instead of vice versa. If you don't think so, that's fine, but you're left with the problem of the Lord and his disciples, together with John the Baptist, not telling the truth. What was the Bible reason that Christ didn't reign in Jerusalem as he and his heavenly Father wanted? The Bible says in Luke: "But his citizens hated him, and sent a message after him, saying, *We will not* have this man to reign over us" (Luke 19:14; emphasis mine).

This brings us to the next point, so prepare to think outside the box! When is the Lord going to return to Israel? We know the Messiah came unto his own, and his own received him not; John 1:11. We also know, because of scripture, when the Lord will return to Israel! No, not the date or calendar year, but the event that triggers Christ's return; *not for the born-again church,* but for Israel. The Lord said concerning his return to Israel, "Ye shall not see me, *until* the time come when…" When what? What must happen to trigger The Lord's return to Israel? Here's the whole verse:

> "Behold, your house is left unto you desolate: and verily I say unto you, Ye shall not see me, until the time come when *ye shall say,* Blessed is he that cometh in the name of the Lord" (Luke 13:35; emphasis mine).

What is the trigger? The Jewish leadership must *say* something! What do they need to say?

"Blessed is he that cometh in the name of the Lord." I see this as a sincere prayer for their Messiah to return. Simply put, the Lord didn't bring in the kingdom at the time it was offered because he was rejected. Furthermore, the Lord won't return until he is *asked* to return. If this doesn't convince you that God is not a forceful God, I don't know what will. Let's consider a corroborating scripture.

> "For I say unto you, Ye shall not see
> me henceforth, till *ye shall say*, Blessed is
> he that cometh in the name of the Lord"
> (Matt. 23:39; emphasis mine).

You may recall that…

Matthew 23 records the *rejection* of the Lord Jesus by the Jewish nation.

Matthew 24 records the *return* of the Lord Jesus to the Jewish nation.

Matthew 25 records the subsequent *restoration* of the Jewish nation or "kingdom of heaven."

The timing of the kingdom age depends upon the prayer of God's chosen nation Israel. On the other side of the coin, God knows the stubbornness of Israel, and we're told that they won't repent nationally until the end of the tribulation period, also called Jacob's trouble.

Are there other Bible events where the timing is changeable depending upon peoples' prayers?

Well, if you believe what the Lord said, yes, there are. Let's examine the aftermath of the abomination of desolation in Matthew 24.

Example 6: "But pray ye that your flight be not in the winter, neither on the Sabbath day: For then shall be great tribulation, such as was not since the beginning of the world to this time, no, nor ever shall be" (Matt. 24:20–21).

Did you see what the Lord said to the Jews? He said "pray." But pray for what? "That your flight be not in the winter, neither on the Sabbath day." The sole logical conclusion is that the Lord will only allow the timing of the abomination of desolation to take place in accordance to the prayers of his people. In other words, if the people of Matthew 24 don't pray responsibly, then their flight will take place in the winter or on the Sabbath day, hindering their escape. However, their faithful prayers can insure a rapid escape. Really folks, if the Lord during the tribulation, can dry up the Euphrates, turn water into blood, shorten the days and perform many other miracles, then how difficult is it for him to restrain or allow the timing of the abomination of desolation according to prayers? All of this makes me wonder about another related subject. That being, if while we're waiting for the Lord to come in the rapture, is it possible that God is waiting too? What would God be waiting for? Possibly, for enough born-again believers to pray as John prayed at the end of the book of Revelation, "Even so, come, Lord Jesus."

Example 7: The great apostle Paul believed that Christian prayers were important and he coveted them.

1. "Brethren, *pray for us*" (1 Thess. 5:25; emphasis mine).

2. "Finally, brethren, *pray for us*, that the word of the Lord may have free course, and be glorified, even as it is with you" (2 Thess. 3:1; emphasis mine).

3. "*Pray for us*: for we trust we have a good conscience, in all things willing to live honestly" (Heb. 13:18; emphasis mine).

And who could forget 1 Thessalonians 5:17, "Pray without ceasing?" Let's study on another question. Who is the greater God? The one who writes the future in stone or the God who sees a future with billions upon billions of variables, decisions and prayers each day, yet sees the future clearly?

To attempt to "prove" the idea that the future is written in stone, I've had friends use verses such as the following examples:

> Example 1: "The steps of a good man are *ordered* by the LORD: and he delighteth in his way" (Ps. 37:23; emphasis mine).

Yes, the steps of a good man are ordered by the LORD. This does not mean that the good man is forced by God to

do anything or has no choice in the matter. The uncompli-
cated understanding of this verse is that a good man will
take his orders from the LORD. If a man doesn't understand
that the LORD wants the best for him and he doesn't see that
it's beneficial for him to obey and have the LORD's blessing,
then he doesn't have to obey. However, a person who does
take his orders from the LORD is a good man, while the one
who chooses not to, isn't so good. The verse is true the way
it's written; the steps of a good man are ordered by the LORD
and a good man will obey God's orders. The good man
willingly *takes* orders from God, but God doesn't force him.

> Example 2: "For as many as are led by the
> Spirit of God, they are the sons of God" (Rom.
> 8:14).

Some may imagine this verse to mean that a person
who doesn't follow the leading of the Spirit of God somehow ceases being a son of God. Of course, common sense
should teach us that this cannot be true. If it were true, we
would need to be saved every day, for who on earth follows
the leading of the Spirit of God sinlessly? The answer is

similar to that of Psalms 37:23. That is to say; God orders our steps, but we don't have to follow unless we want to be good. In the very same way, *every* child of God, i.e., born-again person, is led by the Spirit. This does not mean that every believer *follows* the leading of God's Spirit, but the Spirit does his job and leads each one. Moreover, this verse does not say anything like, "As many as don't follow the leading of the Spirit of God, they cease to be the sons of God."

Example 3: "And why call ye me, Lord, Lord, and do not the things which I say?" (Luke 6:46).

Some have been taught that this verse means that if Christians don't obey the Lord and do the things he says, then they will lose their salvation. This verse is applicable to service and not salvation. As a believer in Christ, if we do not obey, e.g., in church attendance, consistent Bible reading and prayer, we are still a child of God, i.e., Christ is still our Saviour, but not our Lord. We as pastors and church leaders have a tendency to lump salvation and service together and this causes confusion. Christ can be our

Saviour, and we may serve him so minimally that it can't be said that he is our Lord. However, Christ is still our Saviour if we've been truly born-again. By the same token, someone may assume that he is a Christian because he does many good works of service and calls Christ his Lord. Notice the balance between Luke 6:46 and Matthew 7:22–23.

> "And why call ye me, Lord, Lord, and do not the things which I say?" (Luke 6:46).
>
> Many will say to me in that day, Lord, Lord, have we not prophesied in thy name? and in thy name have cast out devils? and in thy name done *many wonderful works*? And then will I profess unto them, *I never knew you*: depart from me, ye that work iniquity. (Matt. 7:22–23; emphasis mine)

The obvious lesson is that all of the good works in the world don't equal salvation. Eternal life comes by receiving Jesus Christ as our Saviour and not by making him Lord. Salvation is knowing the Saviour in a personal way, having received a gift; salvation is not working for a new Lord. Knowing Christ yields eternal life; serving him yields rewards. Trying to serve Christ without receiving him first yields frustration and defeat and no eternal life. Receiving Christ and not serving him yields eternal life and no rewards. Knowing Christ and serving him yields eternal life, peace, joy and rewards in heaven. The proper bottom line attitude is, we need to receive everlasting life as a gift and serve our Lord out of gratitude.

So, let's go back to the future. Is it written in stone? There are events that must come to pass and other events that are subject to change based upon the prayers of God's people. Even though there are events which must come to pass, the timing of some of these events is subject to change based upon the prayers of God's people. When it comes to the subject of the future, instead of saying, "Can God?" We should say, "God can!"

Prayer changes things.

> "*If my people*, which are called by
> my name, shall humble themselves, and
> *pray*, and seek my face, and turn from

their wicked ways; then *will I* hear from heaven, and will forgive their sin, and will heal their land" (2 Chron. 7:14; emphasis mine).

16

The Point System

A point system has been devised to assist with keeping track of the various doctrines within Calvinism. The point system is meant to be applied to the TULIP doctrines which we have considered earlier.

1. *T*otal depravity or total inability of man
2. *U*nconditional election
3. *L*imited atonement
4. *I*rresistible grace
5. *P*erseverance of the saints

We have also established that these are all non-Bible terms, including sovereignty. These terms gender much confusion simply because there are different meanings assigned to these terms by different people. Compounding the confusion is the use of half points and half-truths, as we will see. The way the point system is supposed to work is that each of the letters of the TULIP is to be considered as one point. According to this system, Calvin himself would have been a four-point Calvinist, rejecting point three, the limited atonement of Christ. Another example would be, if someone rejects the election for salvation and irresistible grace, but believes in the other points, he would then be identified as a three-point Calvinist and so on. It gets even more confusing when people say that they believe in half points. Here is how the half point system is supposed to work.

Calvinism a half a point at a time.

1. *T*otal depravity or total inability of man: For example, someone may say that he believes in the total inability of man to save himself, but not to the point that Calvin believed. Calvin believed that man was so depraved that he can't even call out to God. So, if a person says that he believes that a man can't save himself, but that he can call out to God to save him, that would be considered half a point.

2. *U*nconditional election: Under "U," a person may believe in choosing and election, but not to the extent which Calvin believed it. That is, Calvin believed in choosing for salvation. So, if a person believes that God chooses individuals for service and not salvation, that would be another half point.

3. *L*imited atonement: This seems to be an all or nothing doctrine. Either a person believes that Christ's blood is sufficient for all or not. I suppose there may be some kind of a middle of the road, "it is, but it isn't," doctrine, of which I'm thankfully not aware.

4. *I*rresistible grace: Again, a person may believe in the Grace of God, but not as Calvin believed. Calvin believed that God's grace for salvation overpowers or forces people to believe the Gospel. I suppose this is justifiable as grace in some people's minds, because salvation is a good thing. Nevertheless, force is still force and grace is not force. So, if a person believes in biblical grace that is offered and

not irresistible, Calvinistic forced-grace, then that is supposed to be counted as a half point.

5. *Perseverance of the saints:* Finally, the perseverance of the saints the way Calvin believed it was that the believer had to endure to the end. So, if someone rejects perseverance and believes in the biblical doctrine of eternal life, i.e., that children of God are preserved and kept by the power of God, that is supposed to be a half point as well. We have therefore, persons who are labeled one, one and a half, two, two and a half, three, three and a half, four, four and a half, and five point Calvinists. If this sounds confusing to you, then I'm glad; for the Bible declares in 1 Corinthians 14: "For *God is not the author of confusion,* but of peace, as in all churches of the saints" (1 Cor. 14:33; emphasis mine).

This confusing point system and the seemingly endless maze of doctrinal combinations comes from the mind of man and not from God. Briefly stated, Calvinism is so confusing because it mixes man's thoughts with God's thoughts, error and truth. Let's separate fact from fiction.

1. *T*otal depravity or total inability of man:

    Is it true that man can't save himself? Yes! Does this mean that man can't call on the Lord to save him? No!

2. *U*nconditional election:

    Is it true God elects/chooses people? Yes! Does God choose people for heaven or hell? No!

3. *L*imited atonement:

    Is it true that some people will reject God's blood atonement? Yes! Is it true that the blood of Jesus is limited in its saving power? No!

4. *I*rresistible grace:

    Is it true that the Holy Ghost draws people for salvation? Yes! Is it true that people can't resist the Holy Ghost? No!

5. *P*erseverance of the saints:

    Is it true that once a person is born again they have the gift of eternal life and they will never perish? Yes! Is it true that the Bible teaches that they themselves must persevere? No! By its very nature Calvinistic teachings are divisive. The entire point system divides the brethren at every turn. This is contrary to the will of God which is the unity of the Spirit.

> "Endeavouring to keep the unity of
> the Spirit in the bond of peace" (Eph. 4:3).

What exactly is the unity of the Spirit spoken of in the scriptures? No one can say it as well as Paul said it in 1 Corinthians 1:10.

> Now I beseech you, brethren, by the name of our Lord Jesus Christ, that *ye all speak the same thing*, and that there be *no divisions among you*; but that ye be perfectly joined together in the *same mind* and in the same judgment. (1 Cor. 1:10; emphasis mine)

PASTOR KEVIN KLINE

This verse could easily be expanded into a book itself, but we will only consider a few points.

1. In a general way, Paul repeats the same basic concept in one sentence, three times! Sometimes we must read, reread and re-reread before we understand, but when we do understand, it's worth it all.

2. The doctrine of the unity of the Spirit was so important that Paul not only repeated it three times in one verse, but he also pleaded with us to follow it! Did you catch that? Paul used the word "beseech" which means, among other things, to exhort or pray. Paul really wants us to understand this point! But why? Why is this unity thing so important? Well, what's the opposite of unity? Yes, it's needless divisions.

3. Where there is a lack of doctrinal harmony, there is envy, strife and divisions.

"For ye are yet carnal: for whereas there is among you *envying*, and *strife*, and *divisions*, are ye not carnal, and walk as men?" (1 Cor. 3:3; emphasis mine).

Yes, the context of this verse is also doctrine; see verse two. Now, let me ask a question. According to the Bible, what causes divisions within the church? Please don't get upset with me, for I did not write the Bible! Paul knew that the Corinthian church had divisions *and* Paul *knew* the *cause* of their division! What was it? Not according to the author, but according to the Bible, what was the cause of divisions in the church?

The problem:

> "For first of all, when ye come together in the church, I hear that there be *divisions* among you; and I partly believe it" (1 Cor. 11:18; emphasis mine).

The cause:

> "For *there must be* also *heresies* among you, that they which are approved may be

made manifest among you" (1 Cor. 11:19; emphasis mine).

Heresies always cause divisions; the more heresies, the more divisions occur. I would like to elaborate on the Bible concept of unity which is harmony. The prophet Amos taught…

"Can two walk together, except they be agreed?" (Amos 3:3).

A belief structure that has *ten* major divisions based on a system of points and half points will gender unnecessary strife automatically. Not to mention a plethora of seemingly limitless *combinations* of doctrinal points and half points. It's enough to make me pull my hair out, and I can't spare any! On the Arminian side, things are just as bad, if not worse. I have many Amish and Mennonite friends too. If you want to make your mind spin over senseless divisions, please talk to a Mennonite! Ask him about their different sects and conferences and why there are so many. They divide over the most silly things; like the style of a hat, the color of clothes, what technology may and "mayn't," be used. I love my Arminian and my Calvinist friends and I'm not trying to be judgmental or unkind. What do I want? I want people to be made free from religious systems that bring bondage.

> "And ye shall know the truth, and the truth shall *make* you free" (John 8:32; emphasis mine).

This freedom producing truth extends well beyond salvation. In fact, salvation truth isn't the end of freedom; it's the beginning! It makes perfect sense therefore, that there is envy, strife and divisions when there is doctrinal confusion within the church. Without unity and harmony in *doctrine*, a local church *cannot* and *will not* have peace. The Bible says so, thus saith the Lord! This church harmony concept is not an isolated Bible teaching.

> "For where *envying* and *strife* is, there is *confusion* and *every evil work*" (James 3:16; emphasis mine).

Dear reader, you are welcome to believe what you will. I only ask that you consider what you believe in the light of scripture. That is, don't believe what you do just because you were taught it, but because you have studied it out yourself and you have peace about it. The world is full of followers; most Methodists are Methodists because they were taught to be. Most Catholics the same, as well as Buddhists, Muslims and so on. I have read several other "sacred texts," and none other is inspired by God and none rings true like the Holy Bible. I have also studied the theology of the major sects of Christianity. While every denomination has some truth, we should be eager to gain as much truth as possible, regardless of where it takes us. Let's be followers of Christ and not followers of the doctrines of men. Furthermore, when we harmonize all of the Bible doctrines there is true peace and harmony. When we wrest the scripture to make it fit our belief system, we invite strife.

As also in all his epistles, speaking in them of these things; in which are some things *hard to be understood*, which they that are unlearned and unstable *wrest*, as they do also the other scriptures, unto their own destruction. (2 Pet. 3:16; emphasis mine)

Yes, there are things in scripture which are hard to be understood and the Bible warns us not to twist the scriptures, for doing so leads to destruction. When we don't understand the Bible, we can admit our lack and study it out until the scriptures harmonize, or we can take the easy road and twist the scripture to make it fit our understanding. We wrest the scriptures when we say the word "world" in John 3:16 really means "elect." We wrest the scriptures when we teach others that "everlasting" life doesn't really mean "everlasting." We wrest the scriptures when we teach that man has no free will, when the Lord Jesus clearly said he does. We wrest the scriptures when we teach that we obtain, maintain or retain eternal life by our good works. We could go through the five major points of Calvin here and many points of Arminian teachings as well, but this will suffice.

Calvinism and Arminianism are both growing. Calvinism seems to answer some questions which the babes in Christ have asked their unlearned teachers. The teachers, unlearned in pure Bible doctrines, are often, however, very educated with college degrees and very skilled in the TULIP system! They suckle the babes in Christ on half-truths and human reasoning and teach things such as, "a spiritually dead man can't believe anything therefore God must elect him for salvation." On the Arminian side, babes are most often taught to live in fear of losing their salvation, which causes them to either follow the leadership blindly or separate from it. This is true of Calvinistic churches as well, i.e., either persons submit and follow the leadership blindly or *separate* from it, hence the multiplicity of *divisions*. Heresies cause divisions and strife when the unlearned in pure Bible doctrines wrest or twist the scriptures. However, truth leads to unity, harmony and peace.

Review: Heresies cause division.

1. For first of all, when ye come together in the church, I hear that there be *divisions* among you; and I partly believe it. For there must be also *here-sies* among you, that they which are approved may

be made manifest among you. (1 Cor. 11:18–19; emphasis mine)

The unlearned wrest the scriptures.

2. As also in all his epistles, speaking in them of these things; in which are some things hard to be understood, which they that are *unlearned* and unstable *wrest*, as they do also the other scriptures, unto their own destruction. (2 Pet. 3:16; emphasis mine)

The Spirit of God leads us into truth and freedom.

3. Howbeit when he, the *Spirit* of truth, is come, *he will guide you into* all *truth*: for he shall not speak of himself; but whatsoever he shall hear, that shall he speak: and he will shew you things to come. (John 16:13; emphasis mine)

"And ye shall know the truth, and *the truth shall make you free*" (John 8:32; emphasis mine).

I mentioned earlier that both Calvinism and Arminianism are growing. One very large reason for this is that it's easy to adopt a system to follow which seems to answer some of the more difficult questions, but it's extremely labor intensive to study things through and rightly divide the word of truth. In other words, accepting a pre-packaged belief system is easy; building your own on Bible truth takes work. Another reason these systems of man-made doctrines are growing is because we are living in the last days and the Bible told us that people would leave pure Bible doctrines and believe unclean doctrines.

> "Now the Spirit speaketh expressly, that in the latter times some shall *depart from the faith*, giving heed to seducing spirits, and *doctrines of devils*" (1 Tim. 4:1; emphasis mine).

Many babes in Christ, when learning Calvinism or Arminianism for the first time, may see it as new truth, when in fact it's only old heresy. Heresy is confusing and complicated, but there is simplicity in Christ. Anyone can be saved. God wants all to be saved and he gives each saved child the free gift of everlasting life. The differences between what I have presented and what these systems teach may seem very subtle, but they are very important. Please don't allow anyone to corrupt these simple Bible teachings.

> "But I fear, lest by any means, *as the serpent beguiled Eve through his subtilty*, so your *minds* should be *corrupted* from the *simplicity* that is *in Christ*" (2 Cor. 11:3; emphasis mine).

So, let's reconsider the point system. According to a Calvinist, even though I believe all of the Bible doctrines on election, predestination, et. al., I would be a two pointer because I don't believe any of the doctrines the way Calvin believed them. So, do I consider myself a two-point Calvinist? No, I consider myself to be a *zero*-point Calvinist, which is not a Calvinist at all. A very staunch and popular, present-day hyper-Calvinist had this to say about his belief system. He was asked what he called a four-point Calvinist, (usually this refers to someone who rejects the limited atonement doctrine) to which he said, "An Arminian!" His friends thought that was extremely funny, but it wasn't. Think how absurd this statement is; he is calling John Calvin himself an Arminian! You may be thinking that this preacher was just making a joke, but I assure you, he wasn't. He followed up his "funny" remark by saying that hyper-Calvinism (a.k.a. five-point Calvinism) must be taken in its entirety or not at all! I believe this to be the very best advice to date that I have ever received from a Calvinist. If you can't accept all five points of hyper-Calvinism, then reject it all! Hence, my new term, *zero*-point Calvinist.

The Arminian point system.

Arminians have a point system as well! It's not so well defined and clever, yet it is just as persistent. Some who believe they can lose eternal life have lists of sins which a believer may do and not lose salvation, and lists of sins that will result in the loss of salvation. The lists may be written and defined or mental and nebulous, yet they exist. In the extreme case of the sinless perfection crowd, the Bible truth and reality that believers *do* sin is denied! First John was written to born-again believers and the prophet included himself when he wrote:

> "If *we* say that we have no sin, *we* deceive ourselves, and *the truth is not in us*" (1 John 1:8; emphasis mine).

In plain English, any born-again believer in Christ who says he doesn't sin is a liar! I didn't say it; God did, through the prophet. The reason for this sinless perfection heresy stems from a lack of understanding regarding 1 John 3:9.

> "Whosoever is born of God *doth not commit sin*; for his seed remaineth in him: and *he cannot sin*, because he is born of God" (1 John 3:9; emphasis mine).

There are several and varied layers of truth which cannot be explored here for lack of space. However, common sense should teach us that born-again believers *do* sin after salvation. Besides 1 John 1:8, Paul said...

"O wretched man that I am! who shall deliver me from the body of this death?" (Rom. 7:24; emphasis mine).

Please notice that Paul didn't say, "O wretched man that I *was!*" The reality is that I'm not spiritual enough to even be a button on the Apostle's shirt and neither are you. Even an unholy thought is sin. If you are telling me that you've never had an unholy thought since your salvation, then probably one of three things is true. Either you have never had a driver's license, you are deceiving yourself, or you're dead! Of course believers sin; that's why we have a multiplicity of verses such as:

"My little children, these things write I unto you, that ye sin not. And *if any man sin, we have an advocate with the Father,* Jesus Christ the righteous" (1 John 2:1; emphasis mine).

Okay. We realize that believers *do* sin and fall short of God's perfection even after salvation. So, what's the answer to 1 John 3:9? Well, the short answer is that it's not to be taken literally and without the context of many other Bible verses dealing with the same subject matter. First, the phrase "his seed remaineth in him," is a reference to the Holy Ghost which permanently seals and indwells each and every believer. Second, what is the Holy Spirit's job?

1. "And when he is come, he will *reprove the world of sin*, and of righteousness, and of judgment" (John 16:8; emphasis mine)

   After salvation, believers still live in this world! The Spirit of God reproves not just the unsaved in the world of sin, but the saved as well! Do we have any corroborating scriptures? Yes.

2. "Being confident of this very thing, that *he* which hath begun a good work in you *will* perform it until the day of Jesus Christ" (Phil. 1:6; emphasis mine).

   The Spirit of God will not allow you to sin with impunity. There will be consequences for sin! This fact brings us back to 1 John 3:9 and the simple, Bible answer.

3. "Whosoever is born of God *doth not commit sin*; for his seed remaineth in him: and *he cannot sin,* because he is born of God" (1 John 3:9; emphasis mine).

First John 3:9 is saying the same basic thing as John 16:8 and Philippians 1:6, only in a slightly different way. In other words, it's not saying that it's impossible for Christians to sin, but that it's impossible for them to sin and get away with it! There will be consequences, the believer will quench and grieve the Holy Spirit. A paraphrase of 1 John 3:9 in its context, would be something like, "Whoever is born again, can't sin without grieving the Spirit of God, because God's Spirit is sealed within him, so that the believer cannot sin and get away with it like he used to before he became a child of God." Furthermore, the convicting power of the Holy Ghost is one of the ways that we know we are a child of God. This truth is made clear by Hebrews 12:8.

"But *if ye be without chastisement*, whereof *all* are partakers, then are ye *bastards*, and *not sons*" (Heb. 12:8; emphasis mine).

If we can sin and it doesn't bother us, then we have never been born-again! The Holy Ghost *always* does his job, even when we fail. Be advised that sadness, lack of joy, or loss of direction and so on, are part of the chastening power of the Spirit of God. I will share with you a personal experience related to the chastening power of the Holy Ghost in my life almost immediately after salvation. To preface the story: I have never been drunk or even had a can of beer. I've never smoked any tobacco, wacky or otherwise! No, not one puff. I've never had any illegal drugs, which is amazing being born in the fifties and growing up in the sixties and seventies. However, I have done things that I'm ashamed to share. One of those things relates to our Bible subject at hand. Before I was saved, while in Uncle Sam's Air Force, I acquired a foul mouth like my friends and coworkers. One day, after I was saved, I was sitting in my car *alone* and something happened. I have forgotten what it was, but I cursed using my Saviour's name, as was my old occasional habit before salvation. To this day, I get fearful when I recall how my chest tightened up while the words were still in my mouth! I thought I might be having a heart attack at twenty-two years of age! I immediately asked the Lord to forgive me and the tightness went away as quickly as it had come. I have never forgotten that lesson and I still carry a powerful fear of displeasing God. The believer may lose his life, but never his salvation.

Let's return to the Arminian point system and consider its futility from a common-sense point of view. If it were possible to lose everlasting life, which it's not, wouldn't we lose it for the smallest infraction and not just for the *big* sins? Are we to believe that God allows little sins into heaven? The entire idea that sins after salvation can somehow affect eternal life is a doctrine of man and not a doctrine of God. Indeed, it's a heresy which needs to be forsaken. Paul, the self-admitted wretched man, said concerning Christ and the believer's sin…

"Who *delivered* us from so great a

death, and *doth deliver*: in whom we trust

that he will *yet deliver* us" (2 Cor. 1:10; emphasis mine).

Paul knew that he was unworthy of salvation, as we all are, but he trusted not only that God had forgiven his past sins, but his present and future sins too; realizing that a sin can be as simple as a doubt.

"And he that doubteth is damned if he eat, because he eateth not of faith: for whatsoever is not of faith is sin" (Rom. 14:23).

A sin can be as simple as falling short of perfection. If salvation could be lost and son-ship undone, then the believer must live in constant fear of saying or doing the wrong thing. Some "Christians" believe that they need to die in a "state of grace." I put the word "Christians" in quotes because some who call themselves by this name, don't believe the Lord when he said "Ye must be born again." Neither do they understand that the one they call Saviour said, "Except a man be born again, he *cannot see* the kingdom of God." That's right, whether you believe in being born-again or not, whether your church, denomination, pastor or priest believes in being born-again or not. The Lord above all said himself, that if you haven't been born-again, you "cannot" even "see the kingdom of God." Back to the "state of grace" theory. This is a man-made doctrine and nowhere in the Bible do we find such a teaching. However, the way it's supposed to work is that through a priest, pastor or your own confession, your sin is "covered" and you die in a state of grace so your soul can go to heaven. How sad to live your life *hoping* to die in a state of grace. There's a much better way! Receive Christ as your Saviour; trust his saving blood to *take away* your sin, past, present and future!

> "The next day John seeth *Jesus* coming unto him, and saith, Behold the Lamb of God, which *taketh away the sin of the world*" (John 1:29; emphasis mine).

Those who trust Christ and not their own efforts and works can and do have their sins taken away past, present and future, as far as entering heaven is concerned. The futility of trying to keep one's salvation or to die in a state of grace can be summed up in any one of many single verses.

"For whosoever shall keep the whole law, and yet *offend in one point*, he is guilty of all" (James 2:10; emphasis mine).

"Even as David also describeth the *blessedness* of the man, unto whom God imputeth *righteousness without works*" (Rom. 4:6; emphasis mine).

"For the wages of sin is death; but the *gift* of God is *eternal life* through Jesus Christ our Lord" (Rom. 6:23; emphasis mine).

One last question, does your belief system add to the Bible rules or substitute the doctrines of men for the commandments of God? This is error in any context.

"But in vain they do worship me, *teaching for doctrines the commandments of men*" (Matt. 15:9; emphasis mine).

The final thought in this chapter is that God doesn't want you to be confused, but to be at peace in his local assembly.

"For God is not the author of confusion, but of peace, as in all churches of the saints" (1 Cor. 14:33).

Odds and Ends

Starting off on the right foot

In any life venture, it's always important to start off on the right foot. The devil can get us off track on the very first step. He may use our preconceived ideas, prejudices, pride and assumptions to get us off track. Which spiritual foot do you choose to start off on? Intellectual honesty or intellectual dishonesty?

More than once I've had fingers shaking in my face, attached to red-faced, saliva-spraying individuals, insisting that their view of the Bible was correct. The tone of the conversations changed as soon as I asked this one question. "Have you ever read the Bible, I mean, the entire Bible?" Everyone is entitled to their opinion, but please don't insist that your view is correct if you haven't even read the Bible once through! There are two areas of human enlightenment every human being should know. One, there is a God. And two, you're not him! Many years ago, as a child, I came to the realization that I didn't know everything and that I never would. I may not outwardly work alongside those with whom I disagree, but I can still treat them with kindness.

> "And if any man obey not our word by this epistle, note that man, and have no company with him, that he may be ashamed. Yet *count him not as an enemy*, but admonish him as a brother" (2 Thess. 3:14–15; emphasis mine).

We should read the Bible, all of it, even though we don't understand it all. A pastor once told me, "It's not the parts in the Bible that I don't understand that trouble me, it's parts that I do understand!" We'll all get a "real" education on the way up!

I don't believe that either Calvin or Arminius was a devil, but rather sincere men who tried to explain the Bible the best way they could. However, good, honest, intelligent and sincere men can be sincerely wrong. Especially if they start off on the wrong foot or with a false assumption. We will consider more on assumptions later in this chapter. When we apply starting out on the right foot to Calvinism, we can appreciate why it's structured the way it is. If total depravity were true, then unconditional election would be necessary and so on. Calvin's wrong assumption at the beginning caused him to create an unnecessarily confusing system.

Intellectual honesty and Intellectual dishonesty

Intellectual dishonesty explained: We are being intellectually dishonest when we adopt a mind-set such as, I'm going to use the Bible to prove my theology and soteriology. Or, I know Calvinism is correct, therefore anything the Bible says to the contrary must not mean what it says. I will change Bible words and terms to agree with what I already believe to be true. I will change the word "world" to "elect" when it suits me. Likewise, when God says "all men," and it doesn't agree with my preconceived ideas, I will change it accordingly. When "whosoever" doesn't make sense to me, it must be changed as well. When I can't prove what I believe without changing, replacing, or redefining many Bible terms, I will feel justified because I know I'm right. Or, I "know" that salvation can be lost, therefore anything in the Bible that seems to go against this idea must be changed in order to fit with what I believe to be true. "Eternal life" doesn't mean eternal; likewise, I will deny what "everlasting" and "never perish" truly mean. When the Bible declares that eternal life is a "gift," I will either deny it outright or pretend I agree for now and deny it later. I will use the same dishonest scholarship of changing and adding to the Bible words like the other side does, because after all, I'm right and they're wrong.

"Add thou not unto his words, lest
he reprove thee, and thou be found a liar"
(Prov. 30:6).

We have seen in previous chapters that if anyone must change, replace, exchange or reinterpret Bible words to "prove" or make their doctrine understandable, then their doctrine isn't scriptural. If anyone is allowed to change

God's words, then anyone can "prove" anything. When man changes God's words, the scriptures become man's words and not God's. For example, if you and I make a binding contract and I'm able to change the words of that contract, then the contract is worthless to you. Furthermore, God's word can be changed simply by taking it out of context. Remember, any text without a context is a pretext. In other words, anybody can prove anything if he is allowed to take scripture out of context. Further, any Bible teacher must have personal integrity and use intellectual honesty, for we will all face the Lord one day. It's one thing to be sincere, but wrong. And it's quite another thing to know you're wrong and still be unwilling to change and to take scripture out of context. Again, it's much worse to teach error after the Lord has convinced us otherwise.

> "But have renounced *the hidden things of dishonesty, not walking in craftiness, nor handling the word of God deceitfully*; but by manifestation of the truth commending ourselves to every man's conscience in the sight of God" (2 Cor. 4:2; emphasis mine).

"My brethren, be not many *masters*, knowing that *we shall receive the greater condemnation*" (James 3:1; emphasis mine).

The word "masters" here is referring to teachers. If these two verses don't put God's fear in us, perhaps our fear-center is broken. I want the reader to be assured that I believe *all* the Bible doctrines including: man's inability to save himself by works, election, atonement, grace, the soul of man being kept by the power of God, which is eternal life, foreknowledge, predestination and being foreordained/ foreordination. I believe in these Bible doctrines the way the Bible explains them in their contexts and not the popular explanations of some men.

Proving a single doctrine from the Bible is relatively easy, but the challenge comes when we harmonize without contradiction all the Bible doctrines. When we don't understand a verse or passage, do we change the words or grab another Bible version to make it fit with what we believe to be true? Or, do we just forget about it? When we don't understand a doctrine, we should admit it, pray about it and be willing to change our doctrine when it doesn't fit with the Bible. It's important to believe that the Bible doesn't need us to interpret it. That is, the Bible will interpret itself when rightly divided. Another way to say it is, that the Bible doesn't need to be re-translated, reinterpreted or changed to make it understandable, but we need to change our understanding to match the Bible. I've been taught by "my betters" that the Bible is like a lion; we don't need to defend it, just open the cage and it will defend itself! We need to approach the Holy Book as we would God Himself, i.e., as being complete without us, allowing God and his word to speak, without changing anything in it.

I started out reading the Bible at twenty-two years of age, with the attitude in the back of my mind that I would find the mistakes, errors and contradictions that I had been told were there. I found out in short order that the problems weren't in the Bible, but in me. In brief, we aren't supposed to change the Bible, we're supposed to let the Bible change us! Dear reader, don't change the Bible to suit you; let the Bible change you to suit God.

"And be not conformed to this world: but *be ye transformed* by the renewing of your mind, that ye may prove what is that good, and acceptable, and perfect, will of God" (Rom. 12:2; emphasis mine).

Intellectual honesty explained

Intellectual honesty is having a proper attitude and is indeed the way to start out on the right foot. I believe that all the Bible is true. How can all of the Bible doctrines harmonize without contradiction? When I don't understand a verse or passage…

1. I will not change the words to make it fit with what I assume to be true.
2. I will not ignore it and forget about it.
3. I will pray about it and be willing to change my doctrine when it doesn't fit with the Bible.
4. I will not decide what I believe based on my acceptance into a group, fellowship or denomination.

5. I will remember that the Bible doesn't need me to interpret it.

6. I will remember that the Holy Scriptures will interpret themselves when rightly divided.

7. I need to approach the Holy Book as I would God himself, i.e., as being complete without me, allowing God and his word to speak excluding any changes.

Using confusing and non-biblical words and terms

I was confused about Calvinism for many years. It wasn't until I made a detailed study of all the Bible words and non-Bible words associated with Calvinism that the confusion began to lift.

"For God is not the author of confusion, but of peace, as in all churches of the saints" (1 Cor. 14:33).

Let's decide to do something noble and end the confusion. Whether intentionally or not, Calvinism not only adds many non-biblical terms to its teachings, but also changes the meanings of some Bible words and terms. Confusion like a flood is invited in doctrine's door, because all of the five major points of the TULIP are non-biblical terms. The tangled ball of confusing terms, misunderstood Bible words, and shortsighted human reasoning ensure chaos. Without defining the terms in any discussion, the discussion will lead to futility and a waste of time. Why does Calvinism and Arminianism confuse people? It's because with Calvinism, one can never truly know if he is "chosen" or not. Conversely, with Arminianism, one can never truly know if he has sufficient works or not. Both systems become a mixture of truth and error resulting in a non-sequitur, contradictory, "that does not compute," scenario. This brings us to the historical story of Alexander the Great and the Gordian knot. There existed a prophesy in the days of Alexander the Great that whoever was able to undo the Gordian rope type knot would conquer Asia. Alexander, being a man of action, didn't fumble around trying to undo the knot, but rather drew his *sword* and sliced through it! The knot was indeed undone and Alexander did go on to conquer Asia. May we not waste our lives fumbling with a confusing puzzle, but rather may we draw the sword of the Spirit and boldly slice through the knotted ball of man-made doctrine.

> "And take the helmet of salvation, and *the sword of the Spirit*, which is *the word of God*" (Eph. 6:17; emphasis mine).
>
> "For *the word of God* is quick, and powerful, and *sharper than any twoedged sword*, piercing even to the dividing asunder of soul and spirit, and of the joints and marrow, and is a discerner of the thoughts and intents of the heart" (Heb. 4:12; emphasis mine).

The alternative to undoing the knot of Calvinism is to spend an inordinate amount of time and energy virtually rewriting the Bible in an attempt to make it fit.

Things are no better in the Arminian camp. "Everlasting life" doesn't mean everlasting, neither does "eternal life" retain its meaning, nor the term "never perish." A "gift" becomes twisted into something one must either work to get or work to keep. Adding to the confusion, most Arminians have been taught all their lives that "backsliding" means losing their salvation. Have you ever studied the word backsliding for yourself? It's not even a New Testament term, let alone a term directly applicable to born-again persons. It's simply a term used to describe people turning away from God's truth. In modern conversations we most often use the word apostasy. In short, both believers and nonbelievers can turn away from truth. When a believer turns away from truth, he may risk his joy, peace, life, and/or rewards, but never his soul which God purchased. The confusion never stops for a true Arminian, for one can never "know" what sins or how many, may undo God's promise of eternal life. Intellectual honesty comes down to a simple concept. Can you prove what you believe without adding to, taking away or replacing any Bible words or their meanings?

Assumptions: Don't be caught in any of these traps.

1. If Calvinism is wrong, therefore Arminianism must be true.

2. If Arminianism is wrong, therefore Calvinism must be true.

3. If Calvinism has some truth, therefore we must accept it all blindly.

4. If Arminianism has some truth, therefore we must accept it all blindly.

With any two views we may have the following possibilities:

1. One could be right and the other wrong.

2. Both could be right: E.g., one side says Jesus is the Son of man, the other the Son of God.

3. Both could be wrong.

4. Both could have some truth.

There are in fact three main views:

1. Calvin's

2. Arminius'

3. God's

Wrong assumptions often made by some Calvinists

1. If a person says they're not a Calvinist, then they must be Arminian.
2. A spiritually dead person can't do anything, e.g. repent, believe the gospel.
3. God's choosing/election is for salvation. I offer John 15:16 again, because this seems to be every Calvinist's first defense.

> "Ye have not chosen me, but I have chosen you" (John 15:16).

The Bible choosing is actually for service.

> Ye have not chosen me, but *I have chosen you*, and ordained you, that ye should go and *bring forth fruit*, and that your fruit should remain: that whatsoever ye shall ask of the Father in my name, he may give it you. (John 15:16; emphasis mine).

Wrong assumptions often made by Arminians

1. A person may lose eternal life.
2. If a person believes in eternal security, he must be a Calvinist.
3. Service is necessary for salvation.
4. Parables are on par with didactical books and church epistles. Note: Please remember that the gospels were all written concerning events happening *before* Acts 2.

Popular Arminian assumptions and word replacements

When we read the Bible, we must not assume words such as "disciple," "inheritance" and "part," have anything to do with entering heaven.

> "So likewise, whosoever he be of you
> that forsaketh not all that he hath, he cannot
> be my *disciple*" (Luke 14:33; emphasis mine).
>
> "For this ye know, that no whore-
> monger, nor unclean person, nor covetous

man, who is an idolater, hath any *inheritance* in the kingdom of Christ and of God" (Eph. 5:5; emphasis mine).

"And if any man shall take away from the words of the book of this prophecy, God shall take away his *part* out of the book of life, and out of the holy city, and from the things which are written in this book" (Rev. 22:19; emphasis mine).

A person can be truly saved, without being a "disciple." Likewise, a person may be a Christian and have no rewards or "inheritance" in heaven. When God takes someone's "part" out of the book of life, in Revelation 22:19, he is removing their rewards, not their name. When we read the scripture, we must not alter it or change its meaning.

Will you believe this...

"For by grace are ye saved through *faith*; and that not of yourselves: it is the gift of God" (Eph. 2:8; emphasis mine)

Or, will you believe this…

"For by faith are ye saved through *works*; and that not of yourselves: it is the gift of God" (Eph. 2:8; emphasis mine).

Will you believe this…

"Keep yourselves in the *love* of God, looking for the mercy of our Lord Jesus Christ unto eternal life" (Jude 1:21; emphasis mine).

Or, will you assume it means this…

"Keep yourselves in the *salvation* of God, looking for the mercy of our Lord Jesus Christ unto eternal life." (Jude 1:21; emphasis mine).

Will you believe this…

> "Wherefore, my beloved, as ye have always obeyed, not as in my presence only, but now much more in my absence, *work for* your own salvation with fear and trembling" (Phil. 2:12; emphasis mine).

Or, will you believe what the Bible actually says…

> "Wherefore, my beloved, as ye have always obeyed, not as in my presence only, but now much more in my absence, *work out* your own salvation with fear and trembling" (Phil. 2:12; emphasis mine).

The "work out" here is comparable to 2 Peter 3:18.

> "But grow in grace, and in the knowledge of our Lord and Saviour Jesus Christ. To him be glory both now and for ever. Amen" (2 Pet. 3:18).

This is to say that God wants us to "grow" up in our salvation and not remain a babe. This makes perfect sense when we read 2 Peter 3:18 in its context.

> Wherefore, my beloved, as ye have always obeyed, not as in my presence only, but now much more in my absence, *work out* own salvation with fear and trembling. For it is *God which worketh in you* both to will and to do of his good pleasure. *Do all things without murmurings and disputings.* (Phil. 2:12–14; emphasis mine)

The conclusion is that John Calvin was right about some things and not right about others. The same goes for Jacobus Arminius. Neither system of belief, however, is totally correct or biblical. Please feel free to do with this man-made book, as with any of man's works; eat the meat and spit out the bones. Also, be reminded that there were Bible-believing Christians long *before* either Calvin or Arminius.

Assumptions made by most all of us

There is only one definition of the word church. While it is true that the word church generally means a called-out assembly, specifically it has many different meanings. Each occurrence of the word "church" must be defined by its individual context. To assume that the word church is always to be applied to born-again or redeemed persons is to violate scripture. Moses ministered to a "church" of redeemed and non-redeemed persons, as did The Lord Jesus and John, as he wrote to the churches of Asia. Each of these professing churches being separate and distinct from the possessing church. The possessing church consisting of all the born-again believers with no non-redeemed persons. Failure in understanding these distinctions will result in limited understanding of deeper Bible truths.

Next is an assumption most of us make or have made because of Calvinistic influences. When we want someone to make sure of their salvation, do we use this verse?

"Wherefore the rather, brethren, give
diligence to make your *calling* and *elec-*

THE DOCTRINE OF ETERNAL LIFE

tion sure: for if ye do these things, ye shall never fall" (2 Pet. 1:10; emphasis mine).

The problem is that we *may* be thinking of this a little backwards. Do we apply the "election" to salvation? Do we apply the "calling" for service? We have seen that Bible election is always for service and never for salvation. What then is the natural order? Do we find our "calling" for service and then receive the Lord's salvation and assurance of salvation? No, that's backwards. We receive Christ as Saviour and then we serve as the Lord has chosen. We are "called" for salvation and "chosen" for service. The Lord is asking that we make our "calling" for salvation and our "election" for service sure. Also, since believers are called for salvation and called to be servants, we may also understand this verse to mean that God is asking us to make our general "calling" to serve sure and our "election" or specific chosen area of service sure as well.

One last assumption that most of us make or have made because of liberal influences. Please, as quickly as you can, finish this next sentence. If thy brother trespass against thee…

Did you say, "Forgive him?" Here's what the Bible actually says.

> "Take heed to yourselves: If thy brother *trespass* against thee, *rebuke* him; and if he *repent, forgive* him" (Luke 17:3; emphasis mine).

Do you see a process here? The liberals have wrongly taught us to blindly forgive without repentance! Did The Lord forgive you before or after you asked him? After, of course. The process is that the offended party is to go to the offender. The offended party is not supposed to ignore, avoid or tell someone else about the offence, but to go to the offender and tell him. This is a rebuke; telling the offender in love, seeking restoration. When the Bible says "If," that means that there's a condition here; he repents, then you forgive. Notice that the Bible doesn't say, make thy brother feel like dirt or make him apologize ten times. You must forgive him if there is true repentance. This is a social pattern in scripture beneficial to all dispensations. No wonder there are so many relationship problems in churches. If you're a preacher, please preach this Bible process regardless of your stand in other areas; your congregation, fellowship or audience will be blessed.

Observations

If you consider yourself a Calvinist, the observations that I'm about to share may not apply to you personally. These are my general observations and the tendencies of some Calvinists I have known.

Many elements of Calvinism are backwards. A person is supposedly chosen by God for salvation and then they repent and believe the gospel. As we have seen in previous chapters, this is backwards. The Bible pattern being repent and believe before salvation or service. Further, Calvinism teaches "if God" chooses you will be saved, while the Bible teaches 'if you, thou, ye" et. al. will open the door, God will come in.

> "Behold, I stand at the door, and knock: *if any man* hear my voice, and *open* the door, I will come in to him" (Rev. 3:20; emphasis mine).

"I am the door: by me if any man
enter in, he shall be saved" (John 10:9).

You may have been taught that you must wait for God to be saved, but these verses tell us that God is waiting for you to open the door. In Calvinism, the onus, burden and obligation is taken off of man where God placed it and is put back on God where it doesn't belong. This is the reverse of the teaching in scripture. In this concept of salvation, Calvinism is irreconcilably backward. A Calvinist may reason that if God knows that person "X" won't get saved, that this means that person "X," therefore, can't get saved. This also is backward thinking. We have seen that God knowing who will receive or reject salvation has no bearing on the individual's decision to accept or reject God's salvation. Remember, God wants "all men everywhere" to be saved and the Lord Jesus tasted death for "every man," and the Holy Ghost's job is to reprove "the world" of sin, and the Lord Jesus, in the person of the Holy Spirit, will come in to "any man." If person "X" rejects God's gift of eternal life, it's not because God wanted or forced him to. By the same token, if person "X" receives God's gift of eternal life, it's likewise not because God forced him to do so. God "know-ing" the future in no way "forces" our present moment into a fatalistic box. That would be backward thinking.

Along these same lines, I've heard people defending the belief that God chose some people for heaven and some for hell by stating that, since God did it, it must be right. This is more backward thinking. Proper thinking order commands that, if it's not right, then God *didn't* do it! I've also heard the argument that Calvinistic beliefs are a con-tradiction in the mind of man, but not in the mind of God. This thinking is totally backwards, because Calvin's doc-trine is *assumed* to be of God, so we must accept it even if it contradicts common sense. The proper course of action is to put the doctrine itself on trial with the Bible as the judge. If we assume that the teachings of any Bible scholar are correct, and we must wrest or twist scripture (2 Pet. 3:16) to make it fit what the scholar teaches, then we are flawed in our method of reasoning. Using this method of dishonest scholarship, anyone can make any doctrine "fit."

"That be far from thee to do after
this manner, to slay the righteous with

the wicked: and that the righteous should be as the wicked, that be far from thee: *Shall not the Judge of all the earth do right?"* (Gen. 18:25; emphasis mine).

One last backward thought. Does God really only want some to go to heaven and others to hell? If this is so, does God then blind the minds of those whom he doesn't want to be saved?

But if our gospel be hid, it is hid to them that are lost: In whom the god of this world hath blinded the minds of them which believe not, lest the light of the glorious gospel of Christ, who is the image of God, should shine unto them. (2 Cor. 4:3–4)

It seems that in Calvinism God is blinding the eyes of the non-chosen for salvation, while the Bible teaches that Satan blinds men's minds. Needless to say, it's backward and extremely dangerous to accuse God of doing the devil's evil work.

My personal observation of Calvinists is that they have a tendency to be fatalistic. The attitude is often one of complacency, que sera, sera, whatever will be will be, the saved will be saved and the lost will be lost, blah, blah, blah. It's easy to be lazy in regards to soul winning with a fatalist view. Pride creeps in if one has convinced himself that God chose him for salvation. "God chose me for salvation and he made a pretty good choice too, I'll tell you that right now!" Friends, God's law of salvation isn't by God's choosing, but by your faith and repentance.

> "Where is boasting then? It is excluded. By what law? of works? Nay: but by the law of *faith*" (Rom. 3:27; emphasis mine).
> "But *God forbid that I should glory, save in the cross* of our Lord Jesus Christ, by whom the world is crucified unto me, and I unto the world" (Gal. 6:14; emphasis mine).

I've also seen the horns of pride displayed when discussing doctrine with Calvinists. When a doctrinal position becomes rubbery and indefensible, I've been handed the "You just don't understand" card. What is meant by that is "I have understanding, but you don't." Yet for all of their "understanding," they fall back on rhetoric and platitudes. This exact same thing has happened to me with my Arminian friends. The conversation ends with them saying, "I know what I believe," yet they can't defend what they say they believe with scripture.

Calvinists are sometimes judgmental toward the lost. A person in my area, who wasn't ready to receive Christ on the spot, while being visited by a Calvinist was told that he wasn't God's elect and that he would burn in hell. What a great blunder! How many of us didn't receive Christ the first time we heard the gospel? The answer is many.

Backwardness can be seen in both Calvinism and Arminianism in that both systems destroy the simplicity of the gospel with a seemingly endless circle of human reason and life-long rules of bondage.

"But I fear, lest by any means, as the
serpent beguiled Eve through his subtilty,
so your minds should be corrupted from

the *simplicity* that is in Christ" (2 Cor. 11:3; emphasis mine).

Complexity is the reverse of simplicity. Concerning Arminianism, we saw in the previous chapter, that each faction has their own ideas of what rules are to be followed and ignored. The pride factor can be just as strong in Arminian denominations. I've personally seen the pride factor very strongly manifest in the Sabbath-keeping sects. This prideful attitude reminds me of the unjustified Pharisee in Luke 18.

> The Pharisee stood and prayed thus with himself, God, *I* thank thee, that *I* am not as other men are, extortioners, unjust, adulterers, or even as this publican. *I* fast twice in the week, *I* give tithes of all that *I* possess. And the publican, standing afar off, would not lift up so much as his eyes unto heaven, but smote upon his breast, saying, God be merciful to me a sinner. I tell you, this man went down to his house justified rather than the other: for every

one that exalteth himself shall be abased; and he that humbleth himself shall be exalted. (Luke 18:11–14; emphasis mine)

Anyone thinking that he is deserving of heaven because of his good works, no matter how plentiful and grand, may be deceiving his own self, but he's not deceiving God.

"Verily I say unto you, That the *publicans* and the *harlots* go into the kingdom of God before you" (Matt. 21:31; emphasis mine).

Remember Mary Magdalene? Once again…

"Where is *boasting* then? It is *excluded*. By what law? of works? Nay: but by the law of faith" (Rom. 3:27; emphasis mine).
"But God forbid that I should glory, save in the cross of our Lord Jesus Christ, by whom the world is crucified unto me, and I unto the world" (Gal. 6:14).

Conclusions

Starting out on the right foot is starting with intellectual honesty and common sense. I'll share a supposedly true story, which illustrates an important fact. Early in the 1900s, a very educated southern preacher was invited to speak to a small congregation of black folks. The preacher went on for over an hour trying to convince the people, through scholarship, that the devil was chained in hell. After the sermon, the preacher asked a kind, elderly, well-mannered gentleman what he thought of the sermon. The old practical country man with a very thick, unrefined southern accent replied, "Well, if the Dubble be chained in hell, he gots-a m-i-g-h-t-y l-o-n-g chain." Common sense beats intellectualism every time. When it comes to confusing doctrines, a pastor friend of mine has often said, "If it sounds hokey, it is hokey."

Another pastor friend of mine says, "Never mind what the Bible means, what does it say?" Intellectual honesty dictates that the Bible says what it means and means what it says.

All Men Summary

All men are lost in darkness.

The Lord Jesus came to be light unto all men.

Christ died for all men.

Christ's blood is the propitiation for all men.

God's will is for all men to be saved.

God commands all men everywhere to repent.

The Holy Ghost reproves the world (all men) of sin.

The Grace of God that brings salvation is given to all men.

Assurance is given to all men.

"The same came for a witness, to bear witness of the Light, that all men through him might believe" (John 1:7).

"And I, if I be lifted up from the earth, will draw all men unto me" (John 12:32).

"And the times of this ignorance God winked at; but now commandeth all men every where to repent" (Acts 17:30).

"Because he hath appointed a day, in the which he will judge the world in righteousness by that man whom he hath ordained; whereof he hath given assurance unto all men, in that he hath raised him from the dead" (Acts 17:31).

"For this is good and acceptable in the sight of God our Saviour; Who will have all men to be saved, and to come unto the knowledge of the truth" (1 Tim. 2:3–4).

"For therefore we both labour and suffer reproach, because we trust in the living God, who is the Saviour of all men, specially of those that believe" (1 Tim. 4:10).

"For the grace of God that bringeth salvation hath appeared to all men" (Titus 2:11).

Let us agree to use Bible terms as much as possible instead of confusing non-Bible terms. Let us, as Bible students, agree to define the terms we use to help end confusion. Further, let us be willing to ask our teachers the hard questions and not be content with half-answers and nonsensical jargon. Be careful of assumptions, for they can become an inescapable trap. Are we so naive to assume that error couldn't possibly be in my fellowship or denomination?

> "And moreover I saw under the sun
> the place of judgment, that wickedness
> was there; and the place of righteousness,
> that iniquity was there" (Eccles. 3:16).

Methinks the devil spends more time in church than the average Christian! In general, God's ways lead to liberty and man's belief systems lead to bondage and escapism. In the case of Calvinism, it's escapism for we must wait for God to choose us for salvation, so we're off the hook until he does. In the case of Arminianism, we are bound to work for and/or work to keep salvation.

> "Now the Lord is that Spirit: and
> where the Spirit of the Lord is, there is *lib-*
> *erty*" (2 Cor. 3:17; emphasis mine).
>
> "And that because of false brethren
> unawares brought in, who came in privily

to spy out our *liberty* which we have in Christ Jesus, that they might bring us into *bondage*" (Gal. 2:4; emphasis mine).

I hesitate to use the word heresies, but God doesn't. The reality of the situation is that both belief systems cannot be completely correct. When it comes to eternal life being secure without the possibility of being lost, Calvin was correct. Not because believers persevere, however, but because we are preserved. Pertaining to salvation, it is a free will choice of man and not God choosing some individuals. Arminius was right, because choosing is for service and never for salvation. Both men were right about some things and wrong about others. My point is that the Bible is always correct. Furthermore, we would all be wise and receive great benefit if we would return to the fundamentals of the faith and seek pure doctrine. This would result in soldiers of the cross with compassion, making a difference. Instead of shallow, thin skinned babes who expect to hear salvation and tithing every other message.

Ecumenism, which is outward cooperation with compromise, is not biblical, but neither is mean-spirited verbal bashing. How are we to win those with whom we disagree including the lost and the "mal-educated," if not by God's law of kindness?

> "Can two walk together, except they be agreed?" (Amos 3:3).
>
> "She openeth her mouth with wisdom; and in her tongue is the law of kindness" (Prov. 31:26).

If the virtuous woman obeys the law of kindness, should not a virtuous man do likewise? We may be correct in our doctrine, but come across as proud or stubborn, not helping our cause.

> Put on therefore, as the elect of God, holy and beloved, bowels of mercies, kindness, *humbleness* of mind, meekness, longsuffering; Forbearing one another, and forgiving one another, if any man have a quarrel against any: even as Christ forgave you, so also do ye. (Col. 3:12–13; emphasis mine)

And beside this, giving all diligence, add to your faith virtue; and to virtue knowledge; And to knowledge temperance; and to temperance patience; and to patience godliness; And to godliness brotherly *kindness*; and to brotherly kindness charity. (2 Pet. 1:5–7; emphasis mine)

We should be secure in our beliefs and be willing and eager to discuss them openly. We can also disagree like civilized men and women. In all things there is a balance, so on the other side, we are not obligated to be a verbal punching bag for the world or unreasonable men.

"And that we may be delivered from *unreasonable* and wicked *men*: for all men have not faith" (2 Thess. 3:2; emphasis mine).

"Make no friendship with an angry man; and with a furious man thou shalt not go" (Prov. 22:24).

When I talk to those who have been immersed in Calvinism, it seems as if they're on the proverbial hamster wheel. If total depravity is true, then unconditional election for salvation must also be true. If unconditional election for salvation is true, then God must use irresistible grace to call whom he has chosen for salvation. Those whom God has chosen for salvation must persevere and limited atonement makes sense too, and round and round we go. The system is logical to a degree *if* the premise were correct. However, if the premise is not correct then the entire system must fall. We have spent sufficient time in chapter 5 to prove that the premise of Calvinism is wrong. Man doesn't need to be chosen for salvation because he isn't totally depraved to the degree which Calvinism assumes. Truly, man can never save himself, but he can call out to God for salvation. Un-saved man believes the gospel with his God-given soul, which is alive, and not with his spirit, which is dead. The entire system is unnecessary because it proceeds from a false premise. It also leads to bondage and confusion. Please, dear friend, get off the hamster wheel today and don't procrastinate. When the Lord led me to start a new local church work, literally from the ground up,

I was led to name it Victory Bible Church. The reason for the name was simple. I'm tired of seeing good, well-meaning, hardworking, sincere people be in religious systems of bondage. I want them to serve the Lord in victory, without bondage of the mind to any system of man. How does this victory come? From the Bible, of course! First, victory in salvation as a free gift without works and second, victory in service; serving our Saviour with a heart of gratitude, without fear of losing what God has promised to keep.

> "For the which cause I also suffer these things: nevertheless I am not ashamed: for I know whom I have believed, and am persuaded that *he is able to keep* that which I have committed unto him against that day" (2 Tim. 1:12; emphasis mine).

Our church theme verse.

> "But thanks be to God, which giveth us the *victory* through our Lord Jesus Christ" (1 Cor. 15:57; emphasis mine).

18

Questions and Answers

If you have read the entire book to this point, then you should be able to answer these questions and the answers should make sense to you. If you have skipped ahead to read the answers, you have learned nothing. The two sections in this chapter are questions and answers for those of the Calvin and Arminian faiths.

Twenty questions and answers from the scriptures for those who follow the teachings of Calvin.

1. Why was Paul willing to endure all things for the elect's sake so that they may obtain salvation if the elect were already saved?

> "Therefore I endure all things for the elect's sakes, that they may also obtain the salvation which is in Christ Jesus with eternal glory" (1 Tim. 2:10).

The Bible answer: The elect were not already saved. God's choosing is always for service, never for salvation. In other words, God had already chosen the Jews nationally to serve Him as a witness. Paul knew that even though his brethren, the Jews, were already God's elect or chosen for service nationally, they needed to obtain salvation personally, through Christ. Hence, Paul was willing to suffer great things that some of his Jewish brothers might be saved.

> "To the weak became I as weak,
> that I might gain the weak: I am made
> all things to all men, that I might by
> all means *save some*" (1 Cor. 9:22;
> emphasis mine).

God, in the person of Christ, wanted many times to gather Jerusalem and the nation of Israel to himself, but they rejected God's grace.

2. If no one can resist the grace of God, then why aren't all men saved?

> "For the grace of God that bringeth salvation hath appeared to all men" (Titus 2:11).

The Bible answer: The grace of God can be frustrated and rejected. No Bible writer, including Paul, ever said that God's grace could not be frustrated.

> "I do not frustrate the grace of God: for if righteousness come by the law, then Christ is dead in vain" (Gal. 2:21).

Here, Paul is only saying that he did not frustrate the grace of God by trying to add his good works to God's gift. Anyone who does try to do so, does frustrate the grace of God. Moreover, God's grace and will can be rejected.

O Jerusalem, Jerusalem, thou that killest the prophets, and stonest them which are sent unto thee, how often *would* I have gathered thy children together, even as a hen gathereth her chickens under her wings, and *ye would not!* (Matt. 23:37; emphasis mine)

O Jerusalem, Jerusalem, which killest the prophets, and stonest them that are sent unto thee; how often *would* I have gathered thy children together, as a hen doth gather her brood under her wings, and *ye would not!* (Luke 13:34; emphasis mine).

3. If no one can resist the Holy Ghost, why then did Steven, who was full of the Holy Ghost in Acts 7:55 say in Acts 7:51, "Ye do always resist the Holy Ghost?"

"Ye stiffnecked and uncircumcised in heart and ears, ye do always

resist the Holy Ghost: as your fathers
did, so do ye" (Acts 7:51).

The Bible answer: Acts 7:51 is self-evident
and shouldn't need any explanation. People do
resist the Holy Ghost at times.

However, consider this: Is the Holy Ghost performing his job today or is he failing; only doing
a partial job? Of course, the Holy Ghost of God
does everything perfectly and his job is stated in.

Nevertheless I tell you the truth;
It is expedient for you that I go away:
for if I go not away, the *Comforter* will
not come unto you; but if I depart, I
will send him unto you. And when
he is come, *he will reprove the world of
sin*, and of righteousness, and of judgment. (John 16:7–8; emphasis mine)

The point should be obvious to the reader, i.e.,
since the Holy Ghost convicts the world of sin and

no man can resist him, then why isn't the whole world saved? Of course, the reason is because people can and do resist the Holy Ghost.

4. If man has no free will, then why did the Lord Jesus say he does?

> "Then said Jesus unto his disciples, *If any man will* come after me, let him deny himself, and take up his cross, and follow me" (Matt. 16:24; emphasis mine).

The Bible answer: In Matthew 16:24, it should be self-evident that man does have a free will to choose, because the God of creation made man in his own image. Simply put God has a free will and God made man in his image with his own free will to choose. Next is a passage where God, through Joshua, pleaded with people to make the right choice.

And if it seem evil unto you to serve the LORD, *choose you* this day whom ye will serve; whether the gods which your fathers served that were on the other side of the flood, or the gods of the Amorites, in whose land ye dwell: but as for me and my house, we will serve the LORD. (Joshua 24:15; emphasis mine)

Lastly, we have a Bible passage where God, through Moses, is pleading directly with people to make the right choice.

"I call heaven and earth to record this day against you, that I have set before you life and death, blessing and cursing: therefore *choose life*, that both thou and thy seed may live" (Deut. 30:19; emphasis mine).

5. Does God's will always overpower man's will?

The Bible answer: God's will doesn't always overpower man's will. Consider what our Lord said after his will and his offer of grace were rejected by those who had their own will.

> O Jerusalem, Jerusalem, thou that killest the prophets, and stonest them which are sent unto thee, how often *would I* have gathered thy children together, even as a hen gathereth her chickens under her wings, and *ye would not!* (Matt. 23:37; emphasis mine)

This is repeated in Luke 13:

> O Jerusalem, Jerusalem, which killest the prophets, and stonest them that are sent unto thee; how often *would I* have gathered thy children together, as a hen doth gather her

brood under her wings, and *ye would not!* (Luke 13:34; emphasis mine)

God gave mankind his own will and God never forces people to accept him or serve him. Those who choose not to accept or serve him suffer loss.

6. If God is only the Saviour of the elect (or a chosen few), then how do you explain 1 Timothy 4:10 which says that God is the Saviour of all men?

> "For therefore we both labour
> and suffer reproach, because we trust
> in the living God, who is the Saviour
> of all men, specially of those that
> believe" (1 Tim. 4:10).

The Bible answer: God is the Saviour of all men in that he has purchased salvation for all men by the blood of his only begotten Son, The Lord Jesus Christ. God is able to save all men who come unto him through this chosen method of salvation, by grace through faith in the blood of Christ. Hence, God is the Saviour of all men in that he offers the free gift of eternal life to all. To those who have trusted God by receiving Christ, God is their Saviour "especially."

7. Is either the word sovereign or sovereignty found in the Bible?

The Bible answer: No.

8. Does sovereignty mean that God forces some people to be saved and others not to be saved?

The Bible answer: Since the word sovereignty is not a Bible word, the question is invalid. The word sovereignty means different things to different people. However, even if we agree that God rules supreme, this does not mean that God will ever force salvation or service upon anyone. God offers salvation to the world, and even though some people will reject God's offer, this in no way undermines God's supreme authority.

9. According to the Bible, is it God's will that only some men be saved or all men?

The Bible answer: "For this is good and acceptable in the sight of *God* our Saviour; Who *will have all men to be saved,* and to come unto the knowledge of the truth" (1 Tim. 2:3–4; emphasis mine).

Those who believe that God has chosen some for heaven and others for hell are saying that God is willing for some men to perish and not to come unto the knowledge of the truth, which is the opposite of 1 Timothy 2:3–4. The clear teaching of the Bible is that God's will is for all men to be saved.

10. If God only wants a select few to repent and be saved, why would God command all men everywhere to repent?

"And the times of this ignorance God winked at; but now commandeth *all* men every where to repent" (Acts 17:30; emphasis mine).

The Bible answer: God wants *all* men everywhere to repent, just like it says. Please consider:

"The Lord is not slack concerning his promise, as some men count slackness; but is longsuffering to us-ward, not willing that any should perish, but that *all* should come to repentance" (2 Pet. 3:9). Also consider John 3:16, "For God so loved the *world*, that he gave his only begotten Son, that *whosoever* believeth in him should not perish, but have everlasting life."

If you contend that "all men" in Acts 17:30 and 2 Peter 3:9 should read all "elect" men, and the word "world" in Joh 3:16 should read "elect," and "whosoever" doesn't really mean whosoever, then you are guilty of adding to and taking away from God's holy word. Adding to and taking away from God's words is strictly forbidden.

"Add thou not unto his words, lest he reprove thee, and thou be found a liar" (Prov. 30:6).

"For I testify unto every man that heareth the words of the prophecy of this book, If any man shall add unto these things, God shall add unto him the plagues that are written in this book" (Rev. 22:18).

God inspired words, not thoughts. God also promised to keep and preserve his inspired words for ever.

"*Every word* of God is pure: he is a shield unto them that put their trust in him" (Prov. 30:5; emphasis mine).

"*All scripture* is given by inspiration of God, and is profitable for doctrine, for reproof, for correction, for instruction in righteousness" (2 Tim. 3:16; emphasis mine).

"The words of the LORD are pure words: as silver tried in a furnace of earth, purified seven times. Thou shalt *keep* them, O LORD, thou shalt preserve them from this generation for ever" (Ps. 12:6–7; emphasis mine).

Dear friend, if you must add to, take away, retranslate or in some way change God's holy word in order to keep your doctrine, may I suggest that you change your doctrine and keep God's word?

God's will is for no one to perish, but men choose not to listen to God's warnings much like Adam and Eve. Grace is not force. Grace is an offer of help, even if that offer is rejected.

11. According to the Bible, for whom did Jesus die?

The Bible answer: "But we see Jesus, who was made a little lower than the angels for the suffering of death, crowned with glory and honour; that he by the *grace* of God should taste death for *every* man" (Heb. 2:9; emphasis mine).

Every man means every man just like the phrase "the world" means the world in John 3:16. God gave his Son for the world, i.e., every person in the world. To say that every man means every "elect" man and the world means "the elect men" is a violation of scripture.

12. If God chooses people for heaven, why is it the Comforter's (The Holy Ghost's) job to reprove (convict) the world of sin and not just the elect?

> Nevertheless I tell you the truth; It is expedient for you that I go away: for if I go not away, the Comforter will not come unto you; but if I depart, I will send him unto you. And when he is come, he will *reprove the world* of sin, and of righteousness, and of judgment. (John 16:7–8; emphasis mine)

The Bible answer: God does not choose people for heaven or hell. God loves all mankind and sends his Spirit to draw them, but not force them toward the truth. Indeed, if the convicting power of the Holy Ghost were an overwhelming force, then the whole world would now be saved, seeing that the Holy Ghost convicts all men.

13. Does the Bible teach that believers must persevere in order to be saved?

The Bible answer: No. The believer's works neither save him nor keep him.

> Knowing that a man is not justified by the works of the law, but by the faith of Jesus Christ, even we have believed in Jesus Christ, that we might be justified by the faith of Christ, and not by the works of the law: for by the works of the law shall no flesh be justified. (Gal. 2:16)

I know some will say "I know my works can't save or keep me saved, that's all by God's grace." Yes, that's correct; we are saved and kept by the power of God. "Who are kept by the power of God through faith unto salvation ready to be revealed in the last time" (1 Pet. 1:5).

In short, a believer being kept by the power of God is preservation, not perseverance. Do you know the difference? Without a lengthy dictionary definition, know that perseverance is *you* doing something and preservation is *God* doing something.

14. Does man's total depravity to save himself from hell mean that he can't repent and believe the gospel? If so, why did the Lord Jesus tell people to do something that he knew they could not do?

> "And saying, The time is fulfilled, and the kingdom of God is at hand: *repent* ye, and *believe* the gospel" (Mark 1:15; emphasis mine).

The Bible answer: The Bible never says, nor does it express the idea, that man is totally depraved to the point that he cannot repent and believe the gospel. The Lord Jesus commands all men everywhere to repent and believe the gospel because he knows we can. Furthermore, those who refuse to obey God's command will suffer the consequences. Christ gives the individual a choice to repent and believe or reject and perish. Consider these obvious truths in the following scriptures.

"I tell you, Nay: but, except *ye repent*, ye shall all likewise perish" (Luke 13:3; emphasis mine).

"I tell you, Nay: but, except *ye repent*, ye shall all likewise perish" (Luke 13:5; emphasis mine).

"I said therefore unto you, that ye shall die in your sins: for if *ye believe* not that I am he, ye shall die in your sins" (John 8:24; emphasis mine).

While it's true that man cannot save himself from hell, man must choose to repent and believe the gospel or reject it. Keep in mind that the term "total depravity" is a man-made term and appears nowhere in scripture. Calvinism dictates that man was spiritually dead in trespasses and sins, and that he was unable to repent or believe. This misunderstanding of scripture is explained in more detail in chapter nine. The truncated answer is, that even though an unsaved man is spiritually dead, a person repents and believes the gospel with his soul which is alive, not with his spirit which is dead.

15. Is God's election of man for salvation or service? The Bible answer: Service only.

> "Behold *my servant*, whom I uphold; *mine elect*, in whom my soul delighteth; I have put my spirit upon him: he shall bring forth judgment to the Gentiles" (Isa. 42:1; emphasis mine).

This verse speaks of Christ, "the son of man," who was chosen for God's service and never needed salvation.

"For *Jacob* my *servant's* sake, and *Israel* mine *elect*, I have even called thee by thy name" (Isa. 45:4a; emphasis mine).

Election is always for service and never salvation. When it seems otherwise, re-study the context of the scripture.

16. What crucial Bible point did Calvin overlook relating to the election of man?

    The Bible answer: The three parts of man and their proper function. Man possesses a soul which is alive in spite of possessing a dead spirit. This is explained in detail in the chapter 5.

17. Did Calvin believe in the doctrine of the limited atonement of Christ?

The Bible answer: No, because of verses like John 3:16 and John 1:29.

"The next day John seeth Jesus coming unto him, and saith, Behold *the Lamb of God,* which *taketh away the sin of the world*" (John 1:29; emphasis mine).

18. Can you explain the difference between Calvinism and hyper-Calvinism?

The Bible answer: "And *he is the propitiation* for our sins: and not for ours only, but also for *the sins of the whole world*" (1 John 2:2; emphasis mine).

Hyper-Calvinism teaches that the blood of Christ is limited to a chosen few while Calvinism does not hold to this limitation.

19. A follower of Calvin may claim to be a one, one and a half, two, two and a half, three, three and a half, four, four and a half, or five-point Calvinists. Why are there so many variations on Calvinism?

The Bible answer: Dear reader, I am not attempting to degrade anyone with the following explanation of why Calvinism is so confusing. I am, however, speaking the truth in love to help us adhere to Bible doctrines rather than doctrines of men. The answer as to why Calvinism is so confusing is because Calvinism is a compilation of confusing, man-made doctrines and half-truths. If we but separate Bible fact from Calvinistic interpretations of what the Bible is saying, the confusion will dissipate.

"For God is not the author of confusion, but of peace, as in all churches of the saints" (2 Cor. 14:33).

20. If election is for salvation and God only calls the elect to be saved and no one can resist God's calling, then *every* called person must be God's chosen, right? But what does the Bible say?

The Bible answer: "For many are called, but few are chosen" (Matt. 22:14).

How is it possible that "many" can be called, but "few" chosen? According to Calvinism, every "called" person must obey and can't resist the calling of the Holy Spirit, right? So, *every* person "called" for salvation must also be a "chosen" person for salvation. Therefore, there should be an equal number of "called" and "chosen" persons. Is the Bible wrong when it declares that many are called, but few are chosen? No, the Bible is never wrong, only our understanding of it. Choosing in the Bible is always for service and never for salvation. Consequently, few are chosen for service because few answer the call and accept salvation. God calls all for salvation and some accept the call. Out of all of those who respond to the gospel call, only some are willing to serve. Since choosing in the Bible is always for service, God chooses his servants from those who have responded to the gospel call and are willing to serve him. In this way, many are called for salvation, but few are chosen for service, hence:

"For many are called, but few are chosen" (Matt. 22:14).

Twenty questions and answers from the scriptures for followers of the Arminian faith:

Do you believe that eternal life can be lost? Can you answer these questions using scripture?

1. What is the Bible definition of eternal life? The Bible answer:

> That whosoever believeth in him should not perish, but have *eternal life*. For God so loved the world, that he gave his only begotten Son, that whosoever believeth in him should not perish, but have *everlasting life*. (John 3:15–16; emphasis mine)
>
> And I give unto them *eternal life*; and they shall *never perish*, neither shall any man pluck them out of my hand. (John 10:28; emphasis mine)

The Bible definition of eternal life is to have everlasting life or to never perish. By definition, if the life you have can be lost, it's not eternal; it's conditional, temporal or something else. The point should be self-evident that the Bible definition of eternal life is everlasting life or to never perish. *Anyone who believes he can have eternal life (as stated in John 10:28) and still somehow perish, does not believe in the doctrine of eternal life.* That person believes in something called temporal (temporary) life or conditional life or some other kind of life foreign to the Bible. God never promised anything other than everlasting life! All other ideas, concepts and thoughts are doctrines of men and not of God.

2. Is eternal life given by God as a gift or as a payment for doing good works?

The Bible answer: As a gift.

"For the wages of sin is death; but the *gift* of God is *eternal life* through

Jesus Christ our Lord" (Rom. 6:23; emphasis mine).

"For by grace are ye *saved* through faith; and that not of yourselves: it is the *gift* of God: Not of works, lest any man should boast" (Eph. 2:8–9; emphasis mine).

"And they of the circumcision which believed were astonished, as many as came with Peter, because that on the Gentiles also was poured out the *gift* of the Holy Ghost" (Acts 10:45; emphasis mine).

3. Does the Bible teach that born-again believers keep their salvation or that God keeps the believer. The Bible answer:

Blessed be the God and Father of our Lord Jesus Christ, which according to his abundant mercy hath begotten us again unto a lively hope by the resurrection of Jesus Christ from the dead, To an inheritance incorruptible, and undefiled, and that fadeth not away, reserved in heaven for you, Who are *kept by the power of God* through faith unto salvation ready to be revealed in the last time. (1 Pet. 1:3–5; emphasis mine)

For the which cause I also suffer these things: nevertheless I am not ashamed: for I know whom I have believed, and am persuaded that *he is able to keep* that which I have committed unto him against that day. (2 Tim. 1:12; emphasis mine)

The following verses and others like them, are referring to believers keeping themselves pure for God's *service* and have nothing to do with keeping *salvation*.

"Little children, *keep yourselves* from idols. Amen" (1 John 5:21; emphasis mine).

"*Keep yourselves* in the love of God, looking for the mercy of our Lord" (Jude 1:21).

"We know that whosoever is born of God sinneth not; but he that is begotten of God *keepeth himself,* and that wicked one toucheth him not" (1 John 5:18; emphasis mine).

4. Is it possible for a child of God to have no rewards in heaven?

    The Bible answer: Yes.

    "Look to yourselves, that we lose not those things which we have wrought, but that we receive a full reward" (2 John 1:8).

The context here is not salvation, but the things which the believer wrought (made/worked for) and the result is a reward in heaven, not heaven itself. Yes, these things/rewards can be lost!

For other foundation can no man lay than that is laid, which is Jesus Christ. Now if any man build upon this foundation gold, silver, precious stones, wood, hay, stubble; Every man's work shall be made manifest: for the day shall declare it, because it shall be revealed by fire; and the fire shall try every man's work of what sort it is. If any man's work abide which he hath built thereupon, he shall receive a reward. If any man's work shall be burned, *he shall suffer loss*: but *he himself shall be saved*; yet so as by fire. (2 Cor. 3:11–15; emphasis mine)

5. Can God lie?

   The Bible answer: No, it's impossible.

   "That by two immutable things, in which it was *impossible for God to lie*, we might have a strong consolation, who have fled for refuge to lay hold upon the hope set before us" (Heb. 6:18; emphasis mine).

   Since it's impossible for God to lie, then these words are true.

   "That if thou shalt confess with thy mouth the Lord Jesus, and shalt believe in thine heart that God hath raised him from the dead, *thou shalt be saved*" (Rom. 10:9; emphasis mine).

6. When does a believer in Christ receive eternal life?

   The Bible answer: The moment we call upon Christ with a heart of repentance and faith.

"Beloved, *now are we the sons of God*, and it doth not yet appear what we shall be: but we know that, when he shall appear, we shall be like him; for we shall see him as he is" (1 John 3:2; emphasis mine).

7. What does the Bible phrase "never perish" mean?

    The Bible answer: It means never perish! It does not mean "never perish unless…"

    "And I give unto them eternal life; and they shall *never perish*, neither shall any man pluck them out of my hand" (John 10:28; emphasis mine).

8. Can a person pluck himself out of God's hand?

    The Bible answer: No. The Lord further explains what "never perish" means.

> And I give unto them eternal life;
> and they shall *never perish*, neither shall
> any man pluck them out of my hand.
> My Father, which gave them me, is
> greater than all; and *no man* is able to
> pluck them out of my Father's hand.
> (John 10:28–29; emphasis mine)

Relating to eternal life, no one can be plucked out of God's hand. I can't pluck you out, you can't pluck me out, and you can't pluck yourself out! You say what if I...! Hold on friend, are you a man, i.e., a human being? If you believe the Bible, then "no man," not even you yourself, can pluck yourself out of God's mighty hand. Just trust the Bible.

9. Can a believer in the Son of God know that he has eternal life?

The Bible answer: Yes.

> "These things have I written unto
> you that believe on the name of the

Son of God; that ye *may know* that ye have eternal life, and that ye may believe on the name of the Son of God" (1 John 5:13; emphasis mine).

The phrase "may know," means can know. We have permission from God to know that we have eternal life. God does not want his children, who are born into his family and by his Spirit, to guess, hope or feel, but know that we belong to him.

10. What does the word "redeemed" mean?

The Bible answer: It means to purchase, to buy or to buy back.

Forasmuch as ye know that ye were not *redeemed* with corruptible things, as silver and gold, from your vain conversation received by tradition from your fathers; But *with the precious blood of Christ*, as of a lamb

without blemish and without spot.
(1 Pet. 1:18–19; emphasis mine)

God owns his redeemed children entirely.

11. Did God buy us just to throw us away when we fail?

The Bible answer: No.

> "My little children, these things write I unto you, that ye sin not. And if any man sin, we have an advocate with the Father, Jesus Christ the righteous" (1 John 2:1).

> "If we say that we have no sin, we deceive ourselves, and the truth is not in us" (1 John 1:8).

> "If we say that we have not sinned, we make him a liar, and his word is not in us" (1 John 1:10).

No, God doesn't throw his children away, but he has made provision for our spiritual growth and failure. However, even though God has promised every believer eternal life, there is a remedy for outright rebellion; God may choose to push the red button! In brief, God won't take away our promise of eternal life, but he can and does sometimes take away our temporal life.

> "All unrighteousness is sin: and there is a sin not unto *death*" (1 John 5:17; emphasis mine).
> "For this cause many are weak and sickly among you, and many *sleep*" (1 Cor. 11:30; emphasis mine).

Nothing stops a disobedient Christian from embarrassing God quite like death!

12. Did Job and Paul guess, hope, feel or know that they were saved.

    The Bible answer: Know.

"For *I know* that my redeemer liveth, and that he shall stand at the latter day upon the earth: And though after my skin worms destroy this body, yet *in my flesh* shall I see God" (Job 19:25–26; emphasis mine).

"For the which cause I also suffer these things: nevertheless I am not ashamed: for *I know* whom I have believed, and am persuaded that *he is able* to keep that which I have committed unto him against that day" (2 Tim. 1:12; emphasis mine).

13. For which category of sins did Christ die; past, present, or future?

The Bible answer: All.

"Who *delivered* us from so great a death, and *doth deliver*: in whom we trust that he will *yet deliver* us" (2 Cor. 1:10; emphasis mine).

The Lord Jesus died for the sin of the world which entails past, present and future sin.

14. Is there a difference between sins before salvation and sins after salvation?

The Bible answer: Yes.

> "For we must all appear before the judgment seat of Christ; that every one may receive the things done in his body, according to that he hath done, whether it be good or bad" (2 Cor. 5:10).

Yes, sins before salvation block us from heaven, while sins after salvation affect our rewards in heaven and do not hinder us from entering heaven.

> "Verily, verily, I say unto you, He that heareth my word, and believeth on him that sent me, hath everlasting life, and shall not come into condem-

nation; but *is passed* from death unto life" (John 5:24; emphasis mine).

15. What is threefold sanctification?

The Bible answer:

"Who *delivered* us from so great a death, and *doth deliver*: in whom we trust that he will *yet deliver* us" (2 Cor. 1:10; emphasis mine).

God delivered born-again believers from so great a death, i.e., hell, through salvation and does continue to deliver us today from temptations and a meaningless life as we yield to him and will yet deliver us in the future, ultimately unto heaven. To keep it short, God has delivered every child of his from the penalty of sin and delivers them daily from the power of sin and one day from the very presence of sin.

16. Does the Bible make a distinction between salvation and service?

The Bible answer: Yes.

> And whatsoever ye do, do it heartily, as to the Lord, and not unto men; Knowing that of the Lord ye shall receive the reward of the inheritance: for ye *serve* the Lord Christ. But he that doeth wrong shall receive for the wrong which he hath done: and there is no respect of persons. (Col. 3:23–25; emphasis mine)

Colossians is written to believers in Christ, i.e., those who are going to heaven. It's very clear in these verses that some believers serve Christ more than others. Being born-again is one thing, serving is yet another.

17. Does the Bible make a distinction between being delivered from hell and discipleship?

The Bible answer: Yes.

"If any man come to me, and hate not his father, and mother, and wife, and children, and brethren, and sisters, yea, and his own life also, he cannot be my *disciple*" (Luke 14:26; emphasis mine).

"So likewise, whosoever he be of you that forsaketh not all that he hath, he cannot be my *disciple*" (Luke 14:33; emphasis mine).

Yes, there is a monumental difference between salvation and discipleship. A child of God may serve Christ as he should or may not serve as he should. Please notice that the Lord, in these verses in Luke, didn't say "…ye cannot be saved," but "… ye cannot be my disciple."

18. What does it mean to become a child of God?

The Bible answer:

> He came unto his own, and his own received him not. But *as many as received him*, to them gave he power to become *the sons of God*, even to them that believe on his name: Which were *born*, not of blood, nor of the will of the flesh, nor of the will of man, but *of God*. (John 1:11–13; emphasis mine)

A child of God is someone who has received eternal life and is spiritually born into God's family by faith. This is that same concept which the Lord communicated to Nicodemus in John 3:1–8.

19. Can a child once born become unborn?

The Bible answer: No, this is exactly why the Lord compared being saved to a natural birth in John 3. Once a baby is physically born into a family, the baby can never go back, neither can his essence be undone. In like manner, once we are spiritually born into the family of God, we cannot go back; our birth and our destination can never be undone.

> "Let your conversation be without covetousness; and be content with such things as ye have: for he hath said, *I will never leave thee*, nor forsake thee" (Heb. 13:5; emphasis mine).

For more information, please reread chapter 8.

20. Is our will greater than God's promise?

The Bible answer: No, never.

God's promise:

> "That if thou shalt confess with thy mouth the Lord Jesus, and shalt believe in thine heart that God hath

raised him from the dead, *thou shalt be saved*" (Rom. 10:9; emphasis mine).

"If we believe not, yet he abideth faithful: *he cannot deny himself*" (2 Tim. 2:13; emphasis mine).

19

God's Salvation Plan

Faith

Can I go to heaven?

Yes, if you're willing to repent, believe, and receive.

Repent of what?

Your sin; that is being sorry for your sin and having a desire to change.

> "Testifying both to the Jews, and also to the Greeks, repentance toward God, and faith toward our Lord Jesus Christ" (Acts 20:21).

God commands (orders) everyone to repent.

> "And the times of this ignorance God winked at (over looked); but now

commandeth (commands) all men every where to repent" (Acts 17:30).

Repentance is necessary to receive salvation (deliverance) from hell and go to heaven.

"For godly sorrow worketh repentance to salvation not to be repented of: but the sorrow of the world worketh death" (2 Cor. 7:10).

Believe what?

The Holy Bible when it says that you're a sinner.

"For all have sinned, and come short of the glory of God" (Rom. 3:23).

That all sinners deserve hell and the lake of fire.

"For the wages of sin is death; This death is both physical and spiritual" (Rom. 6:23a).

"But the fearful, and unbelieving, and the abominable, and murderers, and whoremongers, and sorcerers, and idolaters, and all liars, shall have their part in the lake which burneth with fire and brimstone: which is the second death" (Rev. 21:8).

That you need to obey the gospel.

"In flaming fire taking vengeance on them that know not God, and that obey not the gospel of our Lord Jesus Christ" (2 Thess. 1:8).

That Jesus Christ is the sinless Son of God who died on the cross to pay for your sins, was buried, and was resurrected from the dead.

"But God commendeth (shows) his love toward us, in that, while we were yet sinners, Christ died for us" (Rom. 5:8).

"That if thou shalt confess with thy mouth the Lord Jesus, and shalt believe in thine heart that God hath raised him from the dead, thou shalt be saved" (Rom. 10:9).

That God loves you and doesn't want anyone to perish in hell.

"The Lord is not slack concerning his promise, as some men count slackness; but is longsuffering to usward, not willing that any should perish, but that all should come to repentance" (2 Pet. 3:9).

Receive what?

Eternal life as a free gift, not as payment for doing good works.

"For the wages of sin is death; but the gift of God is eternal life through Jesus Christ our Lord" (Rom. 6:23).

"For by grace are ye saved (from hell) through faith; and that not of yourselves: it is the gift of God: Not of works, lest any man should boast" (Eph. 2:8–9).

And receive Christ as your Saviour by confessing your need to Him as the only way to be saved from hell.

"But as many as received him, to them gave he power to become the sons of God, even to them that believe on his name" (John 1:12).

"For with the heart man believeth unto righteousness; and with the mouth confession is made unto salvation" (Rom. 10:10).

"Neither is there salvation in any other: for there is none other name under heaven given among men, whereby we must be saved" (Acts 4:12).

The penalty for not believing, repenting and receiving Christ and His gospel.

"I tell you, Nay: but, except ye repent, ye shall all likewise perish" (Luke 13:3).

"In flaming fire taking vengeance on them that know not God, and that obey not the gospel of our Lord Jesus Christ" (2 Thess. 1:8).

If you understand and believe these things from the Bible, you can pray this prayer from your heart and God who promised to save your soul from hell, will.

Dear God in heaven,

I know I'm a sinner.

I believe that I deserve hell for my sin.

I believe that the Lord Jesus died on the cross to pay for my sin.

I believe that Christ arose from the dead and is alive in heaven today.

Dear Jesus, please come into my heart and save me from hell.

May I know in my heart that I'm saved.

Dear God, thank you for saving my soul. In Jesus' holy name, amen.

If you have received the Lord it would be a blessing to hear from you.

People often have other questions not answered here. If you have sincere questions about salvation please visit our website at www.vbiblechurch.com

What to do when the gospel doesn't seem to work. When the gospel of Jesus Christ doesn't seem to work, rest assured that there's nothing wrong with the gospel. The fault is always in us and our lack of understanding, lack of faith or the stubbornness of our own heart.

What eternal life is not.

1. A promise to God that you'll be good...give up bad habits, go to church, etc.

2. "I believe in God." A general belief in God isn't enough. The devils believe in God too.

3. "I believe in Jesus." Believing that Jesus is Holy is necessary for salvation, but it's not enough by itself. The devils know who the Lord Jesus is.

"Saying, Let us alone; what have we
to do with thee, thou Jesus of Nazareth?
art thou come to destroy us? I know thee
who thou art, the Holy One of God"
(Mark 1:24).

"Saying, Let us alone; what have we
to do with thee, thou Jesus of Nazareth?
art thou come to destroy us? I know thee
who thou art; the Holy One of God"
(Luke 4:34).

After many years of showing people what the Bible
says about being saved, I realize that many people have said
a prayer, been baptized and joined churches without truly
being saved. Salvation isn't in a prayer, but in a person, the
Lord Jesus Christ. God wants people to know they're saved;
not guess, hope or feel.

And this is the record, that God hath
given to us eternal life, and this life is in
his Son. He that hath the Son hath life;
and he that hath not the Son of God hath

not life. These things have I written unto you that believe on the name of the Son of God; that ye may know that ye have eternal life, and that ye may believe on the name of the Son of God. (1 John 5:11–13)

Still have questions? Please visit our website at www.vbiblechurch.com

Additional Salvation Information

Salvation is not a process, but an event, just like a new birth!

"Marvel not that I said unto thee, Ye must be born again" (John 3:7).

"For he saith, I have heard thee in a time accepted, and in *the day of salvation* have I succoured thee: behold, now is the accepted time; behold, now is *the day of salvation*" (2 Cor. 6:2; emphasis mine).

"Beloved, *now* are we the sons of God, and it doth not yet appear what we shall be: but we know that, when he shall appear, we shall be like him; for we shall see him as he is" (1 John 3:2; emphasis mine)

"He that believeth on the Son *hath* everlasting life: and he that believeth not the Son shall not see life; but the wrath of God abideth on him" (John 3:36; emphasis mine).

"Verily, verily, I say unto you, He that believeth on me *hath* everlasting life" (John 6:47; emphasis mine).

We can know that we have received eternal life.

"These things have I written unto you that believe on the name of the Son of God; that ye may know that ye have eternal life, and that ye may believe on the name of the Son of God" (1 John 5:13).

Salvation is never by man's works.

> "Therefore by the *deeds* of the law there shall no flesh be justified in his sight: for by the law is the knowledge of sin" (Rom. 3:20; emphasis mine).
>
> "For by grace are ye saved through faith; and that not of yourselves: it is the gift of God: (9) *Not of works*, lest any man should boast" (Eph. 2:8–9; emphasis mine).
>
> "*Not by works* of righteousness which we have done, but according to his mercy he saved us, by the washing of regeneration, and renewing of the Holy Ghost" (Titus 3:5; emphasis mine).

Salvation is by God's grace which is God giving us something which we do not deserve or earn.

> "Being justified freely by *his grace* through the redemption that is in Christ Jesus" (Rom. 3:24; emphasis mine).

Salvation is through faith.

> Knowing that a man is *not* justified by the *works* of the law, *but by the faith* of Jesus Christ, even we have believed in Jesus Christ, that we might be justified by the faith of Christ, and not by the works of the law: for by the works of the law shall no flesh be justified. (Gal. 2:16; emphasis mine)

We are kept by God's grace and power.

> "To an inheritance incorruptible, and undefiled, and that fadeth not away, reserved in heaven for you, *Who are kept by the power of God* through faith unto salvation ready to be revealed in the last time" (1 Pet. 1:4; emphasis mine).

We can have assurance from the moment we receive God's salvation. The great song writer Fanny Crosby wrote a song titled "Blessed Assurance Jesus Is Mine."

The great Apostle Paul gave assurance to *all* of the believers in the church at Rome.

> "Much more then, being now justified by his blood, *we shall be saved* from wrath through him" (Rom. 5:9; emphasis mine).

Paul didn't say we might be saved or we shall be saved as long as we do additional things, but we shall be saved. The apostle John did the same thing as Paul, in that he gave assurance of eternal life to all of the believers in the seven churches of Asia.

> "He that overcometh, the same shall be clothed in white raiment; and *I will not blot out* his name out of the book of life, but I will confess his name before my Father, and before his angels" (Rev. 3:5; emphasis mine).

Every born-again person has God's assurance of heaven. There are no qualifiers here, this guarantee is just for being a child of God and not for being a servant of God.

The gospel comes with assurance.

> "For our gospel came not unto you in word only, but also in power, and in the Holy Ghost, and in much *assurance*; as ye know what manner of men we were among you for your sake" (1 Thess. 1:5; emphasis mine).

Trust God and believe his word.

ABOUT THE AUTHOR

Kevin Kline—author, pastor, and conference speaker—was born in 1958 and is a graduate of Bible Truth Institute. He has served as a senior pastor since 1987, preaching and teaching the Bible. Pastor Kline presently pastors Victory Bible Church in Paxinos, Pennsylvania, a church that he founded in 1996. His simple method of "line upon line" instruction draws listeners and readers in. Pastor Kline has a special gift of teaching complex doctrines in a way simple enough for the average Christian to understand while stimulating the mind of a scholar. He also is an entrepreneur, a USAF veteran, and has been married to his high school sweetheart, Kay, since 1977. Together, they enjoy their two children and six grandchildren.

CPSIA information can be obtained
at www.ICGtesting.com
Printed in the USA
LVHW020723301219
642043LV00001B/3/P